P9-CFO-786

SIGN OF THE CROSS

SIGN OF THE CROSS

The Prosecutor's True Story of a Landmark Trial Against the Klan

John W. Phillips

Westminster John Knox Press
Louisville, Kentucky

Book design by Sharon Adams

First edition
Published by Westminster John Knox Press
Louisville, Kentucky

This book is printed on acid-free paper that meets the American National Standards Institute Z39.48 standard. ♾

PRINTED IN THE UNITED STATES OF AMERICA

00 01 02 03 04 05 06 07 08 09 — 10 9 8 7 6 5 4 3 2 1

Library of Congress Cataloging-in-Publication Data

Phillips, John W., 1954–
Sign of the cross : the prosecutor's true story of a landmark trial against the Klan / John W. Phillips.—1st ed.
p. cm.
ISBN 0-664-22196-3 (alk. paper)
1. Metzger, Tom—Trials, litigation, etc. 2. Ku Klux Klan (1915–)—Trials, litigation, etc. Hate crimes—California—Los Angeles. I. Title.

KF224.M48 P48 2000
345.73′0248—dc21

99-089656

This book is dedicated to my family and friends who offered their loyalty during the difficult times of which I've written, and particularly to my mother who taught me the value of faith and the meaning of parental love.

Contents

Preface

The evil we find in the Ku Klux Klan is an absolute evil inherent in any secret order holding itself above the law. They are ignorant bullies, callous of the harm they know they are doing, and lacking sufficient understanding to comprehend the chasm between their actions and the noble charter of liberties under law that is the American Constitution. Wrapped in myths and misbeliefs which they think relieve them of the obligations of ordinary citizens, Klansmen pledge their first allegiance to their own twisted Konstitution and give their first loyalty to a cross in flames."

U.S. Supreme Court in United States versus The Original Knights of the Ku Klux Klan.

The "cross in flames" cast its harrowing glow throughout America since the aftermath of the Civil War, until 1991 when men came forward in a case destined to redefine the boundary between freedom of speech and freedom from oppression.

I had been a successful career prosecutor when I first began the investigation into a Ku Klux Klan cross-burning conspiracy known as *People of the State of California versus Thomas Metzger et al*. This was the prosecution of fourteen members of the Ku Klux Klan and other neo-Nazi terrorist groups, including national leaders and rank-and-file murderers. They had assembled for a cross-burning ceremony intended to solidify the white supremacist movement nationally and to reestablish the California Knights of the Ku Klux Klan. After they inflamed three towering crosses on a hillside above the San Fernando Valley, we led an unprecedented and stormy legal battle against the legality of this traditional Klan ritual.

From the beginning, legal complexity and personal endangerment made it the case no other prosecutor wanted to prosecute and no judge wanted to hear. The charges were once dismissed, and at this time, bitterly disappointed and disparaged, I resigned my position at the Prosecutor's Office. But two years later the dismissal was reversed on appeal. The District Attorney of Los Angeles County called me back from private practice. I would return as Special Prosecutor for one last trial.

The civilian witnesses, informants, and undercover cops we summoned to testify believe that our neighbors, regardless of their color, have the right to be free from fear. For me it was something more than that. The cross is the Christian symbol of Jesus' forgiveness and love. It wasn't right for the Klan to use that cross in an expression of intimidation and hatred. We hoped this case would set the legal precedent to end forever the ritualistic Ku Klux Klan cross-lighting. And we hoped we could factionalize the white supremacist movement.

But what price was I to pay for pursuing these objectives? Did I simply underestimate the obstacles and risks, or was I completely naive to believe my family would not be threatened by the Klan conspiracy? I could accept the personal endangerment, but I will never forgive myself for the perils to which my wife and children were exposed.

This book is based on the actual testimony, recorded conversations, and reports of cops, Klansmen, informants, and prosecutors. If you find interest in the notorious deeds of the Klan, in courtroom drama, and in trial strategy, or if you want to know the story of a man who fought to stop the Klan from organizing in California, I invite you to read this true story.

Chapter 1

The Sign of the Cross

"Hey, Samuel. Hey, Samuel! Would you please pass the—Robert, would you kindly step on your uncle's big toe and ask him to pass the butter down this way?"

Nine-year-old Robert Gentry also had difficulty hearing his father speak over the commotion and laughter of their family picnic. His dad raised his voice to a level all would hear. "And if that don't work try a mild kick to the shin."

"Now what are you doing provoking this boy to do your ill deeds? You want the butter? You gonna have to come down here and take it by force." Samuel stood and assumed a fighting stance, completely belied by an ear-to-ear smile. The brothers broke into a roar of laughter, joined by the wives, cousins, and friends gathered for one of the precious days of which boyhood memories are made.

On this summer day of 1964 in Atlanta, Georgia, dusk cast shades of violet and purple on clouds adrift in a blue sky. "And may God bless this food. In the name of the

Father, the Son, and the Holy Spirit. Amen." With the sign of the cross, their meal began.

As Robert busied himself buttering his corn on the cob, he noticed his Uncle Samuel had abruptly stopped speaking midsentence. As another moment passed without hearing more from his gregarious uncle, Robert looked up and saw him staring intensely into the distance. The others at the table also felt the sudden stillness. In a soft, humorless tone Samuel then spoke, staring fixedly beyond the faces of his friends and family. "What in hell are they doing?"

Before Robert could turn to see the source of his uncle's consternation, his father cautiously rose, his attention also drawn to the foothills behind Robert. He spoke in a soft but determined voice. "This is our park as much as theirs. The white folk don't even want this park."

Robert turned to see. At the foothills beyond the sandbox, a fire crept up what seemed like a pole. Then, about ten feet high, the flames spread to the side poles as well, forming a fiery cross. Surrounded by dozens of figures in white robes and hoods, the fire fully engulfed the cross and illuminated the Klansmen below it. Some held torches. Others carried clubs or rifles.

Many questions quickly passed through Robert's mind, although he did not speak. He remembers his mother hurriedly reaching for the picnic basket. "C'mon, let's go. There's no further purpose in our being here."

Robert's older cousin Marcus turned to Samuel and demanded of his father, "What are we gonna do about it?"

Samuel paused. A feverish chill passed through Robert as the tip of the flames forebodingly beckoned the heavens. Samuel softly answered his son. "We're not going to do anything about it." He picked up items on the table and moved toward the basket being filled by his wife. "You don't mess with these people. Not here, not now."

"You're backing down. I'm not backing down." Marcus stepped toward the distant flames, but Samuel grabbed his arm. Marcus turned with a defiant glance.

"There's children and the women here. Know your place in this family. We're leaving, and I mean move it," demanded Samuel.

There was no further discussion. They quickly gathered belongings and loaded their vehicles. As they drove away, Robert stared from the car window, his mother and aunt ordering him to look forward. But Robert continued to watch the flames dance and frolic around the cross, mocking the dignity of his family.

Samuel and Cherise drove home with Marcus seething silently in the back seat. When the car pulled into the driveway, Marcus quickly leaped out, stomped into the house, and went to his bedroom. Needing to be with him, to make sure he was all right, Samuel gently pushed open the door and looked at his son. Marcus was lying on his bed, hands folded behind his head, gazing toward the ceiling. The father and son had always been close, making more awkward Marcus's indifference to his father's presence. Samuel gently spoke. "I thought we might go to the harbor sometime this week, get a full-day boat, and see if we catch a yellowtail tuna."

"I don't think so, Dad." Marcus continued to look away. "Seems like there's enough yellowtail here as it is."

Samuel winced at the loss of his son's respect. It was more painful than the indignation he felt as the cross burned. In leaving the park, there was some measure of honor in protecting the family. Now, there was no saving grace. He backed away, and as he closed the bedroom door he became filled with anger.

He walked to the kitchen, finding his wife returning the unused picnic items to their places. She turned toward him, her eyes softening in compassion he did not want. "I'm so sorry about what happened. I'm glad you took us out from there. We—"

"I need to go down to the market," Samuel said. "The cold drinks got put in my brother's car."

"The market?" Cherise said. "We can do without cold drinks for an evening."

"I'll be back in twenty minutes." Samuel started toward the front door.

"You stay away from the park," Cherise said.

Samuel turned, glanced wryly at her, but said nothing as he walked to the door.

"You stay away from that park," she hollered more insistently.

It was there he directly drove, though without any particular intention. It was the memory of the flames and his voided sense of self that drew him. As he approached, he saw a few of his neighbors had stayed, others had come. They stood at a distance as the Klansmen began to leave the park. The robes and hoods were removed. Most wore black tee shirts and jeans. The blazing flames that had engulfed the crosses were now mere embers and flickers. Samuel parked his car and stood amid the silent onlookers. The Klansmen, in a close group, haughtily sauntered past them, then proceeded down the street to their vehicles.

A man standing among Samuel's group angrily called out to those around him. "Is it just okay?" The others looked but did not respond. "I said, is it just okay with all of us?" He held the attention of all in the crowd. The man walked several steps to the position of a rock, bent and took it in hand, and then with all his might cast it in the direction of the Klan. It landed short and skipped to the back of a boot. The Klansman turned.

Samuel glanced to the ground. A rock lay near where he stood. He looked away, afraid to throw it, but his eyes met those of an older man a bit farther from it, looking from the rock to him. Samuel looked back to the rock, bent down, and grasped it. He rose and hurled it with all his strength. They watched its flight to the center of the gathered Klansmen, striking one of the men on the shoulder. The others turned with the man and challengingly searched Samuel's crowd for the perpetrator. A tense moment passed as Samuel glared back stubbornly.

From the center of the Klansmen one of them ran slowly, hand at his side, directly toward Samuel. He stopped ten feet short, and the two men briefly faced each other. The Klansman had a jar in his hand, and he quickly thrust the contents into Samuel's face and chest. He smelled the pungent odor of urine.

Samuel ran in rage toward the Klansman, who scurried back into his group. Several quickly came forward holding clubs, and Samuel could not begin a retreat before he was surrounded. The Klansmen swung the clubs ferociously, striking Samuel on his legs and shoulders. As he slumped, he attempted to cover his head, but a man dressed in black repeatedly struck at him. Samuel fell to the ground, helplessly covering his head with his arms. Now, even the Klansmen stopped and watched as the man struck again with his club, hard upon Samuel's right forearm and the back of his skull. The assailant took a step back, raised his club in a triumphant gesture to his cohorts, and walked away.

Samuel lived, but he could no longer speak fluently or think as sharply. He never returned to work at the lumber mill. His son Marcus wept openly at the hospital, remained his constant companion, and never forgave himself for having chastised his father.

After reviewing witness statements, videotape, and photographs supplied by a surveillance unit of the Police Department, the District Attorney declined to file any criminal charges. He wiped perspiration from his forehead as he offered the media the official explanation. "First, the Klan demonstrators had the right to assemble in the park. That's freedom of assembly protected under the First Amendment. Second, the alleged victim was seen throwing pieces of concrete at demonstrators and then attacked a demonstrator. Other demonstrators who came to the defense of the man being attacked by the alleged victim acted in his defense. That's self-defense."

Chapter 2

Klansmen in the Night

(Twenty-five years later)

Frank stood only five-feet-six-inches tall, but the boots he always wore added another three. With swept-back blond hair and squinted brown eyes, he struck the pose of a man with a severe case of attitude. It was in his talk and in his walk, like a cowboy looking for the calf that just kicked him in the ass.

Silva was his last name, though it was rumored he had changed it from De Silva. His ancestors, he claimed, were recipients of a Spanish land grant, lost when Mexico won its independence from Spain in the 1820s. Frank was twenty-five years old, filling his resumé with odd jobs and short-term ambitions. The land he believed his ancestors once owned was now filled with people he resented, people who owned small businesses or drove nice cars or lived in homes better than his. Worse yet, they were people who didn't look like him, and for Frank that was a problem. On this chilly December night Silva hoped his metamorphosis would be complete. He would be accepted into a new society, a community not of residence, but of race.

His rebirth, and the proclamation of his commitment to the new society he longed for, would come this night through the ritual of the Ku Klux Klan cross-burning. He was gaining notoriety as the leader of a Klan "den." Now he sought a much-expanded role. The cross-burning ritual he orchestrated would be attended by national leaders of the white supremacist movement. He hoped to impress them, unite them, and solidify a growing Klan in California.

The cross-burning ritual became Klan tradition in the years following the post–Civil War reconstruction of the former Confederate states. The Klan was initially organized in response to opportunistic carpetbaggers, but when Southerners regained political and economic control of local government and commerce, a new enemy became the Klan's target. Its resentment of the social standing and the equality theoretically allowed the former slave population was the engine of Klan activity through the turn of the century.

Then came the Industrial Revolution. As immigrants came to the United States and competed for jobs, they too attracted the animosity of the Klan.

A succession of ethnic and religious groups roused the ire of the Klan—Catholics, then Jews, Asians, and Hispanics. Eventually, Klansmen found differences even among themselves, giving rise in the 1930s to neo-Nazi factions of predominant German ancestry, and "Aryan" factions in the 1970s, who favored membership of Northern European descendants. From these originated antitax and antifederal government groups, often in the form of militias. In the 1980s, as a generation gap developed within the neo-Nazi movement, the "skin-heads" came to be.

The aggregate of all these groups is identified with the phrase "white supremacist movement," but historically there has been no unifying leader or coordination of effort. This deprived the movement of national dimension, in both political organization and covert operation. Frank Silva recognized the need for unity. The guests and participants at his cross-burning ceremony would include leaders of several of the most prominant factions within the white supremacist movement. But word of their gathering had spread to their opposition.

"Death to the Klan" were the words spoken by a single, angry voice. The words were repeated; then other voices began to join. The cue for their chant was the arrival of a Los Angeles Police Department squad car with an unmarked police car immediately behind it. The crowd had been milling about in front of Silva's home for the past twenty minutes. A slight drizzle periodically dampened the ground.

Two uniformed officers stepped from the black-and-white vehicle. The first to exit, from the driver's side, was Sergeant John O'Neil. He was a big, burly Irish cop with a ruddy complexion and a voice like a gravel road. He looked first at the crowd, scanning for weapons. Then he turned toward the vehicle pulling to a stop behind his. He gave an affirmative, protective nod to the driver. From within the vehicle, Lieutenant Robinson courteously nodded back. He got out and stood for a moment with his hands in the pockets of his tan trench coat. The chant of the crowd had become increasingly louder since they stepped from their vehicles. Robinson walked alongside Sergeant O'Neil toward the front of the anti-Klan demonstrators.

The lieutenant was distracted by a tall, muscular, middle-aged man in the front of the crowd. Robinson pointed at him, then beckoned him over. As the man approached, the lieutenant addressed him in a determined but unemotional tone. "Fisher, I don't want any trouble here."

"You won't be getting any trouble from us," Irv Fisher said.

"As long as you and your people are here, there's the potential for big trouble," Robinson said. "Now beat it."

"You understand that the national leaders of the Ku Klux Klan are inside this house?"

"What I know is mixing you and them is my bad news. I'm gonna hold them to the letter of the law. If they light a cross, we'll make arrests. Understood? But I'm gonna hold you to the letter of the law, too. Right now your people are in the street. If a car slows down two miles an hour, I'll bust the whole damn bunch of you for obstructing traffic."

As Robinson spoke, twelve black-and-white patrol units pulled into position. Officers wearing riot helmets got out. Robinson turned again to Fisher. "Now, do you want my men controlling *your* group or the one inside that house?"

"You'll make arrests if they burn the crosses?" Fisher asked.

As Robinson looked away from Fisher, he saw the arrival of a CBS news van. He knew from experience that the presence of news reporters and cameras tended to complicate the diffusion of tensions. He then replied to Fisher. "You get out of this and stay out. I'll enforce the law."

With that, Fisher headed back to his car. His eyes met those of the news reporter standing beside his crew. He nodded acknowledgment. The reporter turned and quickly spoke to his cameraman, who focused on Fisher and his men. Fisher raised his fist shoulder high and began repeating, at first softly, "Death to the Klan." The others of his group joined in, with a tone increasingly vehement.

Then they left—all but one, a man in his midfifties of average size, but with a military stature and a short, graying beard. He got back out of his car and walked inconspicuously to the end of the block opposite the news crew. He stopped, took a tobacco pipe from the pocket of his full-length coat, struck a match, and lit it. After exhaling, he looked down the empty sidewalk and inhaled a deep breath of fresh air.

Lieutenant Robinson discreetly approached, stopping ten feet to his rear and facing the passing traffic. The bearded man turned, lit his pipe again, then spoke quietly, almost to himself.

"The news crew eliminates Intelligence Division alternatives three and four." He paused. "Have you spoken with Silva yet today?"

"No," Robinson said. "He didn't come to the station."

"Metzger and three of his boys cruised by for a look ten minutes ago." He exhaled a small cloud of smoke toward the bare branches of the tree above him. "Everyone's getting locked in." He struck another match, lit up, and strolled away.

Robinson crossed the street, approached O'Neil, and beckoned him to follow. They entered the chain-link gate of Silva's front yard, stepped to the house, and knocked authoritatively.

Silva opened the door, wearing a tan cowboy hat and red western shirt. He glared contemptuously at Robinson. The commotion of the dozen men gathered in the living room of the small stucco house quickly ceased. Silva stood in the middle of the doorway with his arms at his hips, waiting for Robinson to speak.

"Okay, Silva, where's the permit?"

"I have it right here." Silva pulled from his shirt pocket a folded paper and handed it to Robinson. As the lieutenant began to read, Silva turned his eyes to Sergeant O'Neil, shook his head, and smirked. O'Neil glared.

"This is for an open-pit barbecue, Silva. You're not covered," Robinson said sternly.

"It's a valid burn permit, Lieutenant, and this cross-lighting ceremony is part of my religious belief, and a constitutional right."

"Where's the cross? Let me see it."

"It's not here."

"Where are you planning to burn it?"

"Just where it says on the permit, sir."

Robinson looked down at the permit for the address: "11970 Kagel Canyon." He looked inquisitively to Sergeant O'Neil for the location.

"Sounds like the mouth of the canyon above Lake View Terrace," O'Neil said.

Robinson turned back toward Silva. "That's a black area of town. Just what kind of crap are you trying to pull?"

"We've rented out the parcel for today and tomorrow. Care to join us for some ribs?"

"Listen here, Silva. I've got some free advice for you and the can of sardines standing back there. Bring your bail money. These permits are no good, and if you burn any cross in this city between now and my retirement, I'll personally bust your ass. Understand?"

"I have to do what I have to do," Silva replied defiantly.

Darkness fell. The officers watched as a bright, shifting light was turned on and off inside the house, casting shadows against the drawn curtains. The front door to Silva's home opened. Out filed the men. One carried a long pickax handle. Others held baseball bats and table legs. They placed the objects in the rear of a red pickup truck parked in front of Silva's home. The source of the occasional bright light from within the home now became apparent. It was affixed to the top of a video camera held by a man in his late thirties, dressed in a red vest and a blue shirt. From the front yard of Silva's house he videotaped the officers. As the other Klansmen entered their cars, the cameraman and Silva remained behind.

"Hey, cut that light," O'Neil commanded. "You don't shine that light in my eyes. Got it?"

The cameraman quickly complied and put the camera to his side. O'Neil approached him, drew his flashlight, and made a point of shining it directly into his eyes. The man squinted and held his hand to shield the glare.

"Okay, sir, I understand."

"What's your name?"

"Peter Lawrence, sir." He looked not at all maniacal or disheveled; he didn't seem to O'Neil like he belonged among the Klan group.

"What are you doing here?" the sergeant said.

"I'm videotaping," stuttered the cameraman.

"I can see that. Why?"

The cameraman paused as Silva hurriedly approached. In his usual style, he took center stage and was quick to steal the lines of the other player. "He's not breaking any law here, officer. We're all on the same side here."

"Don't you be telling me whose side I'm on," O'Neil said as he leaned forward, imposing his massive frame over Silva.

Silva held his ground, chin up. "He's videotaping." Then he turned to Lawrence. "Maybe it's better to set your equipment down inside for a while, keep it out of the mist. Come on." Lawrence was relieved to be extricated from the confrontation.

The rest of the Klan party departed in their cars and began winding their way through Lake View Terrace, a semirural community of older ranch homes and new housing tracts above the San Fernando Valley. One of the hard-liners among them was Randy Evans. He appeared middle-aged, sporting a robust beer belly and a fair, reddish complexion that extended to the top of his head through thinning, blond hair. In fact, he was only twenty-seven.

As his vehicle stopped for a traffic light, Evans stuck his head out the driver's window of his red pickup and yelled to the van behind him. "I gotta get me some gas!"

The character driving the van behind Evans was Stanley Witek, the Director of the National Socialist Workers Party, more commonly known as the American Nazi Party. Witek, in his early fifties, was fully committed to the ideology of his hero, Adolf Hitler. He actually looked a bit like Hitler, except clean-shaven, taller, and a little heavier. This night he wore a jacket emblazoned with the motto "Deutschland Forever." So did several of the Party members with him. He rolled down his window and called back to Evans.

"What?"

"I gotta get me some gas."

"What?"

Frustrated by the communication failure, Evans pointed emphatically to the gas station across the street.

Witek sat back in his seat and shook his head disgustedly. "If Rommel led tank columns like Evans is leading this convoy, we would all be speaking Hebrew today."

A deep, heavy voice answered. "I figured him being friends with Frank, he would know this area. But I guess not." It was Canale. When Mike Canale spoke, they all listened. Not out of respect, but out of fear.

The five vehicles pulled into the gas station. Out the bed of the pickup truck extended three burlap-wrapped crosses, twelve to eighteen feet in length. As Evans stood pumping gas, a Chrysler pulled slowly up behind his truck and stopped at the set of pumps there. Out stepped an older black man.

Evans stood menacingly to the side, waiting for the man to see him. Surrounded by his comrades, he was eager to display his contempt. "Hey, Pops."

The man's eyes turned to Randy's.

"We're gonna have us a little barbecue. You wanna join us?"

Evans's wit won the laughter of a few compatriots. The man shook his head and glanced down at the asphalt. Evans gloated. He closed his gas tank lid and reentered the truck. The Klan convoy rolled toward its destination.

As they approached the cross-burning site, police vehicles pulled behind them. The Klansmen turned into the driveway of a residence at the mouth of Kagel Canyon. A long dirt path led down to a weathered wooden house. Trees surrounded it, concealing it from view. An empty field sloped downward from the back boundary. Beyond it was a large tract of relatively new homes, three to four bedrooms, with neat lawns dotted with palm and citrus trees. The neighborhood was predominantly black.

The residence nearest the Klan was that of Robert Gentry. Eight years earlier, he had moved from Georgia in search of a better life for his children. His Uncle Samuel was now passed away, but his cousin Marcus had also moved to Los Angeles. This evening, Robert Gentry finished dinner and helped his wife Tina with the dishes. He kissed their daughters goodnight, unaware the Ku Klux Klan had gathered only a hundred yards away.

A police helicopter circled against the backdrop of moonlit clouds, drawing the attention of curious onlookers, black and white. A rookie cop inside the chopper intently monitored the communication coming through his headphones, then yelled above the engine noise to the pilot, "The field commander wants us to light 'em up." Lieutenant Edward Fryke reached down and flicked the switch for the spotlight, then peered below as his young partner directed the beam on the Klansmen.

At the front of the property, L.A.P.D. officers assembled in full riot gear. The Klan unloaded its wares. The crosses in Evans's pickup were carried to the field by a short, muscular young man named Brad Riley.

"Hey, what's going on?" a middle-aged white resident asked. He realized the peace of their community was threatened. "We don't need this here."

Two of the Nazi Party members stepped forward. With heavy table legs in hand, they sneeringly appraised the man. He backed away.

Witek stood at the front of the driveway, a long pickax handle in one hand and a flashlight in the other. As cars approached he waived them in as he recognized the driver. Periodically, he walked over to the officers and shouted racial slurs aimed at blacks and Jews. He proclaimed the white working class would be brought together by the bond of its oppression, suffered upon them by what he called the "international Zionist conspiracy." He beseeched the riot-garbed officers to recognize their manipulation by the Jewish influence within their department.

"If we take this one in," remarked one officer, "we'll need a straitjacket instead of cuffs."

Checking arriving cars on the other side of the dirt driveway was Michael Canale. At six-feet-four and 250 pounds, with a heavy table leg in hand, he was a horrific figure. His face was broad, with almost no neck separating his chin and chest. He was revered by his Nazi friends for his fearlessness. Conrad Matlock, an old buddy from the Nazi group, sidled up to Canale, smiling uncomfortably as he tried to start a bit of small talk.

"You're going to like this one," Matlock said.

Canale looked at Matlock quizzically. "This ain't no different, Matty. It's just the same old shit."

"I mean the fire, man. We're gonna light up the sky. They got three big crosses back there, bigger than the house. Man, when they go up," Matlock shook his head wistfully, "it's gonna be beautiful."

"Get back there, Conrad. They're gonna need protection from the southwest corner," Canale said curtly.

"Aren't you coming around back?" Matlock said.

"Yeah, I'm coming. I just gotta get my ass outta here before they light the crosses, so I don't get burned on my parole."

"Oh, yeah. Not allowed within a hundred yards of matches without adult supervision." Matlock chuckled at his own humor, then stopped when he saw Canale's cold, implacable expression. "Hey, man, I'm just joking."

"I did the time," Canale said. "It was a long time. There are people who have yet to pay for how long it was."

Matlock took two steps back as his uncomfortable smile faded. Then he turned and walked quickly away.

A dark blue Mercedes driven by Peter Lawrence pulled to a stop between Witek and Canale. Witek bent down to speak to the passenger, Frank Silva.

"Hey, Frank. Riding in style. Don't worry, Pete. We know you actually own this vehicle. It just *looks* like you're the chauffeur." A green Oldsmobile station wagon pulled in behind the Mercedes, and Witek turned to check it out. "Hey, look what the cat brought home. Are my eyes deceiving me, or is Mr. Metzger going to join in the festivities? Couldn't you guys squeeze him into the Mercedes? He's riding in Winston's junker."

Silva's eyes flashed at Witek. "I said he'd be here tonight, didn't I? Every major leader of the movement is here tonight. Where do you have the pastor?"

"He's inside," Witek said.

"Keep him out of public view," Silva said. "He's a security risk. Where's Tate?"

"Tate doesn't leave his side. Neither does Bentley. They're like Siamese triplets."

"Tate's a quick trigger. He's a backwoods boy who could lose his cool in this environment and freak out. Keep him away from the heat."

"Aye, Captain."

"He's a quick trigger," said Lawrence. "I'll attest to that."

"Come on, park it over there." Canale tapped his table leg on the hood of the Mercedes and pointed to an empty space at the far side of the lot. "You got Metzger sitting back there in Winston's junker. It's bad for his image." Lawrence looked to Silva for approval, who nodded his consent.

Up pulled the Oldsmobile. Canale positioned his massive frame across its path, the table leg at his side. As the vehicle stopped, he stepped to the open front-passenger window and bent down, resting his hands on his knees.

Canale smiled. "Well Mr. Metzger, what a pleasure it is to have you with us tonight."

Metzger looked at Canale, then looked away. His lips pursed together, then he calmly spoke. "What's that you have in your hand, Michael?"

"Batman was hoping we'd have a piñata tonight." Canale looked over to Witek, who broke into a broad smile.

"Yeah, I was," Witek said. He and Canale chuckled.

Metzger smiled patiently and shook his head disapprovingly. He looked back at Canale. "Did you happen to see the two dozen policemen standing along the street?"

"Yeah, I seen 'em," Canale said.

"Well, I'm telling you, these table legs you have could be construed as billy clubs, which is a felony violation. You really ought to be more careful, Michael." Metzger smiled and shook his head again. "Especially with him." He indicated Witek with a nod. "He'd use it."

Lieutenant Robinson walked the length of the property on Kagel Canyon Road with a walkie-talkie in hand. He stopped and looked down a trail along the eastern boundary, then turned to Sergeant O'Neil, who was a couple of steps behind.

"Take twelve men and form a skirmish line on this side. We'll have six men and four patrol units in the driveway. Keep the firemen behind their trucks and off the property until I give the signal for them to move in. And that won't be until we've secured the property and cuffed all suspects. Tell Hanson to keep traffic moving along this road. No spectators. Shut it down the moment the fire is lit. Freeman is going to have to get down into that shrub on the south side with a couple of men and make sure no one passes. I don't want anyone coming up the hill. Keep everyone out. From this point on, no one enters."

"Got it," O'Neil said. "Hey, Hanson," he called, walking toward him to convey the lieutenant's orders.

A scratchy communication from Officer Sanchez in the circling helicopter began to come through the lieutenant's walkie-talkie. "We're beginning to get some activity in the backyard. Do you read me, Lieutenant? Over."

"Yeah, Sanchez. What have you got? Over."

"A suspect in a cowboy hat and red checkered shirt, with the sleeves rolled up to the elbow. Blue jeans. Boots. Over."

"That's Silva. What's his activity? Over."

"He's got two five-gallon red canisters that he's transported to the rear of the property. There are three large crosses lying on the ground. Now he's pouring the contents of one can onto one cross. Must be gasoline. He's got the other one now. Pouring it. Suspect one, Silva, now being assisted by two additional suspects. Suspect two appears to be tall, dressed all in black, long dark hair, white male. Suspect three, average height and build, a red jacket, white male. All three are lifting what appears to be a large cross. It's wrapped in something. Looks like some kind of material or fabric. It's big. Estimate fifteen to eighteen feet in length. The cross section is approximately eight feet in width. Okay. They've got it upright in the ground. Over."

"I want your spotlight on it. Are you okay to come down a little lower? Over." Officer Sanchez conferred with the pilot, Lieutenant Fryke. "Do you read, Sanchez? Over."

"This is Lieutenant Fryke. We have a potential problem with the trees on the north side, and we're getting some swirling winds I can feel pulling on us a bit. I can take it down only about another twenty-five feet or so. But I'm already holding as low a pattern as I can. Over."

"Just let them know we're watching them. Over."

"This is Sanchez. The suspects have lifted the second cross and set it in the ground. Suspects one, two, and three now lifting the third cross. They are really struggling. Got it up. Several other suspects are present, one with a video camera on a shoulder mount appears to be taping. He's got his own light on. They've got all three crosses up now. That last one was big."

Three Los Angeles city fire trucks began moving into position curbside at the front of the property.

As time passed, the officers' anticipation grew. Few of them could see any portion of the backyard where earlier movement had been reported by the air support. The chopper continued to circle overhead. Most of the Klansmen remained inside the small, wooden house. Rumor spread among the officers that one of the suspects was a recent congressional candidate.

Robinson watched what he could from the east boundary where the skirmish line was formed. Suddenly, a bright light shone at them from a distance and bounced with the stride of the person holding it.

The light grew brighter, and the officers shined their

flashlights in return. Two figures became identifiable. Officer Kline turned disdainfully to Sergeant O'Neil. "It's that same guy with the camera again."

"Son of a bitch," O'Neil said. "I told him to keep that goddamned light the hell out of our faces."

The light came closer, then stopped about thirty feet away. Two men stood by it. Peter Lawrence was holding the camera with its light attachment on his shoulder. Next to him was Stanley Witek.

The camera scanned the officers. When the light shut down and the two men disappeared from view, each of the officers jokingly volunteered for the assignment of arresting the cameraman.

Robinson resumed discussion with O'Neil. "We need to take everyone at the same time. If we arrest two or three for individual acts, we leave ourselves unable to secure the whole scene. Word is there are weapons inside the house. I don't want my men struggling with arrests outside until we can go in and secure the house."

O'Neil pensively looked back at Robinson. "So far we've got three or four on possession of clubs. We know the address on the permits is wrong, so we got some kind of providing false information to the fire department. Whoever lights the cross gets an illegal burning."

Robinson listened for a moment to O'Neil, but then interrupted. "We can't do it that way, Jack. We've got two of them going out days in advance and securing misleading permits. We got another few barricading the front driveway and standing around with clubs. There's the guy who lives here allowing it, and everybody gathering here. We gotta go with a conspiracy charge to violate the fire codes. If we arrest for conspiracy, that means everybody goes at the same time. We wait until they ignite the crosses."

"I like it," O'Neil said after a short pause. He shook his head once and gritted his teeth. "It may be a difficult one to get filed. At least on some of these dimwits."

"I'm less worried right now about some prosecutor filing charges than I am about fanatics holed up with shotguns watching the grand tomato get taken down. The D.A. can do whatever he sees fit. And I'm sure he will."

The scratchy, amplified static indicated the renewal of a helicopter communication. "This is Observer Sanchez in air support. Ground command, do you read?"

"This is Robinson. Go ahead, Sanchez."

"We have some new activity originating from inside the house. Coming out through a door on the southeast side of the structure, approximately twelve to fourteen adult male Caucasians. We've got a few wearing robes and hoods. I can't see their faces, but under the circumstances I would think a description as male Caucasians is accurate. One wearing a red robe. One robe is black. Some are in white robes. Looks like a small fire has been set at the northwest corner of the lot."

"How small?"

"Looks like just a ground fire in maybe some type of cooking apparatus. Could be a barbecue. Hard to tell from here. Pretty smoky. Over."

"No crosses, though, right?" Robinson said.

"No, sir. No crosses." There was a short pause before Sanchez's next words. "We've got a suspect standing up by what appears to be a podium, looking like he's making a speech. He's waving his arms around. Same guy who was driving the pickup with the crosses. Wearing a checked shirt, looks like blue ski pants and a blue vest. Over."

"Do you see any weapons? Over."

"Well, I've been making out some possible rifles held down by the sides of a few of the suspects. Could be long clubs. It would be hard to see a barrel from up here. Over."

"Let me know if you get a confirmation on that, okay? Over." Robinson turned to O'Neil, who stood silently beside him, listening. "When it's time to go in, we all go at the same time. Secure the house. Okay?"

"I'm going in there personally," O'Neil said.

The winds began to pick up. Fallen leaves swirled on the street. Passing motorists slowed to view the police activity. Officers waved them along. Still, a crowd of neighborhood residents formed along Kagel Canyon Road, and as it grew in number, people began to edge forward for a better look.

A second, even larger crowd was gathering at the south side of the adjacent empty lot, a hundred yards from the Klan assembly. The residents watched in shock as the Klansmen stood before the three towering crosses. The moonlight gleamed on their white robes and hoods, which moved in and out of shadows cast by the hillside foliage. Occasionally, the spotlight from the helicopter above highlighted robed and hooded Klansmen.

"I'm gonna tell my dad," a young boy said as he ran from the crowd of residents back toward his home. Robert Gentry peered from his bedroom window, first down at his neighbors, then across the empty field. The helicopter spotlight illuminated the Klansmen standing beside a tall cross. His wife stood behind him. A moment later, he heard the footsteps of both his daughters entering their room.

"I'm going down to see what all the commotion is about."

"Robert, stay here with your family," his wife said. "Now is not a good time for you to be leaving. The girls are up. I need you here to keep things under control."

Robert Gentry glanced at his wife, sensing her fear. Recalling the burning cross twenty-five years earlier in Georgia and the tragic beating of his Uncle Samuel, he felt compelled to go beyond the safety of his home. "It's never been a good time. But it's never been a better time than now." He grabbed a jacket and joined his neighbors.

The young boy was returning now, pulling his dad along. It was Charles Walker, the man who earlier that afternoon encountered the Klan at the gas station. He had not yet told even his wife about the confrontation so near home. He found a clear view of the Klansmen at the same moment as Robert Gentry. They knew each other from occasional conversation and PTA meetings.

"What the hell are they doing up there?" Gentry said, knowing but no less stunned.

"Those must be the same fellas I saw over at the Shell station around sunset. Told me they were gonna have a barbecue. Asked me if I wanted to come. I saw the crosses in his pickup. I knew what they were up to."

Charles's wife called to their son across the street. "Boy, you come down from there. And bring your father."

"Aw, Mom, do I have to? You can't see as good from there."

"You get down here now!"

The boy turned to his father. "Do I have to, Dad?"

"You do as your mother tells you, son. Go on." The boy left. Charles watched as his wife wrapped her arms around the boy, still complaining and campaigning to be allowed to rejoin his father and Mr. Gentry. Charles turned back to Robert and spoke softly. "They're gonna burn those crosses up there. Burn 'em for all to see."

"No, they're not," answered Gentry in an unmistakable tone. The image of his Uncle Samuel lying battered and bruised in a hospital bed following the Klan attack filled his mind as he gazed toward the assembly. "God as my witness. They're not burning any crosses in this neighborhood. This is where we live."

A yellow flame began to creep up the base of first one, then another of the crosses. The fire then extended outward as it met the horizontal beam, still continuing upward to the top of the cross. The third cross was lit. Whoops and hollers emanated from the Klan party. A Confederate flag unfurled and flapped chaotically in the hot wind thrown off by the flames.

Robert looked at Charles, then spoke with resolve. "That's enough. I'm going up." He began ascending the slope between their position and the burning crosses.

"What are you gonna do?" Charles said. "What are you gonna do?" As Gentry made his way through the waist-high brush, Charles heard no answer. "Wait! I'm coming, too" he hollered.

The police helicopter continued to circle above the jubilant Klansmen. "This is Sanchez in air support. Come in ground command. Over."

"This is ground command. Go ahead, Sanchez," Lieutenant Robinson said.

"We have all three crosses lit and in flames, sir. Over."

"Okay. Give me another ten minutes up there. No chases. Keep an eye on the structure. Over and out."

Robinson reattached the walkie-talkie to his belt clip, then looked toward the driveway. "Bell," he called. As the sergeant looked up, Robinson waved his arm and pointed toward the backyard.

"Let's go," Bell hollered to his men, and six officers moved quickly down the east side pathway toward the back lot.

Robinson turned to O'Neil. "Okay, Jack, hit it!"

O'Neil ran twenty yards to the back side of the residence, with two officers alongside. In one motion as he approached the door, he raised his right foot and placed his next step solidly beside the doorknob with a crushing thrust. The wooden door and door jam exploded under the force of O'Neil's boot. On the other side of the small living room stood Ron Major, the tenant of the property. He was a big man, about six-feet-three-inches, in his early forties. There were streaks of gray in his long beard. He wore leather pants and a sleeveless tee shirt, exposing a collection of tattoos on his arms. "Hold it right there, friend." O'Neil raised his .38-caliber revolver, leveled between Major's eyes, then motioned to Officer Cable. "Cuff him." The sergeant called to Officer Janss. "Come on with me. Confiscate all weapons." They glided skillfully through each room of the house.

The officers from the skirmish line scrambled down the east side of the property. They saw three large columns of smoke billowing up the throat of the canyon. The spectacle of orange blazes, partially obscured by trees, became clearer with each step through the heavy brush. Flames wrapped around the limbs of each cross. An odor like gasoline, but a bit sweeter, pervaded the air. Intense heat replaced the chill. Long orange and yellow flames reached ten feet from the tops of the crosses, like devilish hands grabbing at the floor of heaven. A man in a black satin robe, hood, and mask with a red satin sash draped from his shoulders stood behind swirls of smoke, facing the officers.

Lieutenant Robinson suspected who this was. He had not seen Frank Silva anywhere else, and it was Silva that Robinson most wanted to find. Simmons grabbed the arms of the masked man, pulled them behind his back, and clamped the cuffs on his wrists. Matches dropped from the Klansman's left hand. His mask remained in place.

Robinson walked over and put his fingers to the top of the masked man's pointed hood. "Hello, Frank." He then lifted the hood, exposing Silva's face.

"Thank you," Silva said. "Now I can see the crosses better."

"You're not a good listener, Silva."

"Just a man of my word, sir."

Robinson nodded his head. "I'm a man of my word, too."

Peter Lawrence was still taping the action when Officer Kline pulled the camera from his grasp. He threw it down an embankment near the burning crosses. "Now, where're my cuffs?" He reached into his utility-belt cuff case and with the ease of a rodeo rider removed them, flung them open, spun Lawrence around, and slapped the cuffs shut on his wrists.

Kline jumped down the embankment, landing with the heel of his boot directly into the side of the video camera. "How'd this get here?" he mockingly said, then stepped hard on it again with his other boot. "Somebody's gonna trip on this."

Sergeant Freeman and six patrol officers entered the

west side of the property. "Take the one getting out of the robe." He pointed toward Richard Butler. Freeman turned, reached for Tate's arms, grabbed him, and pulled down. "Get down. Down I said." Tate looked to Butler, offering no resistance. He submitted to Freeman's second tug.

The others, too, were forced to their knees, arms pulled behind their backs, and wrists cuffed. The flames whipped and extended now even higher, desperately reaching to the heavens. "Bring in the fire department," Robinson said.

Robert Gentry and Charles Walker continued up the sloping hillside, running where they could, now half winded. Perspiration ran down Gentry's brow. As he wiped his forehead with his shirt sleeve, his vision blurred. The crosses, twenty-five yards ahead, dared him closer. All his senses were captured by the conflagration. In his narrow, focused trance he stepped closer, unaware of the young man, a swastika painted on his forehead and table leg in hand, eagerly lying in wait.

"Freeze!"

Gentry was startled. He turned abruptly toward the direction of the call.

"Down on your knees!"

The man awaiting Gentry dropped the heavy table leg. The officer who barked the commands grabbed the man by the arm, pulled back, then pushed down, sending him to the ground.

The firemen aimed a steady stream of water at the crosses until the last flame flickered out. Los Angeles Fire Captain John Stillson pushed with his boot on the charred remnants of the burlap-wrapped four-by-fours. He pushed again harder until the crosses dropped to the ground with a heavy thud, branding the ground with the imprint of the crosses. The arrestees were transported to the L.A.P.D. Foothill Division, booked for conspiracy, and released after posting bail.

Chapter 3

Power of the Cross

I was born in Brooklyn, New York, in 1954. My family moved to Los Angeles when I was eight years old, but I still dreamed of playing center field for the Yankees until a high school southpaw threw me hard sliders quicker than my bat. He became a successful pitcher for the Baltimore Orioles. I became a criminal prosecutor for the Los Angeles city attorney's office.

Monday began its usual way, with me driving four levels below the streets of downtown into an exhaust-filled parking structure. I breathed a sigh of relief when the elevator doors opened to the seventeenth floor of Los Angeles City Hall.

"Hey, John." I was greeted by Tom Andrews, a competent young prosecutor with the office two years now. "Congratulations on getting a conviction on that assault trial. I heard about your beef with Sachs. He would have rather just given it away on a cheap plea bargain, the lazy piece of shit."

We laughed and walked toward our office. I saw Sachs alone at his desk. He was one of the senior prosecutors in the office of the Los Angeles city attorney. Once, he too tried cases. Now he manned the calendar court, where cases went after arraignment in hope of resolution before being set for trial. As I walked past him I waited to say a good morning—not particularly because I wished he had one, but merely to be civil. He did not look up. Conspicuous inattention, I thought, and passed him by.

Andrews walked over to Sachs's desk. "Sachs," he said in a sweet, inquisitive tone, "how do you explain the verdict in that sexual assault trial last week?"

"Big damn deal. He didn't testify. Juries always convict when the defendant takes the Fifth."

"Don't get uptight, Sachs; stay cool. At least you have good backup in the trenches," Andrews said.

"I don't need your backup or anyone else's. You just watch your own rear." He glared at Andrews, who shook his head and walked on.

I was slightly annoyed to see that my desk appeared as though someone had sat there reading a newspaper. It was left open, neatly folded to the bottom half of the second page. As I set my briefcase down, the lead article caught my attention: "D.A. Refers Klan Cross-Burning for City Attorney Prosecution."

A special unit of deputy district attorneys in the civil unrest division had decided over the weekend not to file felony charges on a Klan triple cross-burning in north-central Los Angeles. The matter was being referred to the City Attorney's Office for consideration of filing misdemeanor charges, which was the extent of our jurisdiction Representatives of the NAACP and other community groups were highly critical of the decision. District Attorney Robert Philobosian defensively explained his rationale. The head city attorney, Ira Reiner, pledged a fully committed prosecution.

I creased the newspaper around the border of the cross-burning article, tore it out, folded it, and tucked it into my shirt pocket. When I looked up, my eyes naturally made contact with the only ones watching me. It was Sachs. He smiled uncomfortably, raised his hand in a wave hello, and looked down at a file on his desk.

Moments later, a discussion among several veteran deputies near my desk became increasingly heated. Pam Johnston and Henry Stone seemed somewhat on the defensive. They had seniority in the office, and were entrusted with determining the filings of cases for our downtown branch office. Each stood with arms folded, facing two attorneys in our pretrial unit.

What made this conversation unusual was the presence of two appellate attorneys. Their faces were rarely seen in the trial unit, unless a more esoteric point of law had come into play. They listened to the exchange, as did the supervisor of the trial section, Constance Moore.

"All I'm saying is I wouldn't file a case unless I would be willing to try it myself. I'm not a politician."

Stone raised his voice defensively in response. "I didn't file it. He wanted to know what charges could be filed, and we told him."

Pam came to Stone's assistance, "Ira filed it himself. He signed the complaint."

"Who? Reiner?" Paul said in surprise.

"Yes, Reiner," Pam said.

"Well, then that's another mistake. The city attorney himself never files a case, especially one with political overtones. You mean his signature is actually on the bottom of the complaint?"

"Right there," Pamela said. "We told him outright we didn't want our names on it because of all the problems. You can't just assign a case like this. Someone's got to agree to take it. If no one wants it and we told Reiner we agreed with the filing, one of us would get stuck with it."

"You told him outright you wouldn't sign the complaint?" Paul dropped his tone. "You just really messed yourself up."

"He'll be elected D.A.," said Pamela. "I'm still going to be here and so will this case. I don't want to be stuck with it."

"Well, maybe it's not such an albatross," Constance said. "After all, it *is* the Ku Klux Klan. They're not going to generate much sympathy."

"That's a point. They're despicable," replied Howard, not immediately realizing he had left himself open as the next candidate. I smiled, still at my desk, anticipating the obvious. Sure enough, Constance looked to Howard.

"You want to take it?"

He reflected only a moment. "I'm Jewish. I can't take this case. The Klan hates the Jews. They'll say I took it for personal reasons."

"Well, then it's obvious what we need," Paul said jestingly. "We can't have an attorney who's Jewish do it. We can't have an attorney who's black do it. And we can't have an attorney who's heard of the First Amendment do it."

Unable to pass up such a straight line, I called over to them from where I sat. "The First what?" All but one of my coprosecutors laughed.

"The First Amendment," Webster, the appellate intellectual, politely called back.

"Oh, that. Well, the first amendment I add to my garden soil is generally steer manure." Even Webster laughed at that line, but when it was over, I noticed Constance was just looking at me, waiting to pop the question. As the other prosecutors left for court, she came to my desk. In her sweetest voice she inquired, "I had you in mind from the start, John. You want to just read the report and see what you think?"

"I can't take that case. I'm already too busy with the chronic offender unit I'm trying to run."

"It's a challenging case, John. A lot of very interesting issues."

"I'm sorry, Connie. Can't take it." I picked up the files I needed that afternoon and headed to our records section.

I was directing a repeat-offender program. My caseload was heavy. How could Constance seriously think I had the time for some multidefendant quagmire? It wasn't a case for one attorney anyway. Probably the best move would be two trial attorneys, another from pretrial, and one from appellate all working together on it.

How many arrestees were there anyway? I remembered the folded article in my shirt pocket. I set the case files down and reached into my pocket for the article. As I pulled it out, I felt the weight of a small, heavier object caught inside, but before my other hand could grab it, it fell to the floor.

It was the crucifix my father had given me a few nights before. It had been his mother's and on her death was passed to him as the oldest son. When he handed it to me, he clasped his hands around mine and told me his mother had prayed holding it in times of special need. Perhaps I was less sentimental, but the cross was not so meaningful to me. I didn't remember having brought it with me that day. I must have scooped it up with the change on my dresser. I reached down and picked it up gently from the floor, making sure it had not been damaged.

No, that couldn't have been it. I always put my change in my pants pocket. I must have left the cross in the shirt I was wearing a few nights before when my dad gave it to me. I looked at it closely. It was beautifully crafted. So small, and yet the finest detail of the face of Jesus was visible. I noticed for the first time the marks at the hands and feet and in his side. A crown of thorns was etched across his forehead. I placed it back in my pocket, sat down, and unfolded the article.

Fifteen arrestees, including a former Democratic nominee for a congressional seat in the San Diego area, a man by the name of Tom Metzger. He was also the former Grand Dragon of the Ku Klux Klan in California.

A few other arrestees were also from the San Diego area. Three were from Idaho. Others were from areas scattered throughout California. Only two of the arrestees were locals. Three crosses, up to twenty feet in height, burned in a predominantly black residential area. Two rifles and heavy blunt striking instruments were recovered from the grounds and residence of the cross-burning site.

I went about my business, but my imagination kept returning to an eerie vision of a robed and hooded Klan. It was haunting and evil. The Klan delighted in burning the symbol of Jesus' sacrifice. Then, I saw him walking, struggling beneath the weight of the cross. Blood dripping from the thorns at his forehead. They stood about him, celebratively mocking, laughing as he dropped to a knee.

"What are you looking for, Mr. Phillips?" a sweet Texas drawl inquired.

"Oh. I just needed a file."

"You sure you're feeling all right?"

"I'm fine. Thank you."

"I'm sorry. I didn't mean anything by it. You just looked a little pale. Maybe like you just seen a ghost."

"No. I'm fine." I felt, though, as if I had just awakened from a dream. "Here it is. Thanks, Kathy. I have all I need."

When I returned to my desk I noticed a file sitting atop the stack of other papers with a handwritten note stapled to the front. "Please, just read it. Thanks. Constance."

The afternoon passed too slowly for a man waiting to become a father, and Diane was having some difficulty with her first pregnancy. We were fourteen when we first met, freshmen in high school. I don't recall speaking to her regularly until our junior year, but I had always admired her long, radiant blond hair, blue eyes, and soft features. Diane was my image of perfection, as charming and sweet as she was beautiful. We began dating two years after graduating high school and married a week after I finished law school. She was now eight months pregnant with our first child.

Her obstetrician told her to spend the last two weeks resting as much as possible. I was anxious in my drive home to see her. I stepped quietly through the door of our small, two-bedroom house, anticipating that she may be sleeping. The radio was on—she was probably dreaming peacefully. I opened the door of our bedroom, and there she was dancing by herself to a song on the radio.

"What are you doing?" My question startled her.

"What does it look like I'm doing?" she demanded indignantly.

"You're dancing."

"Look at this thing bouncing around." With both hands she held her stomach from beneath. "He was kicking, so I'm rocking him to sleep."

I struck the pose of a bowler who had just scored a needed strike and then froze my follow-through. "All right!" I said.

"What are you doing?" Diane looked quizzically at me.

"It's a boy," I said.

"It is?"

"What do you mean, 'It is?' You said '*he*' was kicking you, so you were rocking '*him*' to sleep. You must know something."

Diane just looked at me, expressionless.

"The doctors must have told you *something*," I said.

"Yeah. They told me you were a nut."

I straightened up from my bowling pose. "Well, then why did you say 'he'?"

"No girl would have kicked me like that." She walked out of the bedroom.

I struck my bowler pose again and said softly, but with emphasis, "*Yes.*"

Diane came back into the bedroom carrying a load of clean laundry. She dumped it on the bed and began to fold. I pulled off my tie, changed into warm jeans and sweatshirt fresh from the dryer, and began to help.

"Oh, could you be sure that blue shirt I just took off gets into the wash this time?"

"Sure." Diane said. She looked over to the shirt. "What do you mean '*this* time'?"

"I wore it twice without a wash. Saturday over to my folks, and again today."

"That shirt right there? No. I washed that shirt Sunday morning with all the colored things."

"No, actually, I found something in the shirt pocket today at work I had left in there from my folks."

"What, silverware?"

"The crucifix my dad gave me. You know, from his mother."

"Oh yeah, very pretty. No, that wasn't left in your shirt."

We continued to fold the laundry. Neither of us spoke for half a minute. She wasn't right, I thought, and it bothered me for some odd reason. "When I was at work today, the cross came falling out of my pocket. I know I didn't bring it with me. The shirt got hung up without being washed. It's no big deal."

"John," Diane said, slightly annoyed but with an air of triumph, "remember the sauce spot, Mr. Messy Eater, right over the pocket? I put cold water on it and rubbed it out with a little soap, then put it straight into the wash."

I walked over to where I had tossed the shirt on the dresser, then looked back at Diane. "Is there any portion of your testimony that you'd like to change, Mrs. Phillips, before the court examines the evidence?" She folded her arms and looked back, rather confidently.

I examined the shirt, expecting to find the sauce stain intact, and then looked closer, somewhat in disbelief.

"The defense rests," she said. "Motion to non-suit the People, Your Honor."

I handed her the suit I'd worn that day. "Motion granted. No starch, please."

But the levity of our debate made the presence of the cross no less perplexing.

During dinner, my mind wandered to the Klan file Connie had asked me to read. Before I finished eating, I began to review the police report, to Diane's surprise. After dinner I sat on the couch with the file. Diane sat across from me, reviewing a music book for one of her students. I gave the Klan file my most critical look, at least for a first reading. I closed the file and dropped it to the coffee table. "I can't take this case."

"Why don't you want it?" Diane said.

"I didn't say I didn't want it, but the way they filed it is all messed up. They've got all kinds of charges in here. A lot of them don't seem to apply. It's like they didn't know why it's wrong for the Ku Klux Klan to burn crosses. The Klan came to that community to terrorize black residents. That's wrong. The attorneys who first handled this should have just filed an unlawful assembly, illegal fires, and conspiracy."

"Well, you could change that if you took the case."

"I just can't take it. Time is already tight enough, and it's a mess. The evidence against some of them looks quite thin. I want it, though. It's just that it would bog down the rest of my caseload. Too bad. The Ku Klux Klan burning crosses. Imagine that, burning three huge crosses right in the city of Los Angeles, above a black residential community. I mean, what are they trying to start, a race war or what?"

"Sounds like what you always wanted, to prosecute a case like this," Diane said.

"What?"

"Well, what did you learn in our high school chemistry class?"

"I got a 'C' in chemistry. The only thing I learned was that there was a chemistry between you and me."

"No. I mean about yourself. What did you say you wanted to do? To be a prosecutor, right? To prosecute something evil. 'Pure evil,' you said."

I did not respond to her. Instead, I wondered if I was perhaps a step removed from the ideals that had led to my choice of occupation.

"This is the thing that you do better than anything else. Remember what you used to say about how God judges us? Could this be your big test? Is it your Judgment Time?" she asked.

The following morning I got to work a bit before the rest of them. I eased into my chair and stared at the stack of files before me. I opened the first of them and unfolded a rap sheet. Pages and pages of it fell out on continuous-feed computer paper. It was a typical defendant in the unit I was directing.

Other deputies passed by, offering morning greetings. As I mulled through the fifth or sixth file, enough of my coworkers had arrived to convene the usual meeting of the coffee club. You knew when the gossip started by the whispers and snickers. I didn't like to engage in it, but I sure liked to hear it.

"Have they gotten anyone to take that case yet?" Pam said.

"The Klan case?" Sachs said. "I hope Reiner has to take it himself. He filed it. He ought to try it."

"Hey, there's an election coming up. Don't give him any ideas," Frank said.

"Right. Just as long as he can start it before election day and finish it after."

"Oh, you're not saying the filing of this case was politically motivated," Jack said.

"So what if it is political?" my young friend Andrews said. "Is it a good case?"

"Andrews, you need say no more," Sachs said. "Quick, someone get Ira on the phone." He turned back to Andrews and addressed him more seriously. "It's got First Amendment problems that would make Thomas Jefferson turn in his grave. Plus, the principal witness is an observer in a police helicopter. He's spinning around up there and can't hear a single spoken word. I've done chopper cases. They can't make the identifications. Besides, we need those Klan guys. They balance things."

A few rows of desks away sat Bill Coleman, a heavyset black prosecutor in his early forties who had been with our office long enough to know whom he didn't like, and why. He didn't like Sachs. "You're right, we do need those guys," Bill said. "If we didn't have them, you'd be working weekends here."

"Hey, man, those guys are too liberal for me," Sachs sarcastically replied. "They burned crosses. Big damn deal. When they start burnin' churches is when I'd give a shit."

"You call it a big damn deal?" Coleman stood up. "Why, you're wet behind the ears. The message it sends is that no law-abiding citizen, not woman nor child, is safe in that neighborhood after dark if the color of their skin is black. You don't see what a burning cross says to the people living in that neighborhood?"

"That's just it. What it '*says*' is free speech." Sachs turned to the other deputies to ensure they noticed his score in the argument. "Maybe freedom of speech shouldn't exist when we don't agree with the speaker. Who's going to decide, Bill, you or me? How about if we take turns? I'll decide Mondays, Wednesdays, Fridays, and we trade off weekends. Or how about if everybody just has to shut up altogether on Sundays? That's it. I decide on Mondays, Wednesdays, and Fridays. You take Tuesdays, Thursdays, and Saturdays. We all just shut up on Sundays. Is that the way you want it, Bill, we all shut up on Sundays?"

Sachs froze his pose, hands raised chest high, staring belittlingly at the only black deputy in the group. Coleman glared back.

"I'm not sure that Bill would want that, Sachs, you all shutting up on Sundays. I think your wife would like it, though," I said.

A burst of laughter eased the tension. Sachs turned to me, no doubt feeling upstaged. "Okay, Phillips, you got lucky with the pervert who took the Fifth. So now you think you know the First Amendment, too. I don't see you jumping at this case. Go ahead and tell him. Tell him you think it's a piece of shit, too. He's a big boy. He can take it."

He stood waiting for my response. It was a question rather than an answer that came to mind. "How is it, Sachs, that you know so much about this case?"

"Well, don't be offended, Mr. Phillips, but when deputies in this office have problems, it's often me they come to rather than you. I gained the inside track on this case right from the start. Reiner insisted that it be filed. The charges they alleged were the very best that I could find."

"That *you* could find?"

"Indeed," Sachs said.

"Well, what's all this garbage about inciting to riot, failing to disperse, burning in a mountain fire zone?"

"Because those were the only charges to allege they did."

"What was it that you didn't read, Sachs? The laws or the reports?"

"I can't make a round peg fit into square holes. No one can. What would you have filed, hotshot? Nothing other, or nothing at all?"

"I would start with 'unlawful assembly.' That's what it is," I said.

"Shows how little you know. For more than a hundred years the Ku Klux Klan has been lighting crosses in just this fashion and never once has it been established that this is an unlawful assembly. They go to Mount Rushmore every year and light crosses in just this way."

"I don't give a damn," I said. "At least not to dictate what I would do. The Klan burned these crosses to terrorize people living around there. An unlawful assembly is what it is."

"Excuse me," Sachs said, "but this is Los Angeles. The state capitol is Sacramento. If you want to pass a new law, maybe that's where you need to go."

"You know, Sachs, I was up last night thinking about this case. I was up really late. I was trying to find the real reason why I wanted this case so bad. I came up with a lot of reasons. Some professional, some moral. Then finally I just said to myself, 'Hey, if I don't take this case, who's gonna take it?' because I knew you were just going to sit around here all week and try to embarrass everybody out of doing what you knew you could never do. So that's why I've got the file right here, Sachs. And you want to know something?" I leaned toward him and lowered my voice. "I'm going to win."

Chapter 4

Evidence and Inference

Matt Gillis was working at the jail arraignment division that morning. We often worked together on cases I took into our repeat-offender program. He was a good man, a Vietnam vet who spent the first eighteen months in the military learning the Vietnamese language. It wasn't so that he could order in style for the brass at the Cong Hilton. Matt was trained to be an interrogator, and practiced his trade, I'm sure, with the same determination he often showed in court. He stood six-feet-four with a round, bearded face and little granny glasses. He spoke with a slight Oklahoma twang. He was mistrusted by some public defenders and disliked by some judges, but all knew to take him seriously. His friends—and there were a lot of these—saw the gentler side. I telephoned, hoping to lure him in as my co-counsel.

"Hey, Matt, you know that Klan case?"

"Yeah. You're taking it."

"Are you asking me or telling me?"

"Neither. I just knew it, buddy. We go around here looking for the badasses. I said the other day to Al Dawson, 'You just watch; Phillips is gonna take that Klan case. He's gonna be drawn toward it like some magnetic force.' And I told him I'd be on board, too."

"No shit. What did he say?"

"He said we'd be damn fools hung out to dry." We laughed. That was Al all right.

"So this is another of those cases we don't have a chance to win? I like the odds. It means we can't really lose, either."

"Look, how many defendants you got there?" Matt said.

"Fifteen."

"Well, then shit, we ought to be able to convict one of 'em. We'll just call him the leader ex post facto and max his ass out," Gillis said jokingly.

"Matt, let's start at square one. I'm heading to the scene and then the property room at the Foothill Division."

We were on our way before noon.

As I drove, he read the police report aloud so we could get some idea of the physical layout. The neighborhood we entered was a relatively new housing tract of single-family ranch homes, one- and two-story residences, painted in earth tones, blending into the hillsides beyond. The streets were clean. The few automobiles still parked curbside at the noon hour were typical of middle-class America. The only difference, at least to me, was that this Ozzie-and-Harriet neighborhood had black residents watering their lawns, carrying briefcases to their cars, and picking up newspapers from their driveways.

We wound our way up Kagel Canyon into a more rural neighborhood. The housing lots were rustic and much larger. Horses were in some backyards. The homes were distinctive Spanish or Tudor style. Here, the residents were white.

The property where the cross-burning occurred was difficult to find. The house itself was not visible from the road, and the street number was removed from the curb. We drove past it first, realizing our mistake only after seeing the number of the next residence.

We had to assume that defendant Ron Major was present. The police had recovered from Frank Silva a handwritten note in which Major agreed to rent this property to the Klan for a forty-eight-hour period. We knew little more of him, and we could not enter the property without a warrant.

We parked my car and strolled the perimeter of the property, stopping at the driveway. It was a position where we could see into the back lot. The old wooden residence and unkept property were markedly different from the surrounding neighborhood. The driveway was a forty-foot, unpaved road leading to the back door of the shack-like house. Oddly, it was the rear of the house that faced the street. It was much lower than the road above and concealed by wily trees. A broken-down old bus and a car on blocks were parked in a clearing. To our right was a handwritten cardboard sign that read "KEEP YOUR M.F. ATTITUDE OUT."

"Hey, John, look there." Matt directed my attention to the written warning.

"Yeah, well, I sort of woke up this morning and the toothpaste was all pressed out; I couldn't find my keys; traffic was a grind. I guess you could say I've got an 'M.F.'

attitude. Let's go to the station and check out the confiscated property."

We arrived at the Los Angeles Police Department's Foothill Division. We were told the numerous pieces of seized evidence would be brought to an interview room, one in which suspects were questioned.

Three boxes and a number of larger items were placed before us, including a rifle, twelve-gauge shotgun, two five-gallon gas cans, and three heavy table legs. The property officer left us, ostensibly to allow us to talk freely, but I knew listening devices were planted within these suspect interview rooms. I wondered why we had been taken to review the evidence here.

The first box contained two bullet-proof vests, one called "body armor" that covered both the front and back torso. This particular vest had been seized from Metzger, the other from another San Diego resident named Winston Burbage. "What do you make of this?" I said.

"Quite simple," Matt said. "These two guys expected they may be shot."

I examined the body armor more closely. There were minor lining tears and creases. It appeared previously worn. "This guy knew to expect trouble."

From the second box, Matt lifted a shiny, bright red robe. "Well, will you look at this," he said with amazement. As he unfolded the fabric we saw a black cape attached to the shoulders. There were five black stripes at the wrist of the sleeves. He pulled the hood from the box. A mask piece was attached with snaps to the front. There were holes for the eyes.

Matt passed the robe to me. I rubbed my fingers over it. "Satin." The quality and craftsmanship were impressive. "These ain't sheets and pillow cases." I held it up, seeing the length full from ankle to shoulder. Inside the yoke was a label that read "Handmade by Cindy." I looked to Matt, examining a second robe and hood he pulled from the box, identical in all regards except that the colors were reversed; black with a red cape, and a black hood and mask. It was also all satin.

There was a third robe and hood among the recovered property. This one was made from the more traditional white cotton. It was otherwise of the same design as the two made of satin but had no stripes on the sleeves.

"Richard Butler and Frank Silva wore these satin robes," I said. "What inferences can be drawn from this evidence? Butler, sixty-four years old and from Idaho; Silva, the twenty-four-year-old local organizer. Same person made both outfits, from opposite colors though. Silva wears the more sinister black. Seems like he may be trying to walk in the old man's footsteps, but maybe more radically. I'll say this, though. These guys are serious players. Each outfit could have cost a few hundred bucks. As for these stripes on the sleeves, well, my guess is they rank pretty high in their own army."

I unscrewed the cap of the large gasoline can and lifted it to smell the contents. Matt looked at me and smiled. "If you're trying to get high, I can get you a rag from the desk sergeant."

I smiled back. "Take a whiff of this," I said and handed him the can. "Does that smell like gasoline to you?"

Matt breathed in and then took a second smell of it. "Sweeter than gasoline. What does it matter?"

"Well, we're trying to prove a conspiracy. We have to show cooperation, planning, and overt acts in support of the conspiracy. If this is a mixture of gasoline and something else, maybe we can find out why, and who told who to do it that way. Let's have it analyzed."

Matt reached into the next box. "Check these out." He handed me a metal insignia that had stamped on it a sword with a Nazi swastika on the handle and the letters 'A.N.' Also, there were a metal skull pin and a cloth patch. The patch prominently displayed the same letters. "What's this 'A.N.' mean?" Matt asked.

Thinking aloud, I conjectured: "American Nazi; someone's initials? Who were they taken from?"

Matt checked the property report. "Peter Lawrence."

"All three items?" I asked.

"That's it. All three were booked to Peter Lawrence."

"Well then, they're not initials. Is there any other stuff like this in here?" I looked inside the same box and shuffled some papers around, but saw nothing similar. "Well, this guy is either real hard core, or he's trying real hard to look that way. Lawrence. Wasn't he the cameraman?"

"He was the one." Matt looked back down to the arrest report. "Says right here, 'Officer Simmons observed that defendant Lawrence was videotaping the proceedings.'"

"That's the next big question." I looked over to the thermostat on the wall of the interview room. Familiar with the eavesdropping devices routinely secreted within, I put my index finger over my closed lips, leaned close to Matt and whispered, "Where the hell is the videotape? Goddamn central piece of evidence isn't listed. Look at this." I pointed to a section of the arrest report that read, 'The camera equipment was handled as excess personal property.' "They friggin' hand it back to Lawrence as 'excess personal property.' What kind of shit is going on here?"

Chapter 5

Conflicting Agendas

It was five days before Christmas, a festive time of year in downtown Los Angeles, where normally indifferent stares become eyes searching for the warmth of a friendly hello. But for me the holiday joy was dampened by the weight of the task before me.

Particularly problematic were the criminal violations that had been filed. Hoping to please city attorney Reiner, Sachs alleged so many different crimes that the case became unduly complicated without adding to the prospective sentences.

Compounding the legal difficulties were inadequacies in factual proofs. Our primary witness was Officer Sanchez in the police helicopter, and he could not make positive identifications or recall the specific actions of any defendants.

Interviews of the other officers did little to cure the weaknesses. I scolded them for relinquishing the videotape. No one knew who actually returned it to Peter

Lawrence—or if anyone did know, I was not told. When I posed the question to Captain Warmoth, he acknowledged its return was a mistake.

I drove early the morning of the arraignment through the no-man's-land surrounding the county jail. Only bail bondsmen saw fit to locate here. Not even the homeless camped in the lots left vacant since the building of the jail.

Turning the corner from Vignes Avenue onto Bauchet Street, I got my first taste of the rancor that followed the Klan wherever they went. Two dozen L.A.P.D. officers in riot gear attempted to move a hundred, placard-carrying demonstrators from the street. I could hear their chants, led by a man over a bullhorn. "Death to the Klan. Free the land. The police and the Klan work hand in hand." I thought it ironic that the police had arrested the Klansmen and were now being accused of cooperation with them. Did the demonstrators know something I didn't? Closer to the courthouse, another dozen helmeted officers blocked entry to the parking structure. I displayed my identification and was allowed to pass into the eye of the storm.

Our clerical staff were gathered about the windows overlooking the street scene. As I walked into the office, Al Dawson nonchalantly addressed me. "You guys didn't listen to the old sage's advice."

I turned and headed down the hallway to the arraignment division. Scores of angry faces milled about. Television cameras were trained on Reiner. His thick, swept-back gray hair and deep, resonant voice commanded the attention of all. He didn't see me. I slowed to hear a portion of the questions and answers.

"What sentence will you be seeking if you get convictions on these charges?"

Without a second's thought, Ira came back in grand fashion. "Maximum sentences on all counts consecutively imposed. There will be no deals or plea bargains."

I walked past. Seated in the front of the courtroom was a motley group of white men. Their ages ranged from the early twenties to the midsixties. Some wore suits and ties; others dressed casually. One stood with arms folded, facing those behind him. It's got to be Silva, I thought.

I approached Matt, who was seated at the counsel table. "We all ready to go?" he asked.

"Have any of these guys got lawyers?"

"No one has come up to me yet."

I looked for any lawyerly types seated among the defendants. There was one fellow neatly dressed in a red tie, blue suit, and white shirt, attire fully incorporating the patriotic standard of the defense bar. He was seated beside another man, well-dressed but a bit too dapper for most attorneys in arraignment court. Then I noticed that the dapper dresser had a camera strap around his neck. This was no attorney.

The court was filled with an assortment of demonstrators advocating or protesting just about every aspect of the case. Low-pitched jeers and taunts occasionally filtered through the courtroom chatter. News photographers shifted about for optimum angles.

The courtroom doors suddenly swung open. Through them stormed a bearded young man, moving aggressively toward the Klan. He cupped his hands to his mouth and began to yell. "Tom Metzger, you fascist piece of garbage. Death to the Klan. Death to the Klan."

From the midst of the Klan rose Metzger, a middle-aged man in a navy-blue suit. The strident protestor continued toward him until a deputy marshal grabbed him from behind. The young man pulled free. The marshal grabbed the man again and applied a control hold around his neck. The man got off two punches to the marshal's head before the bailiffs dragged him from the courtroom.

The Klansmen stood and watched with amusement. Silva laughed with those around him. Metzger gloated—obviously pleased to have been the object of the demonstrator's contempt. The dapper dresser with the camera rose and photographed the anti-Klan protestors seated behind them. It seemed a symbiotic relationship of hatred.

When calm was somewhat restored, Gillis leaned toward me and asked, "Who's that son of a bitch with the camera?"

"We'll see when they're called up for the arraignment," I said. "My guess is that it's Lawrence, the one with the videotape. Let's not get too annoyed with this guy. We need to strike a deal."

Matt raised a brow.

"All rise and face the flag of our nation, recognizing the principles for which it stands," the bailiff called the court to order. "Division 82 of the Los Angeles Municipal Court is now in session."

Judge David Doi approached the bench, his eyes nervously scanning the restive crowd before him. "The court first calls the case of *People versus Metzger.*"

The defendants filtered down the aisle, through the swinging doors of the mahogany partition behind the counsel table. I read the charges to them and advised them of their rights. It turned out that I had correctly surmised that the defendant with the camera was Peter Lawrence. He was the only one among the defendants to have an attorney present with him. The others requested court-appointed counsel. Metzger wanted the court to appoint the attorney of his choice, which is normally not allowed. He could not articulate special circumstances that would allow for it. I opposed his request, and it was denied. The arraignments were continued until fourteen court-appointed attorneys could be assigned. We gathered our files. Matt looked about discreetly, making certain no one was within listening distance. "You want to cut a deal with Lawrence?" he said.

"As it stands right now, we have little choice. We've got a fairly weak case against most of these defendants. I look at these charges, and I wonder how in the hell anybody could have filed all this."

"I know," Matt said.

"Lawrence has the videotape. Remember O'Neil saw a bright light casting shadows against the drapes inside Silva's home. It must have been the camera light. He must have been taping. He was taping again when the crosses were raised and lit. We've got to get that footage."

"If they haven't destroyed it already," Matt said. "We've got some hard-core Klanners here. You've got to wonder if someone would sell out these folks."

Matt's point was well-taken. Also, we didn't have a very strong case against Lawrence. If he realized this, there would be no reason for him to cut a deal in exchange for the tape.

As we walked from the arraignment court, the lights of television cameras turned on, one after another. I was a stranger to this type of attention and continued to walk, squinting into the lights.

"Mr. Phillips, could we have just a moment please?"

The heat emitted by the camera lights made me uncomfortably warm. No one's face was visible through the glare.

Five or six voices began questions. I heard none clearly. I looked to a reporter who had a microphone closest to my face. "Excuse me. Could you repeat that?" I asked.

"Are you going to make an example of the Klan?"

"It's not my practice to make *an example* of anybody."

"What are you going to do?" he asked. Another reporter followed with "What's your intention?"

"We're going to stop it. We're going to stop this kind of conduct."

I turned and continued to walk down the hallway. As I entered our office, I heard a secretary's voice. "That's him. Just came in." A uniformed officer walked toward me, hand outstretched for an introduction.

"Mr. Phillips, I'm Lieutenant Farell. Captain Warmoth sent me down here. Is there someplace we can talk for a minute?"

We went to a small storage room used by the clerical staff for occasional cigarette breaks. I had Gillis join us. He closed the door and opened a pair of folding chairs beside a few cases of stationery. I asked the purpose of the lieutenant's visit.

He proceeded with a slow, thoughtful choice of words, like a prepared statement: "The Captain has asked me to inform you that there are two informants active in this matter. One is among your defendants. I'm sure you want to know who these people are. That I cannot tell you. They aren't L.A.P.D. informants, but we have a relationship with the source, and we have assured him that we will do nothing to expose their cover. He considers that a life-threatening danger. We trust that you'll cooperate."

I looked over to Matt. We had played the police technique of good-guy-bad-guy before, and he read my glance. He addressed the lieutenant with a hostile tone.

"You know, I should have seen this coming. You make this big splash arrest, do a press conference with every news reporter you can find. You put our asses on the line. And the moment we step out of the arraignment court, you tell us we're knee-high in shit and on our own."

The lieutenant folded his arms defensively. "I'd like to help you. I don't even know who the informants are. This has the potential to make us all look bad."

"Did the district attorney know this before he referred the case here?" I said quietly.

"Yes," responded the lieutenant.

I turned to Matt. "He saw what's coming. This trial could take two months. When it comes out that an informant was privy to defense strategies and interviews, we risk dismissal of all the charges, even if the informant is not directly giving us information."

"I can see to it that you receive no information whatsoever that has been derived from this source," offered the lieutenant.

"And if you were one of their attorneys, would *you* believe that?" I looked back to the lieutenant. "You really don't know who the informants are?"

"I don't. I personally guarantee that."

I probed for more. "So then, one is a defendant pretending to be a Klansman; the other is a Klansman who brought the informant in, but wasn't arrested."

The lieutenant paused. "Did I say that? One was there that night. He wasn't arrested. He left before the crosses were lit. If he hadn't, we would have arrested him too. We didn't know anything about it at that time. I don't know any more."

"When did you find out about it? How long after the arrests?" I said.

"Before they were released, the captain was contacted by another law enforcement agency."

"The FBI?"

"Mr. Phillips, you're working me. I really can't say any more on this."

The lieutenant began to rise from his chair. I rose as well. "Who else knows anything about this?" I asked.

He turned one last time before leaving our cramped, impromptu interrogation room. "The two of you, Captain Warmoth, and myself. That's all." He closed the door behind him.

Matt slammed his fist to the side of a box next to him. "What kind of bullshit is this? Someone's going to come forward eventually, and it's going to look like you and I are guilty of misconduct. They've set us up to be the fall guys."

"Hey," I said, "he's told us enough to get started. Let's get the field IDs on everybody present at the cross-burning. Let's get all the newspaper accounts and see who's in the pictures but wasn't arrested. Have Richards call for copies of the booking photos. Find out if anyone was released without posting the bail. Run rap sheets on everyone we come up with. We'll see who has a probation or parole tail. We'll find the guy with the reason to cooperate."

Matt paused thoughtfully and his anger subsided. "Sounds like a plan."

Chapter 6

The Informants

We met the next week at our office conference room in city hall. Matt had gathered newspaper reports of the cross-burning. We found an independent news photographer who sold pictures taken that night to the local press. Although none of the published photos was helpful, we made an appointment for the photographer, Bill Bradford, to bring in the proof sheets. Richards, our law clerk, obtained the booking photos. I asked Sergeant Hansen to search for the field identifications in the department's report file. They were missing. This told me we were on the right track. But the sergeant did provide a recent follow-up report.

In that report was a reference to a contact from a Kern County Sheriff's Department deputy named J. R. Frank. He heard of the Los Angeles cross-burning and called to report that there had also been a cross-burning in a remote area in his county, about two hours north of Los Angeles, outside the small town of Rosamond. It occurred on

November 12th, three weeks prior to the triple cross-burning in Los Angeles. He did not know if there was a connection between the two incidents. I asked him to fax his incident report.

Indeed, the two cross-burning incidents were closely related. Five of our defendants had been identified by Deputy Frank at the Rosamond cross-burning. The sixth man identified by the deputy, Michael Canale, was not arrested at the Los Angeles cross-burning. The narrative portion read as follows:

Kern County Sheriff's Department

Crime or Incident Report

Received by: Dispatch. Assigned to: J. R. Frank

> I received a call of a burning cross and gunshots by subjects dressed as KKK members. When I arrived, approximately eight men ran from the property into the surrounding hillside. The remaining six subjects were gathered around a bonfire with several high-powered rifles and hand guns.
>
> S-1 Evans told me that they were having a "directors meeting" of the KKK. Evans identified himself as the "Pastor and State Director of the Aryan Nations." S-3 Canale also identified himself as a "State Director" of the Aryan Nation. S-5 Witek identified himself as a "State Director of the American Nazi Party." S-1 Evans also showed me a fire permit issued by the Kern County Fire Department.
>
> I advised all six suspects on the county ordinance 50.50 (illegal shooting). I also advised them on the repercussions of the cross-burning. All suspects were checked for warrants—no hits.

The report then listed the six men by full name and birth date.

I handed the report to Matt and waited as he read, anticipating a comment on the participants. "Same damn bunch as the ones who came into Los Angeles," he said. "All except for this one here who identified himself as part of this Aryan Nations group, Michael Canale."

"Have you heard this name before, in any of your digging around?" I asked.

"No."

"It's got a birth date here, though. Let's run him. What did you get back on the records check for the other defendants? Any active probationers or parolees?"

"No. A couple of minor misdemeanor arrests. No active probation."

He put the booking photos down in a stack before me and left for the computer terminal to call up the Canale rap sheet.

The booking photos were fairly typical, with the usual deadpan and disgruntled looks. Then I came to one oddly different. I wondered how many booking photos I had seen in my years as a prosecutor—several hundred at least. Never before could I recall seeing an arrestee photographed with a grin. He's just been arrested, I thought. What the hell is this one smiling for?

There was a knock at the door. I put the picture down. The receptionist from our front desk told us that free-lance news photographer Bill Bradford was in the reception area. I left to greet him, and we spoke as we returned to the conference room.

He had been present at the Los Angeles cross-burning throughout the evening, after hearing of the Klan activity on his police scanner. Frank Silva had apparently taken a liking to him, or at least he was not opposed to having the night's activity photographed from a distance.

The one caution Bradford recalled was not to photograph "the elderly gentleman."

He removed two proof sheets from a folder. For the first time, we saw photographic depictions of the events of that night. Generally, the quality of the pictures was not good. They were dark, since Bradford used the helicopter spotlight and the Klan video-camera floodlight for his lighting. Most of the shots depicted robed and hooded Klansmen standing around the crosses. Few of the photos showed faces. With the exception of one photograph depicting Witek holding a long pickax handle, the pictures did nothing to improve the evidentiary weaknesses of our case.

In the photograph of Witek there was another man, holding a baseball bat at his side. I was unable to match his face to any of the booking photos. He was exceptionally large and barrel-chested, with a rectangular head. He wore a distinctive flannel shirt, which was recognizable in other photos taken prior to the igniting of the crosses, but not during or after the cross-burning.

Matt knocked once on the conference room door to signal his return, then entered and stood poker-faced before me, holding several sheets of computer printout paper. He raised them to the top of his head and, holding the edge of the last sheet, released them in grand fashion. The connected sheets unraveled from the top of Matt's six-feet-four frame to his size-thirteen shoes.

"Excuse me, Mr. Bradford," I said, "this is my partner Matt Gillis. Matt, Bill Bradford, the photographer who shot the pictures for the *Daily News* article." I turned back to our guest. "Matt is one of these save-the-trees ecology guys. He just hates to see the secretaries waste paper."

I asked Bradford if he would discuss the events he witnessed, but I was not surprised he declined, citing the newsman's privilege not to divulge facts beyond the content of his published material. I told him I would like to purchase a full set of his photographs and, being a freelancer, he agreed to sell them. He then left.

"Is that printout all for the same Michael Canale?" I asked Matt. The computer sometimes accessed several different persons with similar names.

"All the same guy. And guess what, he's on parole."

"For what?"

"Arson. I also got a photoprint of his last driver's license."

He handed me the copy of the license. I looked from it to the Bradford photo of the three men posing beside the Confederate flag. "I think we found our man," I said.

Matt made the comparison. "That mug is unmistakable."

"Let's go." I hurriedly put the booking photos into my briefcase and headed to the door.

"Where are we going?"

"Parker Center, R and I." That was the L.A.P.D. headquarters' records and identification division. "We're going to get the arson report."

The arson of Temple Beth David occurred four years earlier in a commercial district of the San Gabriel Valley, twenty miles east of Los Angeles. It was a dark, moonless night, and the heat and humidity lingered, taxing the pulse of a restless soul. His dented and dirty sedan turned sharply off the main drag and abruptly stopped a short distance from the corner, still leaving a line of sight to the synagogue he had fled minutes earlier. Mike Canale shut down the engine and stepped out of his car. He was two days unshaved, hair and clothing disheveled, wearing the usual long-sleeved shirt to cover the needle marks within the tattoos. He opened the car door, got out, and propped his head on arms folded atop the roof of his car. He stood there gazing through the trance of a heroin fix. The passenger doors on the curb side opened. Canale's two good buddies looked about, then nervously got out when no vehicles were passing their position.

The only motion from Canale's relaxed posture was a slowly broadening grin, then the slow speech of his deep, raspy voice. "Yeah. Look at that. Can you see the glow coming up behind the stained glass windows? It's pretty, man. We should be up closer—front-row seat."

"Yeah, Mike, it's cool. We did good work. Get back in the car. Let's hit it."

Canale stood motionless, still gazing with satisfaction. The faint sound of a siren could now be heard between the noises of passing traffic.

"Fire trucks, Michael." Canale did not move. "Fire trucks are coming, Mike." Still, no movement. "Get back in the car."

Canale still stared at the flames spreading within the temple.

"Get back in the fuckin' car!"

Canale stood straight and glared menacingly at his disrespectful buddy.

An apologetic tone replaced the command. "I'm leaving, Michael. I think it's better to get out of here." The man quickly stepped away. After a few fast steps, he started to jog, then run, full speed. The sound of his boots hitting the concrete pavement became less and less discernible. The street lights along the path of his flight down Clayton Street dimly illuminated his figure until he disappeared into a patch of darkness.

Canale rested his head back onto his folded arms, showing no sign of the apprehension felt by his remaining friend.

"I'm gonna get a pack of cigarettes, Mike. I'll find my way home." Having attempted to conceal his fear, Canale's second buddy turned and walked his way nervously down the boulevard, then quickly around the first corner.

As Canale stood alone, he saw flames begin to come through an air vent on the roof of Temple Beth David. Feeling he had braved the longest witness to their deed and had won the right to tell the best story, he moved from his relaxed posture and reached into his pocket for his keys. Canale was about to get in the car when a flashlight shined on his face.

"Hey, Canale, what are you doing up so late? Isn't it past your bedtime?"

Canale startled and dropped his car keys, then braced himself as he bent to pick them up. It was then that he noticed an unmarked police car had pulled up behind him.

"Whoa, my friend, we're moving in slow motion again. Roll up those sleeves."

The intense beam of the flashlight moved closer. Canale recognized the voice of Jack Streep, a narcotics officer who knew Canale well, both as a heroin addict and as a member of a neo-Nazi group suspected of vandalizing a Jewish cemetery.

"I'm clean, man, I haven't shot in days." Canale's raspy, slow intonation belied his words.

"Come on, Mike, roll up those sleeves." Streep took hold of Canale's arm. The officer's young partner stood with a gun drawn at his side by the open door of their vehicle. The sounds of the sirens from the approaching fire trucks grew closer, then shut down a couple of blocks away. The police radio could be heard making occasional scratchy transmissions.

"What you doin', Canale? You doin' the rag?"

"What are you talking about?" Canale asked.

"You know damn well what I'm talkin' about. You're sniffing gas, man. I gave you more credit than that. You stink of gas."

Streep called over to his covering officer. "Hey, partner, he's on the rag. I don't know if that's up or down for this guy. You got bracelets?"

Another scratchy transmission came over the police radio.

Streep's partner began to answer.

"Hold it!" interrupted Streep, pointing to the radio.

" . . . temple. Possible arson. Any available unit requested to meet the fire units. Code 2."

Streep looked down the boulevard toward the burning temple, then back to Canale. "You been playing with matches?" Canale said nothing. "What have you been up to tonight, Canale?"

Streep turned the beam of his flashlight to the interior of Canale's car. "What's this? You collect gas cans?"

Inside Canale's vehicle were three gas cans that became the central evidence establishing Canale's guilt in the arson of Temple Beth David. He served a prison sentence of three and one half years. He had been on parole for the past six months.

I placed the Canale arrest report into our file. We were surprised that a temple arsonist might be one of the two informants for whom we were searching. "Let's hope not," sighed Matt. "I'd hate to see you argue this guy's credibility."

"He's on parole, so he has constant law enforcement contact," I said. "You know, he wouldn't have gotten parole on something like this unless he had expressed a change of heart. It says in this report that he was a Nazi Party member. But in that Kern County incident report he says he's the state director of, what . . . Aryan Nations?"

Then it hit me. The booking photo confirmed it. It was from Peter Lawrence that the police had confiscated a metal lapel insignia and a cloth patch, both with the capital letters *A.N.* prominently inscribed. *A.N.* stood for Aryan Nations. Canale and Lawrence were connected.

"And check out this booking photo of Peter Lawrence, Matt." I reached into my briefcase and pulled it. "Have you ever seen anybody grin for a booking photo? He doesn't have anything to worry about. He knows he gets to walk."

"Makes sense," Matt said. "And it also makes sense that when Warmoth found out, he let Lawrence keep his videotape. Too bad we can't just call him up and ask him. I mean, him being a defendant. We're still not 100 percent sure, and even if he *is* the informant, we don't know that he would choose to cooperate with us. After all, he's been arrested, charged, and arraigned, and still maintains his cover."

"You're right. We can't just call him up and ask him." For a moment we again felt frustrated that we were no closer to building our case. "How about his attorney, though? I've never seen this guy around the courthouse before. What about you? Do you know anything about his lawyer?"

"I got his card at the arraignment." Matt opened our file to the inside cover where the attorney's business card was stapled. "Roger Olsen. He's with a firm by the name of Conrad, Maslach, and Johnston. His office is in Hollywood on Sunset. It doesn't say what type of law he practices."

"Not a law firm I've heard of before. Most of the big ones have better sense than to do criminal defense. There's nothing to stop us from giving him a call. Let's go back to the office."

"What are you going to tell him?" asked Matt.

"I'm not going to tell him anything. The question is, what is *he* going to tell *me?*"

We walked quickly to our office across the street. Matt sat opposite me, putting his boots up at the corner of my desk. I lifted the telephone receiver and thought a moment before dialing. When the receptionist answered, I identified myself and asked to speak to Mr. Olsen, then was placed on hold.

A minute, then two passed. The receptionist came back on the line. "Is this the same Mr. Phillips as the one at the city attorney's office?"

I looked over to Matt, "Yes, this is the same Mr. Phillips." She asked me to hold again.

She returned quickly. "Mr. Phillips, Mr. Olsen will be with you in just a moment."

"I'll hold."

Matt's face broke into a broad grin. He spoke softly. "They're probably trying to figure out what the hell is going on." I smiled back.

"This is Roger Olsen speaking."

"Good morning, Roger. How are you today?"

"Oh, okay I guess. How are you?" he asked hesitatingly.

"Just fine. Couldn't be better. Say, didn't I see you downtown last month at the Criminal Courts Building?"

"Oh, no. Wouldn't have been me," he readily answered.

"What type of law does Conrad, Maslach, and Johnston mostly practice? I don't think I know any of the partners."

"Oh, they do mostly entertainment law. Occasionally we do some criminal."

"Right. My brother does entertainment law and occasionally he does some criminal too. You know, when one of the clients gets into trouble. Makes sense."

"Yeah. Makes sense."

"Well, I guess it figures here." I realized that if I was wrong about Lawrence being the informant I could make a humorous remark about his having the video camera.

"Oh? . . . Is there something I can do for you?"

"Well. Isn't there something you want to tell me?"

There was silence. I waited for Olsen to speak first. "I think I had better know how you found out," he said.

"I couldn't just let him sit there. I mean with all the defendants," I evasively answered.

"I understand the problem," answered Olsen. "But I think I'd better know who blew Peter Lake's cover."

Peter "Lake," I thought. He had been using an assumed name. I gave Matt a thumbs-up.

"Well, Mr. Olsen, really. You're working me," I answered with the same tone of disdain as Lieutenant Farell, and grinned at Matt. "Who do you think I found out from?"

"Well, I knew he couldn't trust the police. I knew it."

"I guess that's just the way the world is these days. You put your trust in somebody and they blow it for you. I guess that's just the way it is. Police, lawyers, . . . pediatricians." Matt covered his mouth to hold back laughter.

"Pediatricians?" Olsen said. "You have cases against pediatricians?"

"Oh, are you kidding? They're the worst." Matt's eyes opened wide and he quickly spun away from the phone, bursting into laughter.

"Pediatricians," Olsen softly mused. "I guess it makes sense."

"Listen," I said, changing tone to address the business at hand. "Lake doesn't seem like such a bad guy, and maybe I can work a deal for him if he gives us his videotape."

"What kind of deal?" asked Olsen.

"Well, I don't know. Plead to one count for straight probation."

"Plead? You want him to plead? That's not fair."

"Hey, look, I could just subpoena the tape. I'm trying to do the guy a favor."

"He's got the privilege."

I still didn't know enough about Lake to know what Olsen was referring to as "the privilege." I couldn't let it show.

"I know he has the privilege," I answered. "But it's not absolute."

"It is to a prosecutor," Olsen replied. "Look at his intent. He's doing a news story. He doesn't have to give up his videotape."

"Well, if he doesn't, then he's going to have to sit there with the rest of them as a defendant. That's my offer, the tapes for straight probation on a plea to one count."

"You have to dismiss this case."

"The hell I do. If he wants a dismissal, he'll have to testify as well."

"He won't take it."

"That's my offer. Take it to him and let me know." I curtly bade Olsen farewell and turned to Matt. "Well, now we know why this case is getting so much air time."

I watched as Matt's expression changed from mirth to concern again. "Why's that?" he asked.

"We got our hooks into some news show's inside story."

"Oh, no," he sighed, placing a hand to his forehead.

"Come on," I said. "Let's go nail a pediatrician."

Chapter 7

Quest for the Truth

I decided we had no choice but to completely amend the original complaint. As it was originally pled, count one alleged a violation of California's new antiterrorism statute, penal code section 11411. This statute makes it a crime to burn a cross "on the property of another" with the intent to terrorize that person. This statute was inapplicable because Silva had rented the property from Ron Major, who consented to the cross-burning.

I instead alleged an unlawful assembly in violation of California penal code section 408. An unlawful assembly is "the coming together of two or more persons to do an unlawful act, or to do a lawful act in a violent, boisterous, or tumultuous manner." I made it our goal to prove for the first time in American judicial history that a Ku Klux Klan cross-lighting constituted an unlawful assembly.

The conspiracy charge remained count two, but it was modified to allege an unlawful burning—instead of burning a cross on another's property—as the objective of the conspiracy.

The fire code violation as originally alleged also had to go. It prohibited the igniting of fires "where signs clearly stating the prohibitions have been posted." Although the Kagel Canyon area is a "mountain fire zone" according to the fire department, there were no such signs posted near the location of the cross-burning. We instead alleged a violation of the fire code provision (L.A.M.C. Section 57.20.19) that prohibited "open, outdoor fires, without a valid permit issued by the fire department."

Ironically, I learned of this section through Silva. He obtained permits under the ruse of wanting to have an "open-pit barbecue," which was one of the enumerated exceptions for which a permit could be obtained.

Other grounds for receiving a fire permit included "bonfires of legitimate fraternal or civic organizations." But rather than trying to present themselves as a "legitimate fraternal organization," Silva chose instead to pretend their fire was a barbecue rather than the igniting of crosses. When Frank Silva waved his permit in front of the cops' faces, he presented them with the code section on which we would prosecute his Klan.

Reiner and I agreed the charges against Lake should be dismissed. But I did not want the case dismissed unconditionally. I needed the tapes. Lake was not present at the January 10th hearing, but his attorney filed the necessary papers to represent him in his absence. The other defendants were present with court-appointed counsel.

An unusual motion was noticed for hearing by defendant Richard Girnt Butler. It demanded that the charges be refiled as felonies, under an obscure provision of penal code section 17(b)(5). As a practical matter, no defense attorney in his right mind would ever request this because of the increase in the possible maximum sentences. We knew the defendants themselves were behind this strategy.

But there were three benefits the defendants would gain through such a reclassification. First, the Klan would be entitled to a preliminary hearing, a right not available for misdemeanors. Second, jurisdiction was removed from the city attorney and switched to the district attorney's office for prosecution. The Klan knew the D.A. had initially declined to prosecute, and it figured a cheap plea bargain was likely to be offered. Third, if not all the defendants joined in Butler's motion, the case would be split into at least two trials, complicating matters and discouraging witnesses.

The Klan also filed a demurrer to the complaint. This is a legal challenge that claims that even if the charges are true, they do not constitute a violation of law. The demur was scheduled to be heard before the motion to compel the felony prosecution.

Roger Olsen was ill at ease among the Klansmen and their lawyers. He slipped from their company before court was in session. As he stood by the courtroom doors, I had to play my final card to get the tapes.

"Have you spoken to Lake?" I asked.

"He won't give up the tapes," Olsen said. "But he wants out. CBS is broadcasting his story tonight."

I knew I could not continue to prosecute Lake after his story became public. "I must have the tape," I said. "He's withholding evidence. You expect me to just dismiss this case with him withholding evidence?"

"He can't come back here," Olsen said. "They'll kill him. You don't know who you're dealing with here."

I looked aside. "Go along with what the others do today. Come back Thursday by yourself. I'll dismiss his case, but he might as well help us. Even if he doesn't, they'll think he has."

At the time that I told Olsen this I did not realize how true it really was. Klansmen were suspicious of everyone, even those they *must* trust. Newcomers were particularly well scrutinized, and Lake was concerned that inferences of his deception could already be drawn, despite his fairly effortless attempt to befriend them.

Indeed, there were aspects of the Klansmen that Peter Lake had liked. He conversed with them amicably on subjects not political, but they could take any topic to a political threshold. As that threshold was crossed, their violent undercurrent surfaced.

This seemed most true with the elderly leader of Aryan Nations, Richard Butler. He had an uncanny ability to extract quotes from the Bible, usually the Old Testament, to construe the Lord's blessing on his extreme brand of racism. Butler's church was within the twenty-acre Aryan Nations compound in northwestern Idaho.

Shortly after Canale was released from prison, he returned to Aryan Nations and the company of Pastor Butler. It seemed to most of his compatriots that Canale's purpose was to avail himself of the hero's welcome to which the temple arson entitled him. But Canale had come to a crossroads and was deeply remorseful for the destruction of the temple. So much so that he would risk his life to atone. So he brought Lake with him, and they stayed there several days as Butler's guests a month before the Los Angeles cross-burnings. They met the do-or-die soldiers of the movement. Lake accepted the hospitality of Richard Butler, had "broken bread at his table," as he would later put it. This made Lake uneasy, and he stayed in the protective company of his undercover partner. But even Canale feared the vengeance of the Idaho group.

When Tom Metzger heard news media confirmation that Peter Lake had deceived Butler, he telephoned to give the old man a little "I told you so." He had never fully believed that the articulate, sophisticated Peter "Lawrence" was a Klan/Nazi sympathizer. Now, he was anxious about what others may have said on Lake's video. He demanded to know what Peter would do with the crucial evidence in his possession.

Feeling chastened for having mistakenly trusted Lake, Butler agreed to cooperate with Metzger. The Aryan Nations chieftain attached a recording device to his telephone and left a message for Peter Lake to call him.

When Lake received the message, he nervously planned responses to questions Butler might ask. He lifted the receiver and dialed. A male voice answered: "Good evening. Aryan Nations." We later acquired the audiotape, which contained the following exchange:

"Is Pastor Butler there?"

"Yes. Just a moment," the receptionist replied.

"Hello. Butler speaking."

"Richard. It's Peter Lake."

"I understand you did one on us."

"Well, I'm afraid I did," said Lake. "Not much to repay your hospitality; but, there are things that may surprise you that I will do. About the videotape—they're going to have to send me to jail to get it. I'm not the tool of the police department. I'm not going to play ball with the city attorney on it. I frankly don't want to see you in jail."

"Well, I appreciate that. . . . Why? Do you think there is some reason that we may go to jail?" asked Butler.

"I don't know. I don't think they've got a good case. The city attorney wants the videotape. To what end he'll go to get it, I don't know. But your strategy of going up to a felony is either brilliant or crazy. I don't know which. For your sake, I hope it works."

"I have to give you credit, Lake. You certainly did fool me. I guess we're too trusting. And I was very impressed with you."

"Well, I would say as well by you, and I'm sorry to have turned on you if that's how you see it. My intent was not to go and discover what kind of terrible things you were doing, but to really find out whether what you say publicly is what you say privately, and to my mind that is 99 percent the case. Certainly as much as anybody else in public life. You're no hypocrite, Richard."

"I'm afraid not. What about Canale? Were you together on this, Pete, or what?"

"Yes. Michael contacted Irv Fisher as soon as he got out of prison and said that he had a change of heart. And Irv called Hugh Massey, who connected *Rebel* magazine with me."

"We'll have to see how it's going to work out. Eventually, we're going to win. That we believe because we're fanatics. A fanatic is one who doesn't hold opinions, but has an absolute belief. And we do."

"I don't hope so, but I admire your determination. You did treat me well, and as a guest I'm sorry to have abused that. But as far as the tapes aiding your prosecution, there's no way that's gonna happen. So, they'll have to make their case however they can make it."

"I don't think they have a case. Contrary probably to what you believe, there still is a semblance of white freedom, here in America. I say a semblance. But upon that semblance we will build our victory. The Third Reich didn't start off very good, either, as far as the 1922–1923 period. But we do believe that there are still enough white genes left. And according to the promises that are found in Scripture, these white genes will be enough to root out those who are out for the destruction of the Aryan race. And we believe that somehow or other, the Aryan race will live. Of course, on the other side, they're out for our extermination. The battle lines are drawn. Right now your side is winning, but there's a lot more battles to be fought."

Peter Lake did not sleep well that night, for he knew firsthand the nothing-to-lose mentalities of several of Butler's most loyal followers. The gun beneath his pillow was the signature of his insecurity.

As the days passed, I considered our case without additional evidence. The police report referred to "seven male adults carrying billy clubs," with no further description; the helicopter observer saw "several KKK members" pour gasoline on the crosses, with no further description; "three suspects erected the crosses in an upright position in the ground," and again, no further descriptions.

I closed the file, rose from the chair, and turned off the lights in our living room. It was nearly eleven o'clock. There was not a sound in the house. I spoke softly to myself, unaware Diane was near in the kitchen. "I don't have aiding and abetting. I don't even have the principles." I put my hand to my brow, feeling at a loss for what more I could do.

"Were you speaking to me?" asked Diane, as she walked to the doorway.

"I'm afraid the Klan will leave court vindicated."

"Vindicated?" Diane said with surprise. "I hardly think they'll be vindicated. At worse they just don't get convicted."

"No. At worse they'll burn crosses here again, and the police will be obligated to protect them. You'll see."

"No," she snapped, "I won't see. You can't lose hope, John, unless you lose faith."

The moral repugnancy of the Klan burning the cross in proclamation of hatred motivated me beyond all else. And I sat now, considering not only the professional loss but the moral loss as well if we could not be victorious.

Hearing no response, Diane stepped to her jewelry case in our bedroom and returned a moment later with my grandmother's crucifix. "Look." She held it so I could see that she'd attached a silver chain. "Did you know that 'crusade' is the Latin word for 'cross'? It is the badge of all crusaders." Diane reached upward and placed the chain and crucifix around my neck. I smiled, and seeing that I was pleased with her gift, she embraced me.

Immediately noticeable to us both was that she was as pregnant as pregnant gets. The baby was pressed between us. I was leaning awkwardly forward, and Diane held her head far back. We both laughed. Then I leaned forward again, held her by her waist and shoulders, and kissed her passionately. I moved my hand from her shoulders into her soft blond hair. And when I finished kissing her once, I kissed her again.

I awoke the following morning with the chain and crucifix across my chest. The sun was shining and the flowers flourished in early bloom. At least, that was how I imagined the world outside. And when I pulled the drapes apart, it did not seem much different—not to a young man eagerly awaiting the birth of his first child. Whether it rained or the sun shined, to me either was the symbol of a life beginning. Fittingly, the ground was wet with the residue of a pre-dawn rain. Cotton-candy clouds raced low, and between them the morning sun glared, extending a rainbow bridge to a child's future somewhere beyond the morning glories.

Two hours later, I watched Olsen enter through the mahogany doors of the courtroom and sit at the midsection of the gallery, well removed from where he might have contact with me. Court was in recess. It was obvious I would get no cooperation. I might as well prod the messenger.

"Mr. Olsen," I said. "You ever hear the story of a man who yells 'Fire! Fire!' And when the firemen arrive, he refuses to tell them where the fire is?"

"Can't say I have."

"He winds up getting burned."

Olsen glared back. "What's your point, Counsel?"

"My point is simple. Your guy is going into a no-man's-land."

"I'm just the lawyer, Counselor. He is going to assert his privilege under evidence code section 1030."

The bailiff announced court was in session. The judge took the bench. I turned away from Olsen and walked toward the clerk's desk at the front of the courtroom. "Call *People versus Lawrence.*"

She pulled the file from the bin beside her and reached upward with it to the judge. He took the file from her. "The matter of *People versus Lawrence,* case number 31276350. It's just this one defendant today, Mr. Phillips?"

"Yes, it is, Your Honor."

"You have something worked out on this?" the judge asked.

"I wouldn't say we have something 'worked out' on this. There will be a People's motion to dismiss under penal code section 1385."

"In the interests of justice?" the judge asked.

"No, Your Honor. Justice has little to do with this dismissal. Due to the insufficiency of the evidence. Mr. Lawrence was working as a journalist while present during the commission of the crime. We don't believe he possessed the requisite criminal intent to be prosecuted on any counts. Only the intent to do an undercover story."

"Very well, then. The complaint is dismissed in its entirety against Defendant Lawrence. Bail is exonerated. Excuse me, there was no bail on this. This defendant appears to be the only one released on a promise to appear."

I turned to Olsen, who to this point quietly watched the proceedings. "Are you continuing to represent Lake for any purpose?" I asked.

"No. This was it, as far as I know," he answered.

I would now be able to contact Lake directly, I thought.

I stopped to purchase a soda at a grocery store during the drive home that night. As I walked into the market, I glanced at the headline of the evening paper: "Writer Infiltrates KKK." I purchased the paper and a soda, propped my backside against my car, and read the story on Lake by the light of the store sign.

When I returned home, Diane greeted me with a hug. She sensed a bit of distance on my part and knew the reason. "Your case was on the news tonight. They think you dismissed his charges in exchange for some kind of deal," she said.

"I told them that wasn't so. They run what they want."

"You didn't get the tape, did you?" she asked.

I shook my head.

"You're not discouraged?"

"I'm not," I answered. "I have faith that this whole thing is the right thing to do. I just have to go about it the right way." I opened my briefcase and removed the Klan file. "It's time that I convey this to the people whose help is needed, so we work on this together."

Opening the file to the face sheet of the report on Peter "Lawrence," I reclined on the living room couch, lifted the telephone receiver, and dialed his number. After two rings I was connected to a recorded message: "Hello, you have reached the number you dialed. After the message, leave a tone."

I liked his humor.

"Mr. Lake, this is John Phillips calling. I understand you're no longer represented by counsel, and I want to speak with you personally." The receiver was picked up.

"This is Peter Lake."

"Peter, how are you?"

"Relieved today. Thanks for dismissing the charges."

"It was the right thing to do. I was hoping we might talk for a few minutes.

"That's fine. . . . I must say, though, it is rather strange talking to you. Until today you were trying to put me in jail."

"I don't much know that anybody is going to jail off this. One defendant wants out of this now. Roberto Mendez, do you know him?"

"Yes," Peter answered hesitatingly. "He's a Hispanic kid that came with the Nazi group. I never met him before that night. He didn't say much. Seemed out of place with the goings-on that evening."

"He wanted to enter a guilty plea and just cut himself loose from the rest of the bunch," I explained. "So the judge read through the police reports to give his lawyer an indicated sentence. That's typical. What wasn't typical is that the judge refused to take the plea. He told me to reevaluate our case and suggested to Mendez's lawyer that he take the case to trial."

"Can judges do that? I had no idea they could undermine the prosecution like that."

"They certainly can, Peter. It's unusual, but they can. The point is this. You and Canale very courageously infiltrated what appear to be some dangerous extremist groups. You brought to light sufficient information to trigger arrests. But without your cooperation, there's not enough for convictions." I paused, and was relieved that Lake did not immediately refuse my plea. I still had only inferences that Lake was not philosophically in agreement with the Klan. He continued to listen.

"The night of the cross-burning, Peter, you were taping with a video camera. I'm sure there's a lot more than what we've seen on the news."

"The cops smashed my camera," interrupted Peter. "Threw it down and stomped on it. I have the name of the officer."

"What I'm getting at is this. You have a videotape that might provide conclusive proof on many points. If your videotape shows crimes were committed, fine. If it shows crimes were not committed, then that's fine, too. All I'm asking is to know the truth. I cannot do this job fairly without that much."

There was no immediate response. As the silence lengthened I realized there might be more than I expected, perhaps more than he could ever let me know. I almost began to fear his cooperation more than the absence of it. Then he spoke. "Do you have my address?"

"On your booking sheet."

"Come to my house tomorrow night, about 8:30. Be careful. Don't let anyone know I'm doing this until after it's done. There are those who would kill to protect some of the people implicated on the tape."

Lake lived in Los Angeles at the upscale Westside Marina del Rey. His townhouse was located on what is known as the Venice Canals, a series of waterways overambitiously designed in the 1930s to resemble their Venice, Italy, namesake. The project was never fully completed, leaving several sections stark and eerie, especially under the light of a full moon.

As I entered his home I took notice of the books on shelves covering two walls of his living room. I wandered closer to the titles. Philosophical and political works, some with a distinct liberal slant, comprised most of his collection.

Peter was raised in Boston and was still a bachelor as he approached his fortieth birthday. He hoped to settle down and begin a family. His career was adventure journalism—he had written on subjects ranging from the great white shark to jungle tribalism. Tonight, although he seemed trusting, he was far from relaxed.

On the floor beside a television set was a video camera, its cassette holder open and twisted, noticeably damaged. Next to it was a stack of videotapes. I bent down to read the label of the one on top: "Los Angeles Cross Burning." "So this is the tape?" I asked.

"It is," answered Peter. "And the others I've also copied for you. The scope of this whole movement is amazing. It's not just what happened in Los Angeles. What happened here was the coming together of several groups, each very committed, with followers determined to achieve their goals. Look at this." Peter installed one of the videocassettes. "This is in Idaho, up by Hayden Lake. The Aryan Nations group has a compound, forty acres of land, with their own meeting hall, security watchtower, barracks, the whole bit. I stayed there four days. I was eventually sworn in as a member, learned their practices, ate in their mess hall. After a couple of days they drove us out by some dump site. Canale and I thought they were going to kill us. We saw them pack their guns. I had my .45 too, but they told me to put it in the trunk. I couldn't say no. We drove into more and more of a remote area. Then we got to the dump site."

The tape began with the sound of gunfire in rapid succession. Men carrying rifles ran low, moving from makeshift buildings and barricades, then advanced to the next position, crouched, took aim, and fired.

"Recognize anyone?" asked Peter.

"No. Not yet. Was that Silva yelling directions?"

"Yeah, that was Silva. He's tough, a take-control kind of guy." At this point in the tape, a tall young man with midlength red hair leaned around the corner of a shack façade. Within two seconds he raised his rifle, aimed, and fired three rounds. Lake freeze-framed the tape. "You recognize him?"

"David Tate?" I asked.

"That's Tate, all right," answered Peter. "Very dangerous individual. Big, strong kid, living in the backwoods of Idaho his whole life. Hasn't seen any bit of the world firsthand. They get about five television stations up there, seeing the world through stereotypes and inner-city news broadcasts. That's a real bad combination for a poor, uneducated kid. Then a guy like Richard Butler comes along, 'Pastor' Butler they all call him, and tells them from the church pulpit this isn't the way the Lord wanted the world to be. Well, it's easy for a kid like Tate to feel like he's a soldier in the Lord's army."

"Is that what this is?" I asked. "Religious fanaticism?"

"For this Aryan Nations group, a certain brand of religious fundamentalism justifies their goals. At first it didn't seem to make too much of a difference, at least not to me, how they based their beliefs. Then I realized they define who has a soul and who does not. Take it one step further. When you believe there are people who do not have souls, anything done to them can be justified."

"And where do the Nazis and Klan come in?" I asked.

"There is tremendous intermingling here. When I was up in Idaho, Butler spoke of how his grandfather was a Klansman. Silva is Klan and a member of Aryan Nations. The Nazi Party members gravitate to Metzger's group, which he calls WAR, for White American Resistance. Metzger had been the Grand Dragon of the Klan for the state of California. The triple cross-burning, in part, was a symbolic unification of the three groups present, the

Ku Klux Klan, Aryan Nations, and WAR. Each of them has the same goal: an ethnic cleansing. And they want to take a part of the country, the four northwestern states—Washington, Oregon, Idaho, and Montana—as their own separate nation. The danger is that they are willing to take whatever steps necessary."

Peter explained the significance of the unification. "The so-called Church of Jesus Christ Christian, Butler's Church, was founded decades ago but remained isolated. The Ku Klux Klan has been stagnant, almost dead, for many years. Metzger's group, WAR, has been a small-time operation since his unsuccessful bid for the U.S. Senate. But you put these people together, and you have a network of operatives throughout the Pacific coast region. Add to them the Posse Comitatus in Wisconsin; the Cross, Sword, and Arm of the Lord in Arkansas; and Klan groups down South, and the movement has nation-wide dimension. They're already linked through the Internet and are forming alliances. And violence is a fully accepted means of getting their way."

"And so, the police make arrests, and we file criminal charges. Something tells me they aren't feeling happily unified."

"That's right. Metzger was upset with Silva. Very upset. He'd never been arrested before, and he thought the whole evening was poorly thought out. Butler was not talking to anyone except the two who came with him from Idaho. They don't like the idea of coming back to Los Angeles for the trial. And Witek, the head of the Nazi group, he started to get on everyone's nerves with his constant rattling."

"What about this oddball motion of theirs to demand a felony prosecution. What's the thinking behind this?"

"They know the D.A. rejected this case before the city attorney filed it, so they would rather throw it back into his hands. That's half the reason I decided to waive the newsman's privilege. I knew that if I came forward, it would matter to you. But what about their strategy? Can they force you off the case?"

"We don't like the notion of them picking their prosecutors." I paused, looked directly at Peter and said, "You say it was half the reason, our commitment to the case, that got you to come forward. What was the other half?"

Peter smiled and raised his right hand, the thumb and index finger about a half inch apart. "If I had a target that you had to hit to get the tapes, it was only this big. If you tried to force me to relinquish the tapes, I would have gone to jail before giving them up. But it was only the truth you wanted. That much I could give."

Peter reflected a moment, leaned forward in his chair, and continued. "Now they've rallied together again. They've decided to trust each other one more time. If they win, it will solidify their forces. If they lose, it would surely split them apart permanently. These are the national leaders in the white separatist movement. Keeping their groups distant is significant, *very* significant.

"By the way," Peter added, "They don't refer to it as a 'cross-burning.' They call it a 'cross-lighting.'"

"I heard it said that way, once at least." I recalled when Sachs characterized it as such. "What's the difference?"

"They will say a cross-lighting is a display of the glory and power of God."

I realized Lake's analysis could support the Klan's claim of First Amendment protection. I told him why I felt this was too important to pass unchallenged. "The way I sometimes tried to understand why other people did things was by looking at how they did them. Silva lived in the general vicinity of where the crosses were burned, but he didn't burn them at his own property. Instead, he got this two-day rental agreement from Ronald Major for a property that overlooks a mostly black community. They used crosses so damn big for the visibility. They carried table legs and wore bullet-proof vests because they expected to start trouble. I figure they wanted confrontation, not religious expression."

"Oh, I'm sure," responded Peter. "Silva said a couple of times he didn't like the kinds of people that were moving into the neighborhood around him. No doubt they expected some kind of confrontation. Definitely, they were trying to tell people they weren't welcome, to tell them, 'Get out.'"

I probed for more about Canale. He and Peter befriended for the sole purpose of the infiltration. They had nothing in common. Although now in hiding, Canale remained in touch with Peter. He assured me he would pass my phone number to Canale.

Lake also cautioned me that Tom Metzger had worn a recording device and had his own audiotape of the events that evening. I knew immediately that if I were to demand the production of the tape by Metzger I would receive an edited copy that deleted incriminating statements. I saw no advantage in pursuing this.

Peter placed the videotapes in a grocery bag. On top he stacked some Aryan Nations literature. "The tapes run about four hours in all. The one you're most interested in, the cross-burning, is about forty-five minutes." Peter paused for a moment. He looked troubled. "There's another thing. It's not on any of the tapes, naturally. It was something said the day after the arrests."

Again he hesitated, then began carefully repeating the words, “This is it. This is the beginning of the war.” Peter pensively looked up from the package of tapes. “It was a guy who was with the Idaho group. He came in that night. Canale has been saying that their big move would come sometime next year. Now he thinks they’re ready to go. You listen to Canale, and sometimes you just don’t know. Could be he’s fallen for their hype. Then again, maybe not.”

“I have one more favor to ask you,” I said. “You still have a privilege not to testify. It’s your call. I won’t try to force you to testify.”

Peter paused only a moment. “I’ll testify.” He looked right at me and said, “No one can be angry with the truth.”

Chapter 8

A Day and a Life

At moments like this you talk to yourself, moving as fast as you can, telling yourself, "Don't panic; stay calm." Thoughts enter your mind threefold ahead of your action. "Suitcase in the car. Everything's there. Gas is okay. Where is she? There she is." I then spoke out loud as Diane came out the front door. "Are you all right?"

"I'm all right, John. I don't need help to the car."

"Okay. Did you get another contraction yet?

"No, not yet. I'll let you know."

"Let me know." I looked at my hand. "Good, I have my keys. I would hate to misplace my keys at a time like this." I reflected for a moment on this observation. "I just opened the car to put in the suitcase. How could I have misplaced the keys?"

"Are you okay to drive? You're making me nervous."

"God, don't get nervous. Don't get nervous!" I shut my front car door from the outside, went around the car and shut hers, ran back around the car to my side, and my door was locked. I reached into my pants pocket for my keys; not there. I tapped on the window for Diane's attention.

"Check your jacket pocket," she called.

"Right."

Somehow we made it to the hospital well before our son was born.

His name was going to be Joseph. In fact, that's what we called him for the first fifteen minutes of his life. But the more I looked at him, the more he reminded me of my own father. Diane agreed, and so we named him Patrick.

Later that night, as I held my son, I remembered a quotation attributed to John Adams: "A great and good king was once asked if the grandeur of his dominion had brought him a life of joy, and he answered, 'My riches are great and the beauty of my kingdom is boundless, but as I assess my lifetime I can count on one hand the days of pure and complete happiness. And I consider myself fortunate to have had so many.' "

This day I was a king.

Chapter 9

Partner to Be

The night before the hearing on the demur, Diane and I received a social call from a dear friend, Vivian Somosa. Both she and the lucky guy accompanying her this evening, Dale Davidson, were deputy district attorneys. We had known Vivian nearly eight years. They had come to see our baby.

We stepped quietly into the nursery where Patrick slept. My little boy must have sensed our visit. He stirred, let out a soft murmur, and turned to his side. We knew better than to press our luck with a child sleeping so delicately. Dale and I backed out of Patrick's room and took beers from the refrigerator on our way to the back yard. It was a cool, clear night.

Dale started with the district attorney's office a year before I started with the city attorney. He was a physics major as an undergrad, so we talked about astronomy for a while. I looked toward a configuration of stars, wondering at their timelessness.

"What's that around your neck?" asked Dale.

I pulled out the crucifix my father had given me. "I wear this."

Dale looked down. "A cross, huh. That's a nice one. Do you wear that because of your case with the Klan burning crosses?"

I was caught a little off guard. "Vivian told you about my case with the Klan, did she? Don't get me going on that." I smiled. "We could spoil a perfect evening."

"Oh, it sounds like an interesting case." He paused. "Ones like that are tough. Any time you've got a big group of defendants and they're all going to point the finger at the informant," he paused again and looked to me for confirmation. "You do have an informant, don't you?"

His insight impressed me. "Two," I answered.

"That's a good start. But they'll be the fall guys. You'll see. The others will blame them for everything that happened."

"At least what's not shown on video," I added.

"You have the tape?" he asked.

I nodded affirmatively.

"Well, if you don't mind showing it, I think it could be pretty entertaining."

Forgotten was the motion brought by Richard Butler to compel a felony prosecution and the possibility that it would cause a transfer of the case to the district attorney's office. It remained light years beyond our imaginations that fate would one day join our skills in the prosecution.

Chapter 10

The Intemperate Judge

Ira Reiner was elected district attorney for Los Angeles County. He was replaced as city attorney by a politician he did not support, which generally means the new officeholder will clean house of the former city attorney's appointees. Other than the fact that I had handled several high-visibility prosecutions in which Reiner was personally interested, I assumed I had no reason to be concerned with the transition. But in this I was naive.

The following morning, I walked with Matt to the courthouse for the hearing on the demur. As we stepped through the elevator doors on the floor of Judge Malcolm Mackey's courtroom, a flood of news camera lights turned on, forming a hot, blinding path to the court.

Scores of anti-Klan demonstrators lined the hallway. Deputy marshals stood at the courtroom doors, conducting pat-down searches of all entering. "He's okay." The sergeant knew me from other cases. "Let him pass."

"Mr. Gillis is my cocounsel on this," I said.

"Get them in." The sergeant pulled open the door.

The spectator section was filled to capacity. Most were demonstrators. As I placed our file at the counsel table, I listened to a debate at the rear of the courtroom. It was Nazi Party head Stanley Witek and a black demonstrator.

Said Witek, "We don't hate blacks. We don't hate Jews. We seek only to protect the white race from extermination and to restructure society so that the white race is protected."

"We need jobs," answered the demonstrator. "That's what this is all about. Jobs."

I noticed Matt was also silent, listening to the odd exchange behind us. Our case was becoming a forum for issues far removed from what we had intended.

"Don't get too settled down, boys. We're papering the judge with an affidavit of prejudice." We turned to see attorney Brian Pageant. He stood officiously, hands behind his back and a look as though he had just ruined our day. The affidavit to which he referred is a simple declaration by the attorney that he does not believe his client will receive a fair trial from the appointed judge. No showing of actual prejudice need be made. It would have the effect of removing this judge from hearing any aspect of the case. Each side is entitled to one such affidavit.

"Well, why in the hell didn't you do that in the arraignment court where you're supposed to?" demanded Matt. "Now you've got a courtroom full of people that have all been searched to get in here and the marshals are going to have to go through the same thing all over again."

"Now, don't get upset." Pageant raised his hands, backing away. "I'm just letting you know as a courtesy. We didn't have time to discuss this collectively when we were assigned here at the arraignment."

The voice of the clerk boomed above the clamor. "The judge is coming out."

I turned to Matt and asked, "Why would they want to paper Mackey? He'd give them about as fair a trial as anybody."

Gillis shook his head. "No idea," he answered.

Judge Mackey, a handsome Irishman in his late forties, took the bench and called the case. He looked to us and nodded in greeting. "I have been informed by my clerk that an affidavit pursuant to section 170.5 of the Code of Civil Procedure has been filed to remove, on a peremptory challenge, this court from hearing this matter."

Judges generally interpret the filing of such an affidavit as an insult to their objectivity or legal expertise. Mindless of this, Brian Pageant rose to his feet, adjusted his tie, and stood proudly before the courtroom television camera. "Yes, Your Honor. It was I who filed the affidavit. On behalf of my client, Brad Riley, I would ask that this matter be assigned to another court."

The judge looked down at Pageant, peering scornfully above his glasses. "I plan to do that, Mr. Pageant. The courtroom of L. C. Nunley is available. This matter will be transferred to Division 16."

L. C. Nunley, a hard-nosed black jurist, ruled from the gut of his street sense as much as the boundaries of the law would allow. He was popular with neither the defense bar nor the prosecutors, tolerating nothing he considered unfair from either side of counsel table. But I never had a problem with him. In fact, we worked together quite well in cases I'd previously had before him. I thought this was the least favorable judge the Klan could have drawn. Undoubtedly, this was Judge Mackey's way of spiting the defense for affidaviting him.

"Just a moment, Your Honor." Pageant huddled with the lawyers beside him for a half minute as Judge Mackey waited, noticeably impatient. "There will be an affidavit as to Judge Nunley as well, your Honor."

"Your one affidavit for a peremptory challenge is spent, Mr. Pageant," Judge Mackey snapped.

"This affidavit will be on behalf of defendant Hofstadler, Mr. Borowitz's client," answered Pageant.

Disgustedly, the judge's eyes turned away from Pageant. "What's your preference, Mr. Phillips? You have the option of splitting the matter and trying the defendants in two separate groups."

I looked at Matt, and he immediately shook his head no. I answered, "For the sake of judicial economy, we would prefer to keep the cases together. I would say, though, that the defendants' interests are one and the same, and as such they are entitled to only one affidavit collectively."

Pageant responded, "You can't make that representation, Counsel. There are several different political groups involved in this political prosecution, none of which Mr. Reiner may care much for, but they are entitled to individual affidavits."

"Okay. Enough of that," the judge interjected. He turned to his clerk. "What other courts show as open?"

"Division 46, Judge Mary Waters."

One of our favorite places to be. Judge Waters worked well with prosecutors and was a stiff sentencer. Matt and I subtly exchanged approving smiles.

Again Pageant turned to the attorneys beside him. They spoke briefly. Pageant addressed the court. "There will also be an affidavit as to Judge Waters, Your Honor. This one on behalf of defendant Metzger by his counsel, Mr. Kearney."

Judge Mackey exploded in a fury. "I don't know what you're trying to pull here, but we are going to find a court for you, and this motion is going to be heard. Just test me again. I'll invalidate all your affidavits as an abuse of process." He turned to the clerk. "Who else is open?"

The clerk shook her head pleadingly. "Only Judge Cherniss."

I turned quickly to Matt. "That's what it was. They knew they had enough challenges to get the case before Cherniss."

Cherniss had left the regular criminal panel several years ago, having found the steady diet of criminal cases overly stressful. But Matt whispered back a pragmatic analysis. "We can't use our only affidavit now. We may need it later. Besides, he's the only one left."

Judge Mackey finished writing the notes of his order. "Okay. You're off to Division 11." He turned back to his clerk, "Let them know what to expect." He looked disdainfully at Pageant, rose and left the courtroom. Groans of disbelief emanated from the demonstrators behind us.

The hallway crowd had become impatient. As those from the courtroom poured into their midst, misunderstanding of the proceedings incubated a growing tension. We made our way through. "This is bullshit, man," I heard one spectator yell as the camera lights followed our steps.

Many demonstrators reached Cherniss's court by the time we turned the hallway. A handful of deputy marshals denying entry began pushing some backward to close the doors. Shouting erupted. Batons were drawn. The call went out for help.

Courtroom doors swung open as other marshals came to their aid. The news cameras were lifted high to record the conflict. The deputies formed a line in front of

Cherniss's court. With their batons held horizontally, a hand at each end, they began moving shoulder-to-shoulder toward the demonstrators, shoving back those who challenged them.

Matt and I were caught within the wave of bodies. We pushed through an open door to an empty courtroom and waited until the line of marshals passed. The news cameras followed the confrontation like the filming of a Fellini movie. They were all getting exactly what they came for. Gillis and I were reduced to spectators of a circus-like sideshow.

The marshals moved the demonstrators toward the escalator and scattered their number. Away from the cameras, there was no demonstrative behavior. Gillis and I went to Cherniss's courtroom.

Nearly an hour passed without activity in the court on this or any other case. The courtroom seats filled as demonstrators discovered the new location of our hearing. They grew increasingly impatient, and their rancor became more audible. I saw others of their group struggling for position to peer through the small windows of the locked courtroom doors behind us. Occasionally a loud pounding on the door sounded their frustration and contempt. Finally, Judge Cherniss emerged from chambers and tersely called the case. All counsel stated their presence for the record. The hearing began with oral argument from Brian Pageant.

"Thank you. Good morning, Your Honor. As the arrest report in this case indicates, the defendants conducted a cross-lighting ceremony in the backyard of the private residence of one of the defendants. Prior to the ceremony, Mr. Silva explained to police officers that the cross-lighting was part of his religious practice. He further stated that a Los Angeles City fire permit had been obtained.

"The report indicates that the defendants did in fact possess a fire permit, obtained in the name of one of the defendants. The officers told this same defendant that the permits were invalid, that he and his associates would be followed by the police anywhere they went within the city of Los Angeles, and that if they attempted to burn a cross they would be arrested. Silva restated that the ceremony was part of his religious beliefs and that the lighting of the cross itself would last only ten minutes.

"On December 3rd, at approximately 7:40 P.M., the crosses were lighted and the defendants were arrested.

"Now, under the law, a defendant is allowed to demur to the complaint, claiming that the acts, if true, do not constitute a public offense. He may demur at any time prior to the entry of a plea. Two complaints have thus far been filed, and it is my understanding that a second amended complaint will be filed this morning, and we have not, so far, entered a plea to the charges.

"The position of the defendants is that the court is without jurisdiction over the offenses charged, in that the facts contained within the attached police reports establish that the defendants were engaged in the exercise of free speech, religious expression, and free association, all of which are activities protected by the Constitutions of the United States and the state of California. The court should consider the facts of the case, because at the conclusion of the complaint, the police report is incorporated by reference.

"The city attorney's office, through the use of penal code sections that have rarely, if ever, been used for such purposes, has filed charges against fourteen defendants for exercising their constitutionally protected rights. The demur is brought in the hopes of providing a vehicle for asserting the constitutional rights of freedom of religion, assembly, and speech under the First Amendment of the United States Constitution. The actions of the defendants, unpopular as their viewpoint may be, are so protected. And the efforts of the city attorney, clearly motivated by political benefits, should be elsewhere prosecuting criminal activity, not here prosecuting unpopular viewpoints."

Judge Cherniss stared listlessly at Pageant throughout his argument. Seemingly unimpressed, he turned his attention away and requested my response. I stood and began my argument.

"Good morning, Your Honor. The premise of Counsel's argument is that the court is allowed to consider the facts of the case for the purpose of ruling on a demur. That is not what the law allows. A demur is a test of the legal sufficiency of the wording of the complaint. That is its only purpose. According to penal code section 1002, a demur raises an issue of law, not fact, as to the sufficiency of the accusatory pleading. In the case of *People versus De La Guerra,* the supreme court of this state established the longstanding principle that a demur is appropriate only for a legal defect that appears on the face of the complaint. I quote the opinion: 'The sole function of a motion to dismiss the indictment is to test the sufficiency of the indictment to a charged offense, that the sufficiency of the indictment must be determined from the words of the complaint, that the court is not free to consider evidence not appearing on the face of the complaint, and that all well-pleaded facts are taken to be true.'

"Mr. Pageant's argument is based entirely on the determination of factual issues. They argue that a reading of the police reports show that they were engaging in protected

First Amendment activity. But the law commands that such factual issues may not be determined on a hearing on the wording of the complaint.

"The contention that the complaint incorporates the police reports is also just not so. Mr. Pageant bases this claim on wording at the end of the complaint that is there solely for the issuance of an arrest warrant if a defendant does not appear in court. This is standard language contained within every complaint filed by either the city attorney or district attorney offices. It is required language that, if absent, would prevent the arraignment judge from issuing a warrant, because no underlying factual basis could be attested to showing a crime had been committed. As such, this wording merely complies with the terms of penal code section 1427, which requires that a magistrate presented with a misdemeanor complaint see supporting documentation establishing probable cause before he issues a warrant for a failure to appear.

"None of the charges in the complaint allege a crime was committed as the result of speaking, practicing a religious right, or merely assembling. The charges allege such violations as igniting unlawful fires, conspiracy, carrying prohibited weapons, and assembly for the purpose of committing an unlawful act or to disturb the peace of the community. For this reason, the charges themselves do not suggest a prior restraint on constitutionally protected activity.

"If these alleged violations were to be considered now, we would have two trials instead of one. If the defense claims the facts underlying their actions are constitutionally protected, then the law requires this to be raised at trial, and not at this time."

Judge Cherniss lifted his hand, indicating he had heard enough argument to make his ruling. "That is clearly the law, what Mr. Phillips has cited. I'm not here, Mr. Pageant, to make new law or change the law. These complaints include the incorporation of the police report language only so that a warrant can be issued, if necessary. Whom do you think you're dealing with here? I've been on the bench for more than twenty-eight years. Do you know how many times I've seen that language relating to the issuance of a warrant? I'll tell you. I've seen it so many times before I issued a warrant that I stopped looking for it. I just check for it once in a while. It's standard language. On every complaint I see that language. Now you want two trials. You want to carry on and waste court time. I'm responsible to the taxpayers. The demur is denied."

Cherniss continued, raising his voice as he pointed toward the spectators. "Now I'd like to advise all the people in the courtroom that I'm aware there was some sort of disturbance this morning, and as I was trying to do my work I heard banging and commotion coming from inside this court. We will tolerate no disturbance. I'm going to tell you right now that I won't have it. Any person who cannot sit quietly and observe these proceedings will be removed from the courtroom immediately. I will not have things get out of hand. I will not. This had better be understood by all concerned." Cherniss abruptly stood and stormed off to his chambers.

Matt and I were not surprised by his ruling, but the judge's anger made all in the courtroom uncomfortable. Nothing was easy with Cherniss. Not even winning. We served the second amended complaints on each of the defense counsel and court clerk, then returned to the office.

Chapter 11

The Undercover Cop

I sat at my desk the following morning, reading newspaper accounts of the hearing. There had been speculation among some in my office that the American Civil Liberties Union might enter the case as an amicus curiae (a "friend of the court") to support the defense contentions that the Klan activities were protected under the First Amendment. Although it had previously defended Klan demonstrations in other states, the ACLU would never seek the amicus status in this case, probably because of the charges that we alleged. While other prosecutions have been for violations of statutes that deal with terrorism, the statutes on which we based our case were related to unlawful burning, weapon possession, and unlawful assembly. The new antiterrorism statutes incorporate expression of racist views into the violation itself. In those cases, the ACLU has argued that expression of racist views is constitutionally protected speech. In our case, the violations we alleged are long-standing sections of the penal code that have application without the necessity of racist expression.

I received a telephone call from a member of the California Fair Employment and Housing Commission, a woman by the name of Ann Noel. She explained that an undercover policeman for the city of San Diego had testified before the commission on several occasions over the past few years. He had infiltrated the Ku Klux Klan and become Tom Metzger's right-hand man. In his testimony he related that he had attended several cross-burnings with Metzger over a two-year period in areas throughout California. His name was Doug Seymour.

Seymour lived in a rural area outside San Diego. Ann gave me his phone number and told me she let him know I would call. "I've got to warn you, though, he's been put through a lot. He was with Metzger when he ran for Congress. The Klan found Seymour out. He claimed they put a gun to his head to try to make him confess. When the press got hold of it, the San Diego Police Department disavowed him because they were caught spying on a Congressional candidate, even if he was a Klansman. The police department terminated his employment. Later, they acknowledged he was working for them. But the ordeal took a large toll on him psychologically for nearly a year."

"So what kind of witness does he make?" I asked.

"You'll have to be the judge of that. *I* believe him. Every word of it."

I thought a while before phoning Seymour. Our case against Metzger was still weak. The videotape showed only seconds of him, standing thirty or so feet from the burning crosses. If Seymour could demonstrate Metzger's participation in other cross-burnings, it would be strong circumstantial evidence that he was a participant in the Los Angeles cross-burning. This could provide the missing elements of proof we sought on Metzger.

I contacted Seymour by telephone at his building construction company. He had a deep, resonant voice, sounded friendly, and was willing to talk. We agreed to meet the following day. He came to my office punctually, at ten o'clock.

"The San Diego press gives your case a lot of attention," Seymour remarked. "Metzger has been a problem down here for years in various ways."

"Our case is about a cross-burning. Ms. Noel says you've testified before her commission that you've seen some of these."

"I've been to several, six or seven, from the Mexican border on up to Sacramento."

"With Metzger?" I asked.

"He ran them. Got everyone together. Told the membership what to bring, how to prepare the crosses, where to light 'em up."

I recalled the odd result of the lab analysis on the contents of the gasoline canisters. This was an opportunity to test Seymour's credibility. I asked if he knew the content of the liquid used to inflame the crosses.

"That's a mixture of gasoline and kerosene. Metzger had us do it that way because it burns slower than just plain gas."

He was right. The lab analysis had shown a combination of the two fluids.

Seymour continued. "Cross-*lightings*, they call them. The demonstration at Oceanside was particularly bad. A riot broke out. I was caught right in the middle."

I asked if he had any photographs or other documentation.

"Not much. There's plenty of it, though," he answered. "The intelligence units of the sheriff and police departments were at every one. Check also with the police captain at the Oceanside P.D. Smith, I think, Bob Smith was his name. I was standing next to Metzger when Smith came up to him during the riot, and he told Metzger, 'You get your ass the hell out of here.' And he shoved him down, right on his derrière."

In the following week, I followed up on every lead Seymour provided. I traveled to the San Diego Police Department on the southern coast of California, inland to the Fontana Police Department, to the central coast and the San Luis Obispo County sheriff, on up to the Sacramento County sheriff's office. The officers all remembered well Metzger's group descending upon their communities. In Klan robes and hoods, they were an invasion of hatred, openly carrying clubs and shields, brazenly challenging local minorities. They left behind the burnt ash of crosses and smoldering racial tension.

The final stop of my evidence-gathering tour was in the city of Oceanside. Captain Bob Smith welcomed my arrival. He was a tall, stately gentleman in his midfifties, hair graying at the temples. His department was fairly typical of an affluent community. Officers sat around chatting, exchanging information about bike thefts and vandalism at the harbor. Smith and I sat in the roll-call room to see old news broadcasts of the Oceanside incident.

The captain rested his boot on the corner of a desk as he looked up to the monitor. "I'm glad something's finally come back to bite Metzger. We first denied him a demonstration permit, then had to issue it when the city council got afraid we'd get sued. I tried to get this filed. You're gonna see how they beat some man senseless. The D.A. called it self-defense because he'd thrown something into the Klan crowd earlier. What they did to that poor soul *wasn't* self-defense.

"We tried to move in quicker, but we had logistical problems," Smith continued. "Our helicopter noise interfered with our radio transmissions. Then the Klan moved out from the park and began a march down the street. That's where the fighting broke loose. We moved in as fast as we could, but I'll tell you, I took a lot of heat. We're not used to this sort of thing happening in Oceanside."

As the captain began the tape, officers drifted over and sat down behind us. The news footage showed Klansmen arriving with guns, clubs, shields marked "KKK," chains, two Dobermans, a German shepherd and a collie. "Hey, who brought Lassie?" I heard, followed by laughter.

"You see that guy?" Smith pointed to a well-dressed man, center-screen at Metzger's side. "That's a guy by the name of Seymour, undercover San Diego P.D., Metzger's right-hand man. You got to watch out for that guy, though, if you come across him. He had a falling out with his department, and they say he's not all together. I don't know, though. Tried to help us out at the time. Maybe he could help you."

I did not comment.

One of the items Doug Seymour had given me was a copy of the Klan *Arrest Manual.* Among its chapters was a section on how to provoke anti-Klan demonstrators into a physical altercation that will look as though they started it. As I continued to watch the videotape of the Oceanside incident, it appeared the Klan was actually carrying out a well-orchestrated plan that other Klan groups may have executed many times before. They marched in formation out of the park and down a residential street. Counterdemonstrators pelted Metzger and his buddies with trash and other loose items. One of the Klansmen approached the counterdemonstrators and threw liquid from a jar into the face of a middle-aged man. He appeared momentarily stunned, then ran angrily at his assailant. Suddenly he was encircled by club-wielding Klansmen. One of them, wearing all white, I recognized as Stanley Witek. They began striking the man with full-force blows from their clubs about his head and face. Witek repeatedly raised his bat and struck the man across the backside of his head. The man attempted to shield the blows, but to no avail. After his arms collapsed, he dropped to the ground and lay helpless, his body curled into a fetal position. Witek continued to strike with all his might the back of the man's head and shoulders. As the sound of shrill sirens blared closer, Witek paused, then reared his foot back and kicked into the victim's midsection. The man's face was now covered with blood. Witek took a final good look, then walked proudly from his conquest.

The officers were silent during this portion of the tape. "That's not self-defense," Smith repeated softly.

The news broadcast continued with the arrival of the Oceanside P.D. "Now watch this," Smith said excitedly. "That's me right there coming up to Metzger." He pointed to the screen as a tall police figure in a riot helmet approached Metzger, reached out, placed both hands against his chest, and with one forceful thrust sent Metzger flying backwards and down on his rump. The officers burst into laughter at the display of their captain's bravado. He stood and turned to them. "I told him to get his goddamn ass the hell out of here." They all burst into laughter again.

The captain's inadvertent comment confirmed Seymour's credibility. I returned to Los Angeles with two boxes of photographs, films, and tapes given to me by law enforcement agencies across the state. There was much to review with my cocounsel. We spent two days sifting through the new evidence.

Matt raised his right hand in a congratulatory high-five, which I obliged. "John, it's complete! We have it now. All defendants, all elements, all charges! One-hundred-twenty years of Klan cross-burnings is about to come to an end. It's going to be case law. We've got more on the Klan than the Klan has on the Klan."

"Thanks, buddy. Thanks. Nothing stops us now; not heaven nor hell."

Chapter 12

Halls of Injustice

C'mon, wake up, John. You're going to be late for court." Diane gently shook me out of a deep sleep.

"What? What time is it?"

"Seven-thirty," answered Diane. "The baby wouldn't go to sleep. I was up half the night."

I rolled out of bed and moved like a wounded bear toward the bathroom. I pulled my tee shirt over my head and reached for the crucifix to remove it before entering the shower. It wasn't there. I looked down at my chest in surprise, and at this moment Diane came into the bathroom. Our eyes met in the reflection of the mirror.

"Where's your cross?"

I thought a moment. "I don't know. In the car, I think."

"What's it doing in the car?"

"I don't know where it is. Maybe I took it off last night before going to sleep."

"I'll look for it in the bedroom," offered Diane.

"You don't have to look for it!" She was startled by the agitation in my voice. "I'll find it. It's not that important, anyway. I'm trying to get to work on time."

By the time I arrived at the office, most other deputies were also just beginning to settle into work. I began to relax as I sipped a cup of coffee. Then I heard the sound of papers being dropped on to my desk. There was Michael Sachs, his usual unfriendly self, waiting for my attention.

"This brief came in for you last week."

"What is it?" I asked, reaching forward to see for myself.

"Another demur on your Klan case."

I looked at the captions. "This is noticed for a hearing at this morning's arraignment!"

"Don't worry about it. Cherniss already denied it once. This is just a repleading following your last amended complaint."

"How come you didn't get this to me sooner, Sachs?"

"You've been on your traveling junket."

"How about Gillis? Why didn't you give it to him? Now we've got no chance for a written response!"

"It's a repleading, Phillips! You filed a response to the first one. Use the same response as last time."

"Hey, Sachs, you don't know jack shit about my cases, so just butt the hell out!"

"I don't know jack shit about your cases? Well, I happen to be seeing Fran Merrick. I hear quite a bit about this case, and other shit you pull for that matter."

I was surprised by Sach's reference to Fran Merrick. She was a defense attorney frequently opposing our office. I had tried several cases against her, and I knew she viewed me bitterly after I withdrew a plea bargain Sachs offered, then convicted her client at trial.

"Oh, you do. Well, you could kiss my ass before it would matter to me," I said. Sachs turned and walked quickly away, seeking the security of his desk by Constance Moore's office. "You just keep your damn hands off my case. You understand that, Sachs?"

I read through Pageant's second demur. It indeed was a resubmission of the previous pleading. Strictly as a matter of legal procedure, this was allowable because we had amended our complaint, but it seemed the true purpose of bringing the same demur twice was to delay the proceedings. I wasn't pleased. Although demonstrators should not matter, their disruptiveness was increasing, and a further delay could set them off. Having this happen in the courtroom of the capricious Judge Cherniss would be like lighting a match in a tinder-dry forest.

When I told Matt of Sachs's delay in giving us the second demur, *I* had to calm *him* down. Fortunately, he was beyond striking distance of Sachs. There had also been an appellate ruling on a writ affirming Cherniss's denial of the first demur, which should establish the rule of the case.

As we walked to the courthouse, we could see a small band of marshals stationed at the main entry. A crowd carrying signs was slowly passing through the doors. We recognized several of the more vocal demonstrators from the hearing two weeks earlier.

Matt and I took the freight elevator to Cherniss's floor. The hallway was jammed with a startling array of demonstrators. Reporters and cameras clustered around the courtroom doors, where additional marshals waited at a metal detector, though no one else was being allowed to enter.

"Hey, Mr. Phillips, remember me?"

There stood a deputy marshal who worked in the court where I had done the sexual assault trial months ago.

"Malcolm. Of course." I extended my hand to an enthusiastic greeting. He ushered us around the metal detector and through the courtroom doors.

There we found a sea of hostile faces—including the spectators, the defendants, and their counsel. At the side of the courtroom well, a heated argument erupted between Cherniss's bailiff and the news crew doing the main camera feed. "I'm sorry," said the bailiff. "That's the judge's order. All television cameras are out. If you don't agree with it, you'll have to seek a writ."

"Seek a writ? What good is that going to do us today?"

"It may not do you any good today, but this is the judge's place of work, and he has his reasons for not wanting news cameras inside the court."

"Well, that's just not right, deputy. We should have been given at least forty-eight hours' notice on this."

The news crew grudgingly pulled its wires and headed out. As they did, other reporters who were relying on their feed attempted to enter the courtroom. They were stopped at the doorway and denied entry. Behind the news crews stood a hostile crowd, hurling insults at the defendants. When the doors were secured, the bailiff returned to his desk at the side of the courtroom and lifted the receiver of his telephone to speak with the judge. He then announced court was coming to session. Cherniss walked briskly from chambers, plopped into his worn chair behind the bench, and gruffly asked all counsel to state their presence for the record.

The hearing came underway, and I began my argument. "John Phillips and Matt Gillis are present for the People. Good morning, Your—"

I was interrupted by a woman yelling from behind. She was standing on the right side of the spectator section, facing Cherniss. "Tom Metzger is a fascist pig who runs a paramilitary camp in the Cleveland National Forest!"

The Judge exploded. "Bailiff! Silence that woman."

As his bailiff ran through the courtroom well doors, a young male demonstrator stood from the left side of the spectator section and faced the court. He yelled his slogan: "The Ku Klux Klan will not be allowed to exist in a multiracial, free society!"

Cherniss pointed to the demonstrator and called to another deputy marshal. "Do whatever is necessary to remove that man."

A third demonstrator rose, then a fourth and a fifth, each taking his or her turn to yell a prepared slogan. The Klan members stood from their chairs, rather enjoying the notoriety. Cherniss became livid with rage, pounding his gavel repeatedly and with increasing force, screaming directives to the outnumbered bailiffs. The spectacle of the judge broke the orchestration of the demonstration. Cherniss's bailiff and five other deputy marshals struggled to bring the insurgents to the lock-up down the hallway. Order was finally restored. Cherniss's composure was not.

The judge addressed the turbulent crowd. "Okay, now, let's get on with this hearing. I'll have no more of what has transpired here. No more of it. And I'll tell the attorneys now, I don't want to hear any argument from any one of you that has been argued already, in either the written papers or the oral arguments that I heard at the last hearing. It's the same motion. Same arguments. The defense has submitted basically the same papers. So let's get on with it. Who wants to be heard?"

Brian Pageant rose and began to speak, nervously fidgeting with his maroon paisley tie, and apparently incapable of adjusting his prepared oral argument to conform to the admonishment Cherniss had just given.

"Good morning, Your Honor. Brian Pageant on behalf of defendant Brad Riley. As the Supreme Court in the *Kolendar* case has said, we can't have these standardless sweeps by prosecutors or police who wish to pursue their personal predilections. And I would submit that in a case like this, that rule of law is particularly helpful. Because when we—"

Cherniss interrupted irately. "Except in this case. The defendants want me to believe they were acting in ignorance. They were specifically told they would be in violation of an ordinance if they proceeded, so don't argue that point very long. I am going by the facts. In other words, if you want me to read the police report and consider it, these people were told that they could not do this, and they went ahead and did it anyhow. Now don't tell me that you can now argue that the statute is vague and uncertain, because in this particular fact situation, it is not. Go ahead."

I was surprised by the premise of the judge's remark. He had read and considered the police report, as he was requested to do in the defense brief. In doing this, Cherniss would be violating the rule that a demur consider only the wording of the charges. Additionally, if he was going to do this, he would not have the benefit of all the new evidence I gathered. I looked at my cocounsel in surprise. He was equally stunned by the unusual direction Cherniss had taken.

Having been abruptly cut short in his dissertation, Pageant began struggling for words. "It is a violation of equal protection under our laws to single out one group and to enforce laws that are not normally used."

Again Cherniss interrupted. "Counsel, you don't listen very well. I told you at the beginning of this hearing that I was not going to permit a rehash of those points already raised in your moving papers. Now if you have nothing new to say, sit down."

Pageant looked in bewilderment at the other defense counsel sitting around him, then slowly lowered himself into his chair without further comment.

"Will there be anything else from the defense?" demanded Cherniss. There was no response. "Then how about the People?" He turned a cold eye toward me. "Do you have anything to add to your original arguments?"

I rose cautiously. "Good morning, Your Honor. I'll make this brief, because this is a relitigation of a matter that this court has already decided, and because this court's decision was upheld on appellate review of a writ filed last week by the defense. The moving papers again request the court to consider the police report in deciding the demur. And once again, the language at the bottom of the complaint, which incorporates the police report, is there only for the issuance of a warrant in the event that a defendant does not appear for a scheduled hearing.

"A demur hearing is limited to the scope of the four corners of the complaint. There is not supposed to be a review of the facts. If this were not the rule, both sides would be presenting all the evidence they have before a case has been fully investigated, and there would, in effect, be not just one trial, but two. I am not going to waive the right of the People to preserve this rule of law. If I were to do so, this hearing would take many days, if not weeks, and we would then be required to have such hearings not just for the Ku Klux Klan, but for every criminal defendant in every criminal case. I will not establish such a precedent. Beyond that, I have no additional argument to what has already been stated in our responding papers and the oral argument presented at the last hearing." I sat down.

Cherniss dropped the volume of his voice as he began to speak. "We have some problems here. I will make some comments first.

"I ruled the last time that the *Mandel* case did not compel the court to consider the arrest report, because the purpose of that language in a preprinted document, as argued by the People the last time around, is for an arrest warrant, and I thought they had just neglected to strike that language out. I am shocked to see that in the next amended complaint, after knowing the defense arguments, that the language is present again. So I must take it that the People, although they stand to argue in court that this is standard language and that they don't want to incorporate the police reports, don't really mean that because they included the language again. So by including that language in their amended complaint, the court is going to consider the matter set forth in the police report in evaluating these various charges."

I rose quickly, seeing the convoluted reasoning Cherniss was adopting. "Excuse me, Your Honor! There has been an appellate decision confirming—"

"This is not your opportunity! I've begun my ruling, and I've heard your arguments. I am just going to consider it. I have read it and there was no purpose in leaving those . . . that paragraph or that two paragraphs. Now I have considered the police report for each and every one of these charges."

Cherniss continued, determined to rid himself of the case and everything that came with it. "I am going to say at the outset that I have no patience for these people out there and I will not tolerate any kind of demonstration. But I am going to put some harsh words toward most of the people sitting out in the audience because we are supposed to be living in a free country where we have the right to live our lives as we see fit, as long as we don't step on someone else's toes. I don't know what gives the so-called KKK the right to burn crosses or say they are better than anyone else. Who gave them that right?

"So the actions that I read in that police report indicate to me that those who acted as they did that night, the KKK and whoever else participated for them or against them, are slimy, low, and scummy, every one of them."

Cherniss's face became red. His voice thundered; his fist clenched. I looked over to Matt, seated beside me, and asked despairingly, "What is he doing?"

"He's taking himself out of the case," Matt angrily snapped, "establishing cause for his own removal." I looked back toward Cherniss, who had resumed his tirade.

"I am saying it right while I am looking into your eyes. How can you live in this country, this United States? And any time any individual or any group under the so-called protection of the First Amendment uses toward another group derogatory language decrying their color, their race, their religion—whatever—is low, slimy, and despicable, and you have no right to be in the United States. You ought to go somewhere else.

"Now, we have the First Amendment, which allows one to speak his mind, but you shouldn't speak your mind to where you decry your neighbor. In burning crosses, these people demonstrated a completely un-American attitude, and the point is the police operated completely properly as I can read from this police report. They were faced with these jerks, these low-minded scum, going out to burn crosses. Big-deal yellow-bellies, that is what I say, all to your faces, all of you. You have all descended to a terrible level, and it has no place in this United States. Any group that calls another names, makes threats, burns crosses, they do it for one reason—to stir other people up. What gives you that right? Nobody, nothing anywhere gives you that right to stir up other people like that. You ought to look at yourselves in the mirror and look at what terrible people you are.

"I don't know that I have any great wisdom, but I do have a fundamental understanding. This is a great country where you have the right to speak out and say things, but you don't have the right to cry 'fire' in a crowded theater. You don't have the right to go out and stir people up. What does it do for you? What does it make of you? Well, I'll tell you. You are yellow-bellies. Every one of you that pulls that nonsense on either side.

"I have considered the police report in this matter, and I have read all of the counts in connection with the police report, and the People have failed to state a cause of action. There may have been some crimes committed that night. I am not saying by this ruling that I am giving any credit to those people who did what they did that night. They have no right whatsoever.

"What you did cost the taxpayers a lot of money, to have helicopters come over and fly about and to have the police come out and endanger themselves to take action, because where action isn't taken, then you stupid people get together and you start fighting and somebody gets hurt or killed. Are you big men? You are yellow-bellies. Any one of you individually would not be able to handle himself at all. You get in a crowd, and you call other people names. That is terrible, slutty, terrible.

"The demur is granted as to each and every count in the complaint. I will not allow the complaint to be amended. The case is dismissed as to all defendants. Bail is exonerated."

After denouncing the Klan's actions and ruling the First Amendment did not protect their conduct, Cherniss had suddenly dismissed the entire case. He quickly walked toward his chambers.

Astonished gasps filled the courtroom.

"Hold on, Judge!" I hurried toward the side of the courtroom near his exit. "I demand an explanation of how you reason—"

Cherniss turned and pointed his finger as he began to yell. "Your Mr. Reiner blew it right from the top!"

"I want to know your reasoning! Put on the record your reason why the conduct was inciteful and was not constitutionally protected, and then tell us why they can't be prosecuted!"

Cherniss scowled angrily, then turned and slammed his chambers door behind him.

"Come out here and put on the record how there were crimes, but that you're not going to give us a chance to put it to trial!"

The door to the judge's chambers burst open and slammed against the wall with a crash. Cherniss stood in the threshold, again pointing his finger, his mouth quivering in anger. "One more word out of you, Phillips, and you're in contempt. One more goddamn word!"

"If it gets me your explanation of how crimes can be committed, but that you're granting the demur."

"That's it! You're in contempt!" With Cherniss's regular bailiff having gone to remove demonstrators, Malcolm Jefferson remained as the only deputy marshal. Cherniss motioned him toward me. "Go ahead, deputy. Take him to lock-up."

The courtroom suddenly was entirely still, and a feverish chill ran through my body. I looked over to Malcolm. He looked at me. His eyes were steel cold and he stood motionless, arms at his side. He looked back to the judge.

"I told you take that man into custody!"

Malcolm remained motionless. He held his glance to Cherniss for a moment. I watched, not knowing whether to run or surrender. Then Malcolm looked again to me, but he did not take a step. His mouth tightened. He said nothing.

I heard a whisper from close behind. "John, let's get out of here." Matt tugged lightly on my sleeve in a direction toward the rear exit. "Come on, man."

I backed up several steps, exchanging glares with Cherniss, then turned and began to walk, with Matt still beside me. The spectators remained silent. Some stood. Through them I looked to see Malcolm, beads of perspiration glistening in the distance, watching me as I exited through the hallway doors.

Chapter 13

Race Warriors

We filed an appeal of the dismissal of *People versus Metzger* the following day, but the defendants were long gone from Los Angeles by week's end. Some had returned to Idaho, others to San Diego, a few to places dictated by their newly formed legion, which they called "The Order."

◆ ◆ ◆ ◆ ◆

Nothing much to speak of ever happened in the city of Ukiah, a midsize town in northwestern California. Babies got born, the price in the wheat market rose, and the local newspapers were content to report these stories to their quiet, homegrown community. A small sheriff's station handled the neighborhood disputes and occasionally made a drunk-driving arrest. Once in a while, there was a shoplifting call from the only downtown department store. Residents were comfortable with the night air flowing through their open bedroom windows. Only eight days had passed since the dismissal of *People versus Metzger.*

A Brinks armored car rolled along Interstate 20 early that Saturday morning. Its driver watched a field of golden alfalfa bend in breezy waves. The passenger guard struggled with a thermos of coffee, negotiating his cup with the gentle sways in the roadway. They didn't take much notice of the rented moving van that pulled from a side road in front of them. They hadn't seen the pickup truck behind them slow its speed, creating a break in traffic.

As they approached another turn in the road, the moving van began to slow, then came to a sudden stop. Another rental van positioned itself behind the armored car. With only one lane in each direction of the undivided highway, the armored vehicle could not safely pass, or so its driver thought, unaware traffic had been blocked in both directions. Sensing danger, the driver of the armored car stopped his vehicle twenty feet behind the moving van. To his amazement, the van barreled backward in reverse, slamming into the front of the Brinks truck. Almost simultaneously, they were struck from behind by a second moving truck.

Sandwiched by the two vehicles, the driver instinctively pressed the accelerator to the floor, attempting to push the first truck and enable their escape. But the moving truck would not budge. Men from the adjacent wheat fields emerged with automatic rifles. They raised their weapons and began shooting out the tires of the armored car, then shattering the windows with repeated blasts.

The firing stopped. Helplessly, the Brinks guards lay on the floorboard, covered with broken glass, and pleaded for mercy from the eight assailants swarming their vehicle. The guards discarded their weapons as ordered, stepped from the cab with hands raised, and relinquished their keys. Within moments, the rear door to the armored car was opened, and all $3.6 million of its cargo was removed.

◆ ◆ ◆ ◆ ◆

In the broadcast booth of radio station WKOA in Denver, Colorado, sat a talk-show host, impatiently waiting through an auto-dealership commercial. He tapped his pencil several times, then turned to his screener and abruptly asked, "The next call. Come on. What's the next call?"

"Pro-environmental on the Wilderness Act," his young assistant responded.

He tossed his pencil to the side of the broadcast desk and leaned back in his chair. "There's a doozy. Pro-environmental. Come on. Get a firebug on the line who wants to burn that parkland to cinders. We need pro-lumber industry, Peggy. Hurry. Move the lines." The commercial ended.

The host leaned forward in his chair and punched line four. "We're back on the air. This is Alan Berg. Who am I speaking with?"

"Hi, Alan. This is Larry. I enjoy your show very much."

"So do I, Larry. I listen to it every time. What's on your mind today?"

"Well, this Wilderness Act before Congress. It's very important for our area."

"But does it go far enough, Larry? More forest land will burn each year than this bill affords for purchase. Isn't this just a look-good attempt by our boys in Washington?"

"Gee. I hadn't looked at it that way. Are any additional appropriations possible?"

"Additional appropriations are always possible with a government spending more than $3 trillion each year. Priorities. That's the issue. They're all messed up." Berg could see his screener indicating line three with her fingers, mouthing the word "Klan."

"Thank you for calling, Larry. Let's see if we can get the boys in the ivory tower to stop building bombs and start planting trees."

"Yeah, really. Nice speaking with you, Alan."

"You, too." Berg punched line three. "Let's see who we have here so patiently waiting to travel the air waves. You're on. Who's this?"

"Dave."

"Where are you calling from, Dave?"

"The United States of Jewmerica."

"Oh. We have a scholar on the line. You must have advanced degrees in linguistics to come up with so clever a phrase."

"I don't need no advanced degrees to know what's going wrong with this country."

"And what is wrong with it, Sir? Did some big meany take your ball away?"

"The blacks and the Jews."

"The blacks and the Jews took your ball away?"

"The blacks take the safe streets away. The Jews take the fair media away. And you're a good example."

"Well, I am a good example because I let people like you on the air to vent out your Neanderthal views. Would you do the same if the situation were reversed?"

"When are you going to let up on the Klan and the New Right?"

"I asked you a question. Would you let me on the air if you had the show and I was the caller?"

"I want to know when you're going to stop badmouthing the Klan."

"Answer the question. Do you just believe in free speech for yourself? Is that free speech?"

"I'll answer yours if you answer mine."

"Well, I asked mine first. Would you let me on the air if it was *your* show?"

"Not on your cheap life."

"Now I'll answer yours. Not till the day I die will I stop badmouthing the Ku Klux Klan or any group like them, for the very reasons you make so apparent. This isn't the kind of country that you and those like you belong in, and there hasn't been one since the fall of the Third Reich. Why don't you go to the library and learn something about what your mentality brings about? Or better yet, join a church."

"I have a church, you son of a—"

"Or better yet, get a lobotomy."

"You got a big, wise mouth."

Berg pushed the button to abort the call. "On that positive note, I'll say farewell to our caller, Dave. At least we agree that some part of me is wise. Wish I could say the same for him."

During the following weeks a series of bank robberies plagued the Northwest states. Other than for video images recorded by the in-bank cameras, no name identifications were made. Still unknown to law enforcement was the connection between the heists and the white supremacist extremists. "The big move," of which the seemingly uncreditable Mike Canale had warned, had begun—its first stage, the procurement of capital. And in the minds of those comprising The Order, there was no better source than "the Jewish-controlled banks insured by the Zionist Occupational Government." Then came stage two.

He finished his show, removed the headphones, and wearily left the broadcast booth. It was the evening of July 23, and like most nights after work, Alan Berg planned only to return to his townhouse and await calls from friends needing company.

Berg drove to his quiet suburban residence, pulled his car into the driveway, stopped the engine, and removed his keys. Tired from the drive home, he got out slowly, closed the door with a push from his forearm, and walked toward his front entryway.

It was then he first noticed a figure moving toward him, silhouetted by the bright floodlight above his front door. Then a frozen, odd smile became visible. The man kept his right arm to his side. Alarmed the man had come from his front property, Berg slowed his pace to a stop.

"Mr. Berg?"

"Yes."

"I'm a big fan of yours."

As the figure walked closer, Berg saw a long metallic object extending from the man's right hand. Then he recognized the silencer. Berg stepped away, turning toward the street. A second man stood in his path. A rapid succession of pops matched with white flashes propelled Berg backward toward his car and onto his back. Burning sensations filled his chest. Lying helpless as he looked up at his murderers, his last vision was into the barrel of the small automatic rifle. His life ended a second later, as the gunmen mercilessly emptied the clips of their weapons.

Berg's killers were part of The Order, formed only weeks before the Los Angeles cross-burning and consisting of hard-line extremists from various white supremacist organizations. Among their ranks were several of the Los Angeles defendants, including Frank Silva, Randy Evans, David Tate, and Tom Bentley. Each of them swore an oath of allegiance to their cause and comrades, the penalty for its violation agreed as decapitation.

By mid-September, the FBI had completed an extensive manual search through dealers' records of sale for a converted automatic rifle recovered from the Ukiah armored car. It had been sold to an Idaho resident by the name of Andrew Berringhile. Berringhile was a loner. None of his acquaintances had seen him for months, but they remembered well his favorite topic of conversation—the salvation of the white race. A neighbor believed he was a survivalist, having noticed him in military camouflage clothes carrying what looked like a rifle case as he packed his car one morning. It was enough of a lead for the assigned agents to visit Los Angeles to review evidence gathered in *People versus Metzger*. They left with copies of the videotapes Peter Lake had taken at the cross-burning and inside the Aryan Nations compound.

When the Brinks guards viewed the tapes, they immediately spotted one of their assailants, then another, and others until nearly all eight had been identified. Bank tellers also made identifications. A dozen federal agents were assigned surveillance of the Aryan Nations compound.

One of the frequent visitors to the compound was Stewart Scarborough. His gaunt face was largely obscured by a scraggly red beard and long, messy hair.

He lived almost like a hermit in a small, wooden house down the road about a mile from the compound. Money was not a problem for him now, so he had time to hang out and keep a watchful eye on his surroundings.

The late-model Corsica easing down his road was an uncommon sight. Eyeing it closely as it passed, Scarborough guessed right that the driver and passenger were federal agents. He loaded his automatic rifle, boarded his jeep, and slowly followed the direction taken by the Corsica. Spotting it parked several hundred yards ahead, he went off-road to a high point. Scarborough stepped out of his jeep and peered down at the two men. They were walking through a group of large pine trees to a clearing that allowed a direct view of the Aryan Nations compound. Their backs remained to him.

Scarborough grabbed his weapon and moved swiftly, hunching over and staying low. About seventy-five yards to their rear, he found a clear line of view to the two men. They were stopped and viewing the grounds ahead through binoculars. Scarborough's suspicions were confirmed.

He raised his rifle and adjusted the scope. His finger moved to the trigger. His targets remained stationary for the moment he needed, and he slowly squeezed his finger until the rifle burst into a rapid succession of pops and jolts. Losing the perspective through his scope, he looked ahead and saw the two men dashing for cover. He squeezed the trigger again, this time firing from his hip. A long series of blasts sprayed about the small clearing. Scarborough stopped firing and looked again. "Damn!" The agents had taken cover behind two large pine trees. Neither had been hit. He ran toward his jeep, threw the rifle in back, and sped away, never again to return to his Idaho home.

Indictments were issued and a nationwide roundup began. One by one, members of The Order were captured. One of the few remaining at large was David Tate, the quick-trigger country boy who served as Butler's bodyguard at the L.A. cross-burning.

◆ ◆ ◆ ◆ ◆

Missouri State Police Officers Mike Linagar and Steven Price had each sought the excitement of a career in law enforcement but were finding early assignments a dull routine of ticket writing and traffic-accident reports.

Officer Linager stood outside their patrol vehicle, parked roadside, listening to the sounds of insects flying above the dry prairie. Price sat inside. They were conducting spot checks of vehicle registrations along a stretch of remote highway about twelve miles south of Joplin. Thinking about the first fishing trip he was planning for his two little boys, Linagar mechanically raised his hand to a brown van and motioned its driver to the shoulder. The vehicle pulled slowly to a stop about forty feet on. Linagar walked toward the driver's door.

The van door opened. Out stepped David Tate. He saw the officer's hands empty. Believing the officer would discover his fugitive status, Tate reached back, drew his weapon, and fired a burst of rounds from his MAC-10 automatic rifle. Each hit its target, plunging into Linagar's chest. The first four rounds lodged harmlessly into his bullet-proof vest, but as he spun sideways with the force of the slugs, the next three rounds entered his body.

Officer Price grabbed the shotgun from the bracket inside his patrol vehicle. He pulled himself low along the front seat to slip through the door on the passenger side. He pushed the door open and attempted to position himself behind it to exchange fire.

Tate crouched, adjusted his aim, and fired another burst of rounds. Price was thrown backward. He felt burning, piercing sensations in his leg and side, then saw a deep red stain spreading around a hole in the right leg of his uniform pants. He began struggling toward the back of his unit for cover. Tate reentered his van and sped away. Officer Linagar lay dead.

There followed the largest manhunt in the history of the state of Missouri. Tate's van was discovered about six miles down the road, driven into heavy brush beyond a small hill. A ten-mile search radius was set up. Every farmhouse, barn, and haystack were searched. All passing cars were stopped, and trunks were opened at gunpoint. Helicopters scoured the area for movement by any creature on two legs. But after three days and nights, there was still no sign of David Tate.

On the morning of the fourth day, the search dogs were taken again along a path that ran southeast from the abandoned van. Since it had been left on the north side of the highway, the paths leading to the north side were the first to be covered. It was not until the second day that the south-side trails were checked extensively for scents and clues.

Six miles into the hills the dogs began barking ferociously, pulling toward a patch of heavy brush sixty feet off the fire path. Confident in their animals, the K-Nine officers took cover and radioed for backup. A small battalion responded.

Through a handheld public-address system, Tate was ordered out. They assumed he was there. No response.

The captain announced his preference to Tate: to shoot up the shrubs, then search for his body. Still no response. The captain gave the order. The guns cracked and the hillsides echoed for a full minute. Two hundred rounds were fired. Silence fell. On command, the officers cautiously moved toward the patch of brush, the dogs in the lead.

The leader of the pack stopped and snarled, and the officers dropped down. All guns were aimed into a thicket of brush ten feet ahead. Still, no person was visible. The captain yelled his loudest and gruffest. "Get the hell out, Tate, or die here! Now!"

A shrub rustled, then hands raised from behind a mound of soil. "Don't shoot. Don't shoot." Tate was swarmed by the officers, cuffed, and dragged down the hillside to the state police vehicle.

Chapter 14

Picking Up the Pieces

A year and a half passed since the capture of David Tate. He was convicted of the murder of Missouri State Trooper Michael Linagar and assault with intent to murder Officer Price. The state of Missouri, which had no death penalty, sentenced Tate to two consecutive life terms. Frank Silva, Randy Evans, and Tom Bentley were also captured. Silva and Evans were tried and convicted of federal racketeering charges for their participation in activities of The Order and sentenced to twenty years in the federal penitentiary. Bentley received eight years as an accessory to murder.

During that time, many changes occurred in the two Los Angeles prosecuting agencies. Ira Reiner moved from the top spot in the city attorney's office to the district attorney for Los Angeles County. Gil Garcetti became his chief deputy. Bob Bohrer was now the city attorney for Los Angeles. With him came a number of new people to the office. Surprisingly, one of these was

Fran Merrick, who was appointed chief deputy of the criminal division. She in turn promoted Michael Sachs as her chief assistant. They remained very close companions, though they were unpopular with nearly all the deputies they supervised.

One of the bright spots of Fran's day was the social call from Sachs she received like clockwork when the others were busy with work. It usually came around ten in the morning, but today Sachs was a little late. Fran was upset. Her coffee was getting cold, and she was down to her last cigarette. She opened her office door and peered down the hallway. There was Sachs coming toward her, trying to smile as the coffee in his own cup spilled from side to side, burning his fingers. She gave him a disapproving look, pointed to the clock, and shook her finger. "Bad boy. Forty-five minutes I waited for you. Get in here." She closed the door behind them.

"You won't believe what's happened," said Sachs.

"There's no reason good enough to keep me waiting."

"I know. I know. But we have a problem."

"A problem? There's no problem we can't solve. Let's hear it, Michael."

"Good news and bad."

"Oh, what fun already. I always like to hear the good news first."

"Well. The good news is that our Gerald Webster has once again proven himself to be a very fine appellate attorney."

"Yes. And what's the bad?"

"The bad news is that he's done it by resurrecting the Ku Klux Klan cross-burning case that was dismissed almost two years ago."

"That was Phillips's case," said Fran softly.

"Indeed it was."

"And where is our dear Mr. Phillips these days?"

"Private practice, I hear. The dismissal didn't sit well with him," responded Sachs. "Never one of my favorite people."

"Nor mine," said Fran. "Well, let's just put the case back together and have someone do it."

"Put the case back together? No way. It's trashed for one thing. For another, that case could *never* be won. They're burning crosses on their own property. It's First Amendment activity."

"What do you mean, 'it's trashed'?" asked Fran.

"When Phillips left the office, I took about four big boxes of his old garbage and trashed it, threw it out."

"The Klan materials—you threw them out?" Fran was surprised.

"The case had been dismissed! It should have stayed that way. How was I to know?"

"Shit! Didn't anyone talk to Webster before he did his arguments on the appeal?"

"To do what?" he said.

"To set him straight, that's what. Didn't you talk to Webster?"

"You don't talk to Gerald Webster for that kind of thing. He's not one of us."

"Get him in here." Fran stormed over to her office door and opened it, motioning her hand for Sachs to bring the appellate lawyer to her.

"You want his head on a silver plate?" Sachs snidely asked.

"Just get him."

Webster was a forty-four-year-old career prosecutor who found his niche in the appellate department of the city attorney's office. Indeed, he was not one of the "in crowd" within this or any previous administration. Like most appellate attorneys, he was more intellectual than personable. He didn't read people well, which is likely the reason he gravitated away from trial work. But he was sincere and ethical, and I had always respected him.

A few minutes passed before Fran heard the sound of voices approaching her office door. She stood to greet them, fixed a smile, and waited as they came into view.

"Gerald. Congratulations on the decision."

"Thank you, Fran. The law was in our favor. These always are work, though."

"Well, you did your usual great job. Is there no limit to what you can do?"

"Oh, I'm sure there are limits."

"Come in. Sit down." Gerald and Michael waited for Fran, then sat in the chairs before her desk. Michael made himself comfortable, leaning back and folding his hands behind his head. Gerald remained a bit ill at ease, ever apprehensive in the presence of the unpredictable pair. "I'm sure there must have been plenty of press for this one. Am I right?" asked Fran.

"There's still a lot of interest. Especially since some of the defendants got wrapped up with the terrorist faction. It seems like the press was waiting for the decision."

"Did any of them ask what we'll be doing next with the case?"

"What do you mean? When the trial will be?" asked Gerald.

"Or *if* the trial will be," Fran laughed as if she were only kidding.

"I told them it takes about a month for the decision to become final, then the case gets sent back to court for trial." Webster paused and looked curiously toward Merrick. "You say *if* there is a trial. Do you mean you may drop the case?"

"Oh, we can't drop the charges on something as political as this. Not that we would have wanted to, of course. How long do we have to get it ready for trial?"

"It's usually several months."

"Several months. That's plenty of time. Michael, who do we have that might be able to take this case?"

"I don't know." Sachs paused a moment in thought. "Matt Gillis was on it with Phillips."

"Let's get him in here."

◆ ◆ ◆ ◆ ◆

There was a knock on the door. "Come in," called Fran. The door opened, Matt greeted Sachs, then caught sight of Gerald.

"Hey! There he is, the man of the hour. Good job. I knew all along you'd get that magilla reversed."

"Thanks, Matt," answered Gerald, smiling for the first time since entering Fran's office.

"Sit down, Matt," interrupted Fran. "We've got some planning to do."

"How can I help?"

"We have to get this case ready for trial now."

"You gotta have Phillips for that."

Fran was surprised by Matt's definitive response. "Well, we don't have Phillips. You worked on the case. Didn't you?"

"I worked on the case with him, but it wasn't my case. He knows the witnesses. He's got the angles. The case can't be won without developing the background on this, and there're witnesses up and down the state. Informants, surveillance officers, ex-Klan members. They don't just come to court. You have to work with these people, assure them things are being done right. Otherwise they don't come forward to put their asses on the line."

"Okay. Thank you, Matt. You can go too, Gerald. We'll have to see what we do." Fran stood, abruptly curtailing the meeting, and came out from behind her desk to Gerald Webster. "You let us know what you're working on. I want a list of all your cases."

Sachs remained behind as the other two lawyers left. As the door closed behind them, he turned to Fran. "We can't have Gillis working on this."

"Why not, other than the fact that he doesn't want to work on it? I could still tell him to take it."

"He's just been promoted to branch office supervisor. Also—" Sachs looked behind him at the closed door and lowered his voice to a hush—"he's gonna know a lot of shit is missing."

"Oh. So I'm supposed to cover your ass." Fran smiled at Michael. "I guess that comes with the territory."

Sachs returned Fran's smile. "Besides. We don't want someone connected with this administration taking the fall."

"How do you mean?" asked Fran.

"I always thought the case couldn't be won. Now, after all this time, it's certain. If we can farm this case out to someone outside the office, then we make him responsible. Politically, I mean. 'Hey,' we say to the press, 'This was always Phillips's and Reiner's case. If they screwed it up, they screwed it up.' We've got to disassociate ourselves from this case."

Fran sat back in her chair. "You mean, we try to bring Phillips back? I thought you couldn't stand the man."

"I can't. Even more the reason. Just deserts."

"He won't come back to the office. Not with you and me here."

"He will. For this case, he will."

Chapter 15

Prosecutor for Hire

In the Westside business district of Los Angeles was the law office of my brother, Kenneth M. Phillips. When he opened his doors five years earlier, the shingle he hung read "Phillips & Associates." He used his last name in the hope we would someday practice our trade together. I had always looked up to him, both as a brother and a lawyer.

In the interim of the appeal, Diane struggled through her second pregnancy. I was with her when she delivered, as I was for the birth of our first child. This one was a girl—a beautiful, angelic girl with blond ringlet curls. We named her Jessica. When I held her it seemed my life was complete, but of course it never really is. I wondered what, in life, I would be able to give her and my son. The limit of my ability was far less than the bounds of my love.

I had my fill of the city attorney's office, and the dismissal of the Klan case engulfed me in a sense of failure despite an otherwise enormously successful career. My brother Ken encouraged me to rent an open office in his suite, and

I decided to make the transition to private practice. It was new and challenging. But my sense of self was not the same.

I stayed in touch with the witnesses on the Klan matter. Some had been frustrated before with stalled investigations involving the Klan. As news of the defendants got press coverage, I would usually receive a fresh batch of calls from the whole group.

Lake remained friendly. Mike Canale occasionally phoned or came around. He once asked me to represent him on a minor civil matter. I declined, hoping that somehow I might be involved with the prosecution again, and referred him to my brother.

One morning in early June 1991, I interviewed a potential new client, twenty-one years old, in and out of college, and unable to find any meaningful direction. He'd been arrested for the statutory rape of a fifteen-year-old girl and was there with his mother. I sat and listened to his explanation of the events leading up to his arrest. I did not like the looks of this young man.

He finished his presentation, crossed his arms and looked across my desk. "So what do you think you can do for me?" he asked.

"You told all of this to the police?" I inquired. When I was a prosecutor, full confessions such as his always amazed me. Now I got to hear them firsthand.

"Yeah. Like I said. They gave me my rights and I told them. I figured it might help, but now I just want to beat the whole thing. Did I make a mistake?"

"You made a mistake by being with a girl six years younger than you. Being honest with the police is not necessarily a mistake. In fact, it may be a good start to correcting the situation."

"But can you still get me off?"

"That would take a trial. I would have to call not only the girl a liar, but the police also. Do you think a jury would believe that?"

"Maybe. Anyway, I don't want to go to jail."

"If you want me to represent you, I would do it in the way that is most in your interest. You're looking at a possible state prison commitment of four years. I would minimize it. Because you've been honest so far, I could make a good case for probation."

"What would we do?"

"We would go in right at the arraignment and negotiate a plea."

"You mean plead guilty?"

"We would treat this case as a sentencing matter. Do a thorough job on the sentencing report with the probation department. It comes before the plea. We put your best foot forward. The court will respect the fact that you're acknowledging a mistake. You're young. They'll cut you slack. If you do otherwise, you're likely to lose, and then you have no negotiating leverage."

"I thought you were gonna try to get me off?"

"What I can do is get you off as much as you could hope for."

The young man turned toward his mother. "He just wants me to plead."

She looked sympathetically to him, then turned again to me. "I think we had better consider this. We'll give you a call if we decide to go with you." She thanked me and they left.

I knew I would not hear from them again. I sat back down at my desk. The phone rang. Mary, our receptionist, told me Fran Merrick was on the line.

I was not surprised to receive a call from the city attorney's office. I had gone to the courthouse early on the morning of the appellate decision to read the tentative ruling taped to the courtroom door. But I was surprised that it was Fran Merrick who called.

"Hello, Fran. How are things with your new job? I understand you're running the criminal division."

"Yes. Always busy. Always problems. Funny how our situations are reversed. Now, I'm the prosecutrix. Did you hear about the Klan case getting reversed?"

"Let's see now. The Klan case? Oh, yes. I heard something about it. How about that."

"How about it is right. There's going to be a lot of work needing to go into this. Michael Sachs and I are taking the case, but we think we can use your help."

"How so?"

"With the trial. I have clearance from the top to arrange for you to come back to the office, on a temporary basis, to work on it. If you think you might be interested, we should get together to discuss your fee."

Throughout the remainder of the day I tried to sort through conflicting feelings about returning to the city attorney's office. Diane listened during dinner, distracted by the attention required by our two little ones. After they were asleep, she joined me in our living room and tucked herself into the far corner of the couch.

"So this is what you wanted," she said half questioningly. "You get to do the case. This is good. Right?"

"I'm bothered that it was Fran who called. It just doesn't make sense. And Sachs? This ain't real."

"What harm could they really do?" she asked. I looked at her with a slight air of exasperation. "Would you try the case or them?" she asked.

"Oh, I wouldn't put Humpty Dumpty back together again for Merrick and Sachs to play egg toss. I would try the case."

"Then how could they mess it up?"

"By a comment. By a rumor. Doing any one of a hundred little things."

Two days later, I met with Merrick and Sachs.

"Come in, John. Good morning." Fran officiously approached and we shook hands. The pretense seemed strained. Next there was Michael Sachs, smiling over in the corner as though he and I were old friends.

"So you and I may be working on this together," I remarked cordially.

"The pleasure would be mine," Sachs answered.

Fran sat behind her mahogany desk. "Michael's been good enough to volunteer his services. There've been a lot of changes since you were here."

"How many defendants remain charged in this thing?" asked Sachs. "I can't seem to locate the file."

"Thirteen," I answered. "But four of them are serving federal time. Two on racketeering charges, another two for murder."

"Which ones are they?"

Sachs wrote the names down on a notepad, then asked the length of their commitments. I knew his interest was to rationalize a dismissal of the charges against them.

"I wouldn't dismiss all those guys out of the complaint," I offered.

"I didn't say I was going to." He paused and puckered his lower lip. "Why wouldn't you cut them loose, anyway? They're doing more time than we can get them to trial by."

"If Silva and Evans are defendants, then they have Fifth Amendment rights not to testify. A federal magistrate would not issue a removal order for them to be transported out of state to testify here. If you dismiss the charges, Pageant will subpoena Silva to testify, and then he'll take the blame for everything to shield Metzger. That's why."

"Well, I'll think about it. I don't know what we'll do."

"How long do you think it'll take to put the trial on?" Fran asked.

"The People's case in chief, the defense case, and then our rebuttal evidence, I would anticipate, should take about five weeks in all," I said.

Fran nodded in apparent agreement. "Five weeks. I can offer you one hundred dollars per hour for five weeks of trial, and an additional two weeks assisting in the preparation. Let's see. That's 280 hours. Twenty-eight thousand dollars in reserve for the time you bill. How does that sound? It would sound good to me if I were still in private practice."

"Who would actually try the case?" I said.

"Does that matter?" replied Fran. "This is a large sum of money."

"I would like to try the case. If that's agreeable, I'll take the job," I said.

Sachs stood and acted conciliatory. "There's no problem with that." He looked to Fran and smiled slyly.

"You do know it's a political case?" Fran asked.

"Very political," Sachs added.

"We wouldn't want anything to go wrong," Fran said.

"Of course not," I said. I thought a moment. It suddenly hit me where I was, who I was with, and what I was doing. "You may not have to prosecute this case."

"What do you mean by that?" Sachs eagerly inquired.

"They have a motion pending to compel a felony prosecution. It looks like a strategy ploy to move the case over to the district attorney's office."

"A motion to compel a felony prosecution?" Sachs said. "Very interesting."

"We'll get in touch with you after we get a date set," said Fran. "In the meantime, I'll get final approval."

Weeks passed with no word from Merrick or Sachs.

I was driving home from court after having spent nearly the entire day away from my office. It was late in the afternoon. I telephoned my office for messages. None seemed particularly important. Then Mary read one from my friend at the D.A.'s office, Dale Davidson, which he said was urgent. I called immediately, completely unable to guess his purpose in trying to reach me.

"You're not going to believe what a small world it is," Dale began. "Do you know two city attorneys by the names of Fran Merrick and Michael Sachs?"

"They're not to be trusted. How did you come across them?" I asked.

"Get a load of this." Dale exhaled, then began. "We get a call from Division 50 that a case has just been transferred to our office. They don't tell us anything about the case. They just tell us the city attorney no longer has jurisdiction, and that the district attorney's office has to assume the prosecution on the case."

I listened without comment, wanting to know the perspective of the district attorney's office on just how they came to assume the prosecution. I knew Sachs never really wanted this case, right from the start. I was glad he and Merrick were out, but I wondered if I was out,

Tom Metzger, former Grand Dragon of the California Klan, was the principal figure at the San Luis Obispo cross-lighting and elsewhere throughout California until his arrest in Los Angeles County.

Photo Courtesy Stephen Laferney

Stan Witek, front left, and Mike Canale, far right, were among Nazi Party members providing security at the "cross-lighting ceremony."

Photo Courtesy Peter Lake

Richard Butler in Klan robe with bodyguard David Tate inside Major's home.

Photo Courtesy Stephen Laferney

The Klan allowed Peter Lake to tape the ceremony, believing it would preserve their claim to First Amendment protections.

Photo Courtesy Stephen Laferney

LAPD officers swoop down the hillside to arrest the Klansmen. Moments later they smash Lake's camera.

Photo Courtesy Stephen Laferney

Lieutenant Robinson is transfixed by the blazing crosses as newsmen approach him.

Photo Courtesy Peter Lake

Phillips questioning Peter Lake at the preliminary hearing.

Photo Courtesy Court TV

Judge J.D. Smith was determined to preserve the integrity of the trial.

"You can choose to ignore racism today, but you can't choose the victims of racism tomorrow."

Photo Courtesy Court TV

Dale Davidson questions Metzger regarding Frank Silva's prison will.

Photo Courtesy Larry Bessel/LA Times Syndicate

Tom Metzger beside lawyer as jury renders verdict.

Photo Courtesy Court TV

The press got its long awaited interview with prosecutors only after the trial concluded. The case had enough complications without our fueling the media frenzy.

Frank Silva: leader of a Klan den and member of Aryan Nations and "The Order"; convicted of RICO violations serving twenty years.

Thomas Bentley: member of Aryan Nations and "The Order"; serving eight years for aiding and abetting the murder of an Aryan Nations member.

Tom Metzger: Grand Dragon of the Ku Klux Klan and founder of W.A.R.; convicted of unlawful burning.

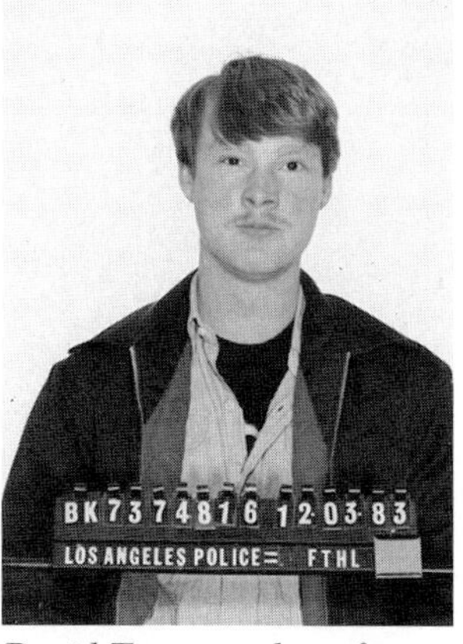

David Tate: member of Aryan Nations and Butler's church, convicted in the machine gun shooting of two state troopers. Serving two life terms for murder.

Booking photos courtesy LAPD

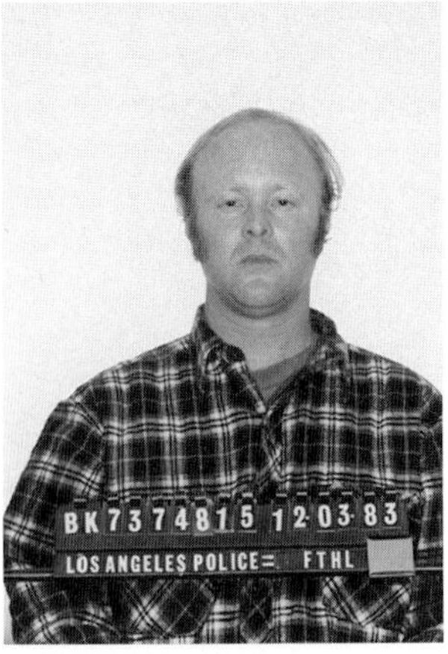

Randy Evans: member of Aryan Nations and "The Order"; serving twenty year sentence for RICO violations.

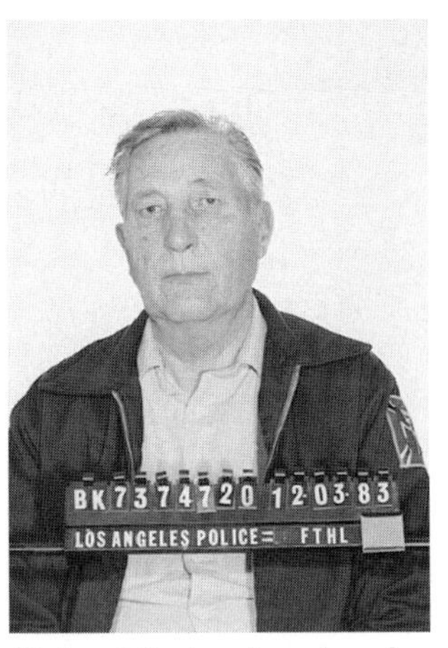

Richard Butler: founder of Aryan Nations and high priest of the Church of Jesus Christ Christian: fled prosecution.

Peter Lake, a.k.a. Peter Lawrence: the telltale smile in this booking photo was my first clue he was the unknown informant.

Booking photos courtesy LAPD

Stanley Witek: head of the American Nazi Party; convicted of conspiracy, weapons possession and distribution.

too. Dale continued to explain how the transfer occurred, sometimes seeming disgusted, at other points sounding excited.

Gil Garcetti, now chief deputy to the district attorney, and Davidson's supervisor, Bob Kuhnert, had gone to court to meet Fran Merrick and Michael Sachs. As Garcetti and Kuhnert walked down the hall, Merrick and Sachs stood waiting at the courtroom doors, holding a small folder of papers. They introduced themselves. Garcetti inquired of the business at hand.

"We got removed from a case," replied Sachs. "You'll have to take over for us."

"Why was the removal ordered?" asked Kuhnert.

"The defendants demanded a felony prosecution," answered Sachs. "We had no choice."

"Did the defense attorneys give you notice that they were bringing this motion today?" asked Garcetti.

"Yes."

"How come you didn't let us know in advance of the hearing?"

"We really thought we could handle this without you," Merrick interjected. "We read and understood the law. And we did the best job we could."

"So, you opposed the motion?"

"Of course we opposed the motion," answered Merrick indignantly. "We would not just willingly relinquish a case like this. We were looking forward to trying it ourselves."

"Then what's that in your hand?" asked Kuhnert as he looked down at the folder Michael carried.

"It's a copy of the whole case file. I brought it with me to give to you."

"I'll take it," said Kuhnert. "What's this case about, anyway?"

"It's the Klan cross-burning case," answered Fran. "You may have heard about it."

Kuhnert opened the folder. "This motion was filed over two years ago, before Reiner became district attorney. You mean they still want the D.A. to take the case? Doesn't make any sense."

"Well, anyway. If you need any help on the case, your best bet is to contact the city attorney who was assigned the case back then. He's in private practice now, but he'll work with you. His card is stapled to the file." Merrick attempted to be as pleasant as possible as she bade farewell. She and Sachs walked quickly away. Garcetti and Kuhnert couldn't believe the manner in which the city attorneys handled the motion. They entered the courtroom.

Busy as usual, this was a calendar court where cases were either assigned elsewhere for trial or a guilty plea was taken. Neither of the D.A.s could figure why a complex motion would have been litigated here. Garcetti approached the court clerk. "Can I see the pleadings on the Klan motion this morning?"

She found the file and removed a single document from the top. "Here you go."

Garcetti viewed the heading. "This is just the defense brief. Let me see the opposition papers from the city attorneys."

"There was no opposition brief," the clerk replied.

"No opposition brief? They offered only oral arguments?

"They didn't actually argue against the defense motion. It was really more like they joined in the motion. But they wanted the record to reflect that they only submitted."

Dale professed that he had never seen such backhandedness between the two L.A. prosecuting agencies. "But, wait," he said. "The silver lining to this cloud shines bright. The case gets sent to the organized crime, antiterrorist unit. And guess who it gets assigned to."

Half in hope and half in disbelief, I asked, "You?"

"Me indeed. And guess who they want to hire as special prosecutor."

"We're going to work together?"

"If you decide to take the job. If you don't want it after all that's gone on—"

"I'm in."

Over the next several days, I met with Gil Garcetti to work out the details of my contract as special prosecutor to the Los Angeles County district attorney. The D.A.'s office had never before hired a private attorney to come in for the prosecution of a special matter. I took the oath of office, repeating an unceremonious reading by the director of personnel to uphold the Constitution of the United States of America and the laws of the state of California.

After nearly a year away, working on my own, I found my heart had not changed. After leaving the city attorney's office, I had difficulty accepting that I would never again work in law enforcement. But then, I knew the background of this case was too complex for anyone to dare step in cold. I believed that the dismissal would be reversed and the case would come back to me. But at the time that I left the city attorney's office, I feared that the hundreds of photographs, hours of videotapes, and stacks of documents would be mishandled or lost during my absence. The trial could not be won without them. Also, the legal ramifications of *any* missing evidence could lead to a dismissal of the charges in a criminal prosecution, particularly if it is perceived that the evidence had exculpatory value and was deliberately discarded. For these reasons, I chose to personally safeguard the Klan evidence I'd gathered, and I took it with me when I left the city attorney's office to begin private practice. In its place I left behind some old boxes marked "Klan" with duplicate reports, news items, and copies of other materials.

The morning of my return to the Criminal Courts Building, I carried a storage box full of the original evidence containing photographs, videotapes, reports, and booklets. Dale met me at the reception desk on the seventeenth floor. We sat at the desk in his office.

"Is all this stuff on our case?" asked Dale, a bit overwhelmed by the volume.

I began pulling out stacks of photographs. "They build the case." There on the top was a picture of a robed and hooded Klansman holding a shotgun, acting as the guard for a speaker standing at an outdoor podium. I placed the photo in front of Dale. "This is the Grand Dragon of the Ku Klux Klan in Georgia. He came to California when Tom Metzger was running for office. Metzger put this function on at Fontana."

As I spoke, Dale paged through other photos. His attention was drawn to a cross-burning demonstration outside Sacramento. Klansmen dressed in white robes and hoods set a towering twenty-five-foot cross ablaze.

"These pictures were taken from an apartment window overlooking this area." I continued. "Look at this shot right here. All four of these guys were carrying guns or rifles. And so were another few in this picture. And looking at the photographs from San Luis Obispo, Oceanside, San Diego, or wherever else that Metzger's Klan was present, you see more of the same."

"Well," Dale began to surmise, "If I remember correctly, Metzger appears only briefly in the video of the L.A. cross-burning. You see him eating a sandwich as the police enter the property to make the arrests. Sort of like Nero, but not much to say as far as aiding and abetting. Is Metzger present at the other cross-burnings where the guns and clubs are being carried openly?"

"Not just present," I answered. "We have a witness who'll testify he organized them."

"Any physical proof?" asked Davidson.

I pulled from a file a letter from Metzger to Doug Seymour, inviting him to the cross-burning at San Luis Obispo. "It's not just Seymour's testimony; there're photographs and videotapes. The case against Metzger is makeable."

"He's like the spider behind the web," Davidson mused. "We need to convict him."

In the afternoon we prepared the felony complaint. Merrick and Sachs had dismissed all charges against the four defendants convicted of the federal racketeering offenses. We would proceed in this trial against the four remaining defendants who demanded felony filings, and on four charges. We worked each day for the following three weeks, until the arraignment in superior court.

◆ ◆ ◆ ◆ ◆

The mahogany-paneled courtroom was spacious and ornately decorated with oil paintings of jurists that once presided there, lending an august aura to the commencement of the morning proceedings. The defendants were seated closely together, conversing and projecting a transparent air of confidence. Metzger wore a dark blue, pin-striped suit. The four defense counsel stood away from their clients, by the end of the empty jury box to the side of the courtroom. I indicated them to Dale.

"I want to see their jaws drop when they see you're back on the case," Dale said softly with a smile. "I'm sure they figured they got rid of you."

We continued toward them. Those facing us looked at me but said nothing, appearing quite surprised. Dale came up behind Pageant and Borowitz, still unaware of his presence.

"Good morning, gentlemen." His voice boomed above their chatter. "I understand you're here on the Klan matter."

Around turned Brian Pageant. "Are you the district attorney?" he asked.

"Yes, I am," Dale answered.

Pageant looked over, seeing me for the first time in two years. "What are you doing here?"

Dale responded boisterously. "My co-counsel, of course. Who are you?"

"Brian Pageant, attorney for Brad Riley." Pageant nervously adjusted his tie.

"You're the one who authored this bullshit motion to compel the felony prosecution?" Dale said.

"Well, I would hardly call it bullshit."

"I'll tell you what," quipped Dale, "You tell me by the time these guys go to jail why that isn't a bullshit motion, and I'll call it something else, too. Right now it just seems like a fool attempt to pick your prosecuting office. I'll tell you right now you picked the wrong one."

"We have our reasons, Mr. Davidson. Perhaps those will become apparent to you."

"Well, now that you're here, you're going to get felony defendant treatment," Dale said. "We would hate to think we didn't cover one of your reasons."

"I would have it no other way, Counsel," sniped Pageant. "Who's trying this case, anyway? You or John Phillips?"

"Oh, I don't know about that just yet. From what I've seen of the defense tactics so far, a cub scout troop could convict this group." Pageant moaned in exasperation. "I guess we'll just have to wait and see who wakes up on the right side of the bed. The other one of us will try the case."

"Then I guess we know who it'll be," mumbled Rudolf Borowitz, defendant Hofstadler's lawyer.

"I wouldn't be so sure, Counsel," Dale said.

"Why not?"

"Because you haven't guessed anything right so far." Dale turned away from the defense lawyers. Facing only me, he brandished a sly grin as we walked to the clerk's desk. "We're going to have us some fun trying this thing."

The judge called the case, and a plea of not guilty was entered on behalf of each defendant. The case was set for trial in the courtroom of Judge J. D. Smith. Dale was pleased with this assignment. I did not know Judge Smith, but I trusted Dale's assessment. The case would finally be put before a jury.

As I left Department 100 I heard my name called. I turned to see one of the defense counsel approaching. I knew this man well from years back, and we had a mutual respect. He looked concerned and waited to speak until we were alone. "Why have you come back for this case?" he asked. "Didn't the FBI contact you about the list?"

I paused a moment, but I didn't want him to know I had fallen outside the circle of information. "Yeah. They sent an agent. But that was a long time ago."

"The Klan wants you off the case," he said. "Why do you think they had us bring the motion to upgrade the case to felonies? It sure isn't my strategy. They'll do whatever to get you off this case."

Chapter 16

False Accusations

Three years had passed since the inception of the case, and my measure of time was my children's progression through the toddler stage. It was five minutes before nine, our starting time in court. Dale and I felt ready to walk the plank. Out we went.

As we rounded the corner from the elevators, the throng of jurors, spectators, and media crews came immediately to view. Cameras turned in our direction. Lights glared in our pathway. In a discreet tone to my partner I remarked, "Out of the kitchen and into the soup."

"Just keep walking," responded Dale. We had agreed not to become part of the media show.

There were no empty seats in the courtroom except for those reserved for the jury panel. As we walked to the counsel table, Brian Pageant approached with a brief in hand. He curtly bade a good morning, then handed Dale the pleading. He avoided eye contact with me, which I thought odd because, if nothing else, he was usually an amicable character. Judge Smith took the bench promptly at nine o'clock. As the jurors entered, Dale kept to himself as he read through Pageant's motion. I was curious but waited for Dale to review it.

"You're not going to like this." Dale smiled, but there was a hint of disgust as he looked down and continued to read.

"What is it?" I asked.

"It's a motion to remove the district attorney's office as the prosecuting agency. Now they want the state attorney general to step in."

"What grounds?"

"Basically, they're claiming that you represent Mike Canale in a civil matter and that your prosecuting a criminal case in which he's a witness would be a conflict of interest."

"That's a lie. I don't represent Mike Canale." I tried to keep my voice low.

"I'm sure you don't," answered Dale. "But he's trying to make it seem like you do. And look at his precious timing, on the morning of trial."

The motion was calculated to remove me from the prosecution. If the judge found a conflict existed, there was no alternative for the district attorney's office but to dismiss me. They would otherwise be compelled to transfer the case to a third prosecuting office, which would be embarrassing and wasteful.

We remained in jury selection throughout the day. When we concluded, Hofstadler's attorney, Rudolf Borowitz, approached the bench and asked that we begin opening statements. The prosecution always goes first, so this seemed intended to hurry us into it.

"That's too much pressure—for the prosecutor to go straight from jury selection to opening statement," answered Judge Smith. "I want to give you guys a chance to organize your thoughts. We'll do it tomorrow." And the judge, who knew nothing of me other than what he would read in Pageant's moving brief, scheduled the hearing on Pageant's motion first in the morning.

Judge J. D. Smith had been a police officer for sixteen years. He worked his way through law school, practiced eight years, and was then appointed to the superior court bench. In many ways he remained more of a police officer than a judicial officer. The word was, "Do not cross J. D." He had a large, imposing presence, was temperamental and sometimes volatile, and was both feared and respected throughout the legal and law enforcement communities.

Mike Canale, always in and out of trouble, had cut deals for testimony in the past. Was it possible that J. D. Smith knew Canale as a police informant?

I sensed a coldness in the treatment I received in court for the remainder of the day. I felt isolated. I prayed I had not come this far, only to be discharged and embarrassed.

Later that evening I went out with Diane and the children for dinner, but I had no appetite. I was weary with anticipation of the hearing in the morning. The prospect of being accused of misconduct in open court was bad enough, but knowing the proceedings would be carried live on *Court TV* and reported by news stations made me feel dismal. I could barely converse with Diane, except to tell her how ironic I thought it all was.

As we drove home, Patrick and Jessica began to quarrel in the seats behind us. "Will you two stop it back there," Diane ordered. She then turned to me. "This motion is just their way of trying to make you look like you've got a personal relationship with a witness. They'll do it again when he testifies."

The little ones continued struggling. "Hey, what are you guys doing back there?" I looked into my rearview mirror. "They're fighting over something. Get it from them, Diane."

She reached behind. "Hey, what do you have here, Jessica? You're not supposed to have something so small." Diane pulled it from Jessica's grasp, looked at it, then held it for me to see. It was my grandmother's crucifix. I hadn't seen it in nearly three years.

"Take up the cross," said Diane adamantly. "The badge of the crusaders."

Chapter 17

The Trade-Off

Any other morning of the trial I would have stopped at Dale's office before going to court. Not this morning. The irony was that I now felt more a burden to the prosecution than an asset. But there was no place to hide.

Department 106 looked more like a television studio than a courtroom. A camera crew busily attached microphones and taped down wires. There were reporters from all the local press and wire services. What a completely imperfect day to be the subject of alleged impropriety.

Dale was standing up front, arms folded, his fixed stare unaffected by the tumult of his surroundings. As I approached, he looked up. He was angry.

"This is pure bull, just a smear. It's the style these days to turn the attention away from the defendants; put the prosecutor on trial." He paused and asked how I was.

"All right," I replied mechanically.

"I told the clerk I want the hearing in chambers to try to keep the allegations against you from becoming a public spectacle," Dale said.

I shrugged my shoulders, almost resigned to an inevitable fate, and glanced at the sea of reporters in the courtroom. "If I'm off the case, I'm just going to walk out of here, and that'll be it."

"Don't worry, John. You ain't going no place. I've thought about this and—"

The clerk's voice interrupted. "Gentlemen, the judge will see you in chambers now."

"I'm the one with the options," Dale continued. He turned and smiled with a sincere air of confidence and, more importantly, friendship.

The four defense attorneys filed into the judge's chambers ahead of us. Three sat on the leather couch at the side of the judge's desk. Pageant sat in one of the two chairs before Smith. Dale sat to the right of Pageant. The setting had the appearance of a miniature courtroom. I took a chair behind the others. The judge held a copy of the motion. He addressed Dale.

"I'll tell you right off the bat that I'm concerned about this. I don't know Mr. Phillips. He may be a hell of a nice guy or whatever. But I know characters like this Canale. They muddy things up. He's muddied your Mr. Phillips. And if it's going to look like he's done some private work for Canale, I'm telling you right now I don't want this trial going off on some sideshow. I'm going to protect the integrity of this court and the trial."

"Judge, hold on," interrupted Dale. "You're accepting allegations that are not true. At least have Mr. Phillips respond. The court will see there is no connection here, certainly not as claimed."

"All right then," the judge addressed me. "What do you have to say about all this? You've read the motion."

I took a breath and looked J. D. Smith squarely eye to eye. "I have never represented Mike Canale. And I've been very careful about this. This is the type of case where you have to stay in touch with your witnesses. Especially where everything is taking so long to get to court. That's the only contact we've had. He came to me about a year and a half ago and asked me to take this civil matter. I told him, specifically, that I would not take it because I thought I might be involved with the prosecution of this case again. I told him he could speak to my brother about it. He wound up representing him.

"My brother and I share the rent on a group of offices, along with another attorney. I do not work for my brother. He does not work for me. We have worked together on cases, but I never worked on this one. In fact, Canale's case was resolved over a year ago. I did not even know this until last night." The judge lit his cigar as he listened to my statement, took a puff, and blew the smoke into a ring. He turned to listen to Dale.

"Judge, you can see there never was a conflict. The case is over. This is just a red herring issue for the defendants to try to pick their prosecutor."

The judge raised his hand to curtail Dale. "It may not be a conflict, Mr. Davidson. I didn't say that's what I'm worried about. What I'm concerned about is that there are areas of inquiry, legitimate or otherwise, that are presented by this involvement, and I'm not going to allow this trial to become unnecessarily sidetracked or prolonged."

Dale stood in a manner characteristic of a prosecutor who had yet to finish, demanding the opportunity to conclude his argument. At the judge's first pause, Dale spoke.

"I will say this. I've prosecuted many murders, many serious crimes. But this trial is more important than any single one of them. That's because what this trial is all about is the Ku Klux Klan getting started in California. The cross-burning is their call for new membership. And if we let them root in California, a lot of bad is going to follow." He captured the judge's interest.

Dale continued vehemently. "Now, I'm also going to tell you this. John Phillips is more important to the presentation of this case than any witness. He's been on this case since the beginning. He built the investigation. He knows the evidence. That's why they want him off this case, and that's the only reason why."

Dale sat back down as he continued speaking, now firmly in hold of the judge's attention. "So this is my offer. We *don't* call Mike Canale as a witness. John Phillips stays on the case."

The judge leaned back in his chair, drew another puff on his cigar, and looked to Brian Pageant. "Sounds agreeable. You knock out a primary witness. All of this civil representation stuff becomes irrelevant and no one makes any mention of it."

"But what if we want to call Canale as *our* witness?" responded Pageant.

"What the hell would you do that for?" the judge angrily retorted. "Just to impeach him by introducing your bullshit claim of conflict? I wouldn't allow you to do that under those circumstances."

Pageant leaned back and said nothing further. The other defense counsel confirmed the agreement with Davidson's offer. We stood as they began to leave, then walked a short distance behind them. Dale was the last to depart.

The judge called to him as he passed through the doorway. "Hey, Davidson." Dale turned and faced the judge. "I'm sorry to have put you through a motion right before your opening statement. I would have rather let you go into it with a clear head instead of having your cocounsel on the hot seat."

Dale looked expressionless at Smith for a moment, then said, "I'm not doing the opening statement, Judge."

I turned back toward the courtroom door, took a paper towel from my pocket, and mopped the sweat from my forehead. From behind me I heard Dale. "He is."

Chapter 18

Opening Statement

(August 20, 1991)

The jurors were seated as we reentered the courtroom, no doubt wondering what happened in the judge's quarters. I approached my seat but remained standing as the judge stepped to the bench. The bailiff announced court was in session.

I was as numb as a boxer who'd survived a standing eight-count. There was a nudge on my forearm. It was Dale. "You all right?" he asked.

"Fine."

"I can do it if you want me to."

"I'm okay."

The judge addressed me. "At this time, Mr. Phillips, I believe you are going to make an opening statement on behalf of the People."

"Thank you, Your Honor. Yes, I am." I stepped forward and looked into the eyes of the jurors before me. I placed my notepad on the podium. I noticed small ovals of perspiration where my fingers held the tablet. I looked at the jurors again, wondering if my frayed nerves were apparent. They waited expectantly. I turned to my right and was about to begin with the usual generic comments about what an opening statement is when my eyes met Metzger's. His eyes were fixed on me, and his smirky little grin suggested he knew what had occurred in chambers. Then it seemed so clear. It was Metzger's mind game. He wanted me to hate, to become angry. It was the reaction he wanted to provoke in the people into whose neighborhoods he brought his Klan cross-burnings. But not this time. I dropped my notes onto the counsel table. Davidson looked up intently, questioningly. I stepped away from the podium, lifted my eyes to the jurors, and walked toward the center of the courtroom.

"Criminal intent. We began studying it the first day of law school, and the ones who knew it right then and there were the ones who were blessed with God's greatest gift—common sense. The rest of them studied it to the day they put on their caps and gowns. They dissected it, read psychiatric reports, tore apart Supreme Court opinions about it. But no matter how many law review articles they could quote, or how many cases they could cite, if they didn't have common sense, they could never understand criminal intent.

"The intellectuals were always the easiest to be confused by criminal intent. The reason was quite simple. The intellectuals could not put themselves in the place of the criminal mind. They were too elevated in their thinking to understand something so simple, so self-defeating. They couldn't understand why anyone would deliberately engage in crime, so they believed the crime must have been unintentional, or misguided.

"But there *are* criminal intentions, and there *are* criminal minds. Sometimes they are smart, sometimes not, but one aspect is common to all. Each crime has its correlating, passionate vice. To theft there is greed; to assault there is anger.

"So what crimes are alleged in the trial *you* are about to decide? The defendants are charged with conspiracy, with setting unlawful fires, with unlawful assembly, and Witek is also charged with the possession of illegal weapons. And the vice that underlies all these crimes is that of *hate.*

"Their attorneys will say you cannot convict a man merely for his beliefs. They will tell you it is the right of the defendants to get together and set these fires as a religious rite. They will tell you their clients had no criminal intent.

"So how can a prosecutor, in any case, ever possibly show the *intent* with which another man acted? How can a prosecutor show what another man was thinking?

"Actually, it's easy. And it's done every day in this courthouse. In this particular case, showing that the defendants acted from hatred and that their intent was to cause conflict is going to be very easy."

At this point I had walked toward the front of the jury box, close to the witness stand. I turned toward Metzger, my face turned away from the view of the jurors. Our eyes locked. This time, I smiled confidently. He glared angrily back as I continued speaking, maintaining our eye contact.

"Because hatred is *very* hard to conceal. The more they hate, the more apparent it is. They can't mask it, not with robes or hoods, or convoluted explanations of what a burning cross means."

As I slowly turned back toward the jurors, I noticed the reporters in the front rows of the courtroom busily writing notes. My attention to them was fleeting. What they, or Metzger, or even Judge Smith thought of me was not important now. My only concern were the twelve jurors. The first to whom I directed my address sat forward in his chair, his brow furrowed. As was my practice, I would establish visual contact with each juror, in random order, making sure that each one knew I was interested in personally communicating.

"We're going to take a journey into the minds of these men. You're going to see what it was that they saw. You're going to hear what it was that they heard. We're going to prove that they burn crosses to frighten innocent people and to start violence. Why? Because if they can frighten, if they can provoke, it puts them in control. It makes them feel superior. Most important, it satisfies their hatred.

"How will we prove the charges against them? The presentation of the case is going to begin with testimony from a gentleman by the name of Peter Lake. He was a journalist, but Mr. Lake used a false identity and pretended to be sympathetic to their beliefs.

"The Klansmen were generally eager to find new friends and document their activities, and Mr. Lake was able to bring a video camera with him to their gatherings. On a December day three years back, Lake had his video camera during a cross-burning at Kagel Canyon in the city of Los Angeles. You will see this incredible video footage."

Just as Davidson and I had made a tactical determination to confine the overt acts of the conspiracy to what the videotape showed, so also would I confine the factual representations of my opening statement to what the videotape showed. In my early trials as a prosecutor, I learned that a skilled defense lawyer will take detailed notes of the prosecutor's opening statement. At the conclusion of the case, the defense counsel will highlight in argument any representation made during the prosecutor's opening statement that was not proven during the trial. The defense tactic makes it appear that the prosecutor thought the case was stronger than it actually turned out to be, and that even the prosecutor must be disappointed and surprised. By confining my factual representations of the overt acts in support of the conspiracy to that which is conclusively demonstrated on the videotape, I ensured that my opening statement could not later be used to our disadvantage.

"Now about count one of the complaint, the charge of unlawful assembly. It can be either of two things. It is either the coming together of two or more persons to commit an unlawful act, such as the setting of illegal fires; or it can be the coming together of two or more persons to do a *lawful* act in a violent, boisterous, or tumultuous manner."

I believed it was important to establish this distinction and to let the jury know that even if the defendants believed they had a valid permit and that their conduct was lawful, they could still be convicted of unlawful assembly for having set the fires in an attempt to provoke a violent reaction.

"We will prove unlawful assembly by showing the circumstances the defendants created that evening, and by presenting evidence and testimony of persons at similar events in Sacramento, San Luis Obispo, Oceanside, San Diego, and Fontana.

"At each of these incidents, ladies and gentlemen, the Ku Klux Klan assembled with their former Grand Dragon of the state of California, Tom Metzger, for the purpose of burning large crosses—crosses placed sometimes in parks, sometimes in recreational areas, sometimes on the property of a Klan sympathizer, but always in select locations, in racially mixed neighborhoods. And they had weapons in hand should local residents take exception to their conduct.

"We will add to this proof the opinions of qualified expert witnesses who have walked within the dark hallways of the Ku Klux Klan, attended cross-burnings, and studied their activities. These witnesses will testify to the underlying intent of the Klan in coming into neighborhoods not their own to conduct their so-called 'cross-lighting ceremonies.'

"We will present the testimony of police officers and fire department officials. A fireman will testify that he issued a burn permit to Frank Silva and Ron Major, but that permit was strictly for an open-pit barbecue. The Los Angeles municipal code section that we are dealing with, 57.20.19, allows a burn permit for an open-pit barbecue. Another allowable fire under this section is for 'the exercise of a legitimate fraternal organization' wanting to have a bonfire.

"You will learn that the defendants did not apply for their burn permit as a fraternal organization wanting a bonfire; instead they acted under a deceptive ruse, in an attempt to disguise their activity.

"You will hear testimony from the captain of the fire station that the type of fire set by these defendants was absolutely not covered by the permit they held; and that the swirling winds, nearby brush, and wood structures created a significant danger that the fire might spread from these three, fifteen- to eighteen-foot-high, wood, burlap-wrapped cross configurations.

"You will hear testimony from Sergeant John O'Neal, the investigating officer. This case initially came to his attention a couple of days before the cross-burning. He and Lieutenant Robinson sought out the individuals they knew were responsible. Sergeant O'Neal will testify that he went to them and said, 'Go ahead, have your meeting; say what you want to say; get together with whomever you want to get together with; but just *don't* do one thing, don't burn the crosses.' He was told by Frank Silva that the Klan had a permit. O'Neal asked to see it, and it was shown to him. He told Silva, 'This doesn't cover the burning of crosses.'

"There was a lot of discussion among the Klan, Nazi, and Aryan Nations members that night about whether they should go ahead with the cross-burning. And there was a lot of police interaction with the defendants. You will find that the defendants knew full well what they were doing. They acted with complete knowledge of the illegality of their conduct."

I had now covered the application of the facts to the law, which in theory is the limit of an opening statement. I needed, though, to introduce the human element. Saving this for the end is most effective, but a prosecutor does not want to risk having objections sustained and being cut short at the conclusion of an opening statement. It had to be passionate but direct.

"Is this the only reason that this prosecution was undertaken? No. We are not here just to prove a point, or to establish a precedent. The full reason will become apparent when you hear the testimony of Robert Gentry.

"Mr. Gentry is one of the residents who lived close to these burning crosses, in a neighborhood he will describe as being of predominantly black families, an upper-middle-class neighborhood. It is a nice neighborhood. It is a neighborhood that has no reputation for much other than people raising families, trying to help their kids through school.

"Mr. Gentry will testify that from his bedroom window he and his wife could see plainly what was happening, the men in the robes and hoods, the crosses being inflamed. He will relate the impact this had on him and on his daughters. They are not named as victims in the complaint, but these people and their neighbors are the true victims of the defendants' hate-inspired conduct. They have a right to walk the streets of their neighborhood at night and to do so free from the fear that was created by this conduct.

"As for the issue of constitutional rights, the boundary of free expression was clearly passed by the lighting of these fires. You will be convinced that when these men staged the cross-burnings on the night of December 3rd, it was done as a provocation to violence.

"The constitutional rights of the residents of that neighborhood must be protected by this jury. And you will be convinced of what your verdict should be at the conclusion of this trial."

I returned to my seat.

As is often the case in criminal trials, each of the defense counsel waived opening statement. Judge Smith put the trial in recess and asked that we call our first witness after the noon hour. Davidson placed his hand on my shoulder in a gesture of satisfaction with the opening statement. When the courtroom cleared of the media and jurors, I heard Judge Smith call, "Mr. Phillips." I turned and looked at him. There was a pause during which neither of us spoke. He seemed to search for words, then said, "Well done."

I waited to say my piece to Davidson until we were returning to his office via a back hallway cargo elevator. "I really appreciate what you did to keep me on. I've lived with it too long, worked on it too long. You put yourself on the line for me. I appreciate that."

Dale shook his head. "This is a two-prosecutor case. We either do it together or not at all."

Chapter 19

The People's Case in Chief

This morning we would begin the presentation of our case against the Klan. The jurors, attorneys, and defendants were seated. The judge perused the courtroom from the perch of his bench. It was also my practice, and Davidson's, to be mindful of who was seated behind us, and how close. I remembered the early days of the proceedings, years ago, when the anti-Klan demonstrators were the primary spectators in the courtroom. As disruptive as they were, they posed no threat to me or my witnesses. Now, our audience had noticeably changed. Skinheads, some in army fatigues, came early to get seats. Particularly today, when our first witness would testify, they made their presence felt. Eight of them in the hallway tried to stare down Peter Lake. Like everyone else, except me and my cocounsel, they had to pass through a metal detector before entering the courtroom.

Two rows behind the skinheads sat two conservatively groomed men, in their early thirties, in gray suits. I'd seen them introduce themselves to the courtroom bailiff, showing ID from their wallets. My guess was that they were FBI, but as I looked at them they avoided eye contact with me. I normally had no trouble getting the attention of the person I sought in the courtroom. These two were reluctant, which I thought strange for apparent law enforcement types.

I turned forward in my chair. The judge's eyes came to rest on us. "Call your first witness."

"The People call Peter Lake."

Peter rose from a seat in the audience behind me. He was dressed in a dark blue sweater-vest, with a lavender shirt and red tie. I remembered the first time I'd ever seen him. He was a defendant, sitting next to Metzger and Butler, and I was his prosecutor.

I remembered how I resented Lake bringing a camera into the court, photographing the counterdemonstrators, and how he seemed to enjoy the hatred and hostility that surrounded him.

Circumstances were different now. His friends had changed, and so had his enemies. He wasn't smiling and cocky as he was back then. More than anything, he had a look of resolve about him. He was going to do this and not back down. After all, as he had once said, how could they be angry with the truth? He was sworn in by the clerk.

Lake was a career journalist, not an infiltrator with a chip on his shoulder. My initial questioning of him developed his lack of preexisting animosity toward the Klan. He summarized his professional experiences with a long list of adventuristic enterprises, from parachuting into the Peruvian jungle to swimming in the midst of great white sharks. Although his past work conveyed a fearless, almost reckless personality, Peter came across as a likable, credible witness. He sensed the jurors were receptive to him and seemed a bit more at ease than before he began to testify. But as my questions moved to his infiltration of the Klan, he shifted noticeably in his seat, and his facial expression became drawn and serious.

"Until three years ago, had any of your work ever involved the Ku Klux Klan or any white supremacist group?" I asked.

"No. I knew very little about them prior to this job," answered Lake.

"Did you have an opinion regarding the Ku Klux Klan?"

"Not really. I had an opinion about them, but it was an uninformed opinion."

"Did someone contact you regarding the activities of white supremacist organizations?"

"Tom Kaplan. He was a producer at CBS I knew from the Writer's Guild of America. He asked if I would like to infiltrate a neo-Nazi organization. There was a former member of the American Nazi Party who had burned down a synagogue, had done time in prison, and wanted to atone by helping expose the groups involved. I wanted to go ahead with the project. I met with a magazine editor for a publication called *The Rebel*, and I met with a reporter and a producer at CBS. We made an agreement that I would infiltrate this organization and take videotapes of their activities, and if CBS liked the substance and quality of the tape and I adhered to their ethical standards, they would negotiate for a purchase."

"What were the ethical standards the producer wanted?"

"They demanded that I not affect the outcome of any events in any way. I simply had to be a witness. I couldn't direct any of the action."

Lake's testimony that CBS required he not affect the outcome of any events, and that his videotapes would not be purchased if he did, was particularly important. I expected that the defense would claim that Peter had directed the defendants' actions, perhaps to dramatize the video to sell it. By having him testify, almost in passing, that the tapes would neither be purchased nor broadcast if he directed the Klan in any manner, I hoped to undermine the anticipated defense tactic before it started. I then asked how he began his effort to infiltrate the Klan.

Lake related that he rented a post office box and had stationery printed under the alias of Peter A. Lawrence. He took the identity of a tropical fish importer.

"I knew a lot about tropical fish, and I made the assumption that the people I was going to be with didn't. It turned out to be correct," Lake explained.

"Who was your next contact?"

"I met with Mike Canale. He brought me to a Ku Klux Klan rally in the San Fernando Valley. It was there that I met Frank Silva, Randy Evans, and some of the others present at the December 3rd cross-burning."

"What was happening at that rally?"

"It was a demonstration against a defendant by the name of Kevin Cooper. He had escaped from prison and killed some people, a whole family. I drove out with Stan Witek's Nazi group. I was actually in the van with Witek, which I learned was a place of honor among the Nazi members because Witek was the head of the American Nazi Party. He and Canale were wearing Nazi uniforms. When we parked, the whole group of us marched in front of the courthouse. Witek and Canale carried signs about Jews and blacks destroying the country. They had a stuffed chimpanzee suspended by a noose. And in the van we drove down in, there were table legs."

I took a heavy table leg from the evidence box. It was nearly three feet long, of stained mahogany, with angular ridges at the wider end. I held it for Lake to see.

"Is this one of the table legs you saw at that first Klan demonstration?"

"Yes, it is."

"Were any comments made about the table legs inside Witek's van as you drove to the demonstration?"

"I asked what they were."

"Anyone reply?"

"Yes, Stan Witek."

"Do you see Stan Witek present in court this afternoon?"

"Yes. He's the individual in the dark blue suit, seated at the far left end of the counsel table."

I glanced over to Witek. Oddly, as I had never before seen a defendant do, Witek raised his hand in a gesture intended to identify himself. He had a little smile on his face, enjoying the notoriety.

"What did he say about the table legs when you first saw them?" I asked Lake.

"His words were, 'If we needed them we would bash some skulls.'"

"After that day, did you ever have occasion to see these table legs again?"

"Yes. At the cross-lighting demonstration at Kagel Canyon. Stan Witek brought them again."

The perception of Witek's American Nazi Party became that of a bullying band of thugs. I then focused Lake's testimony on the Aryan Nations group and their fast-developing tendency toward hyperviolence. If we could later tie these together with the publications and other items of physical evidence, such as Metzger's bulletproof vest, we hoped to establish the defendants' intent to incite terror, which constitutes the definition of an "unlawful assembly." I asked Lake to describe the Aryan Nations compound.

"In a very rural area of northwestern Idaho, at the end of a dirt road, you come to a guardhouse," said Lake. "It has a sign on it that says 'Whites Only.' There's a number of wooden buildings, a guard tower, chapel, assembly hall, a couple of houses, and several trailers. They have a print shop where they manufacture and sell their own literature. They conduct religious services. Not like what one would imagine. Highly racist. And there were also political gatherings among the men, where we all expressed our beliefs to unite in a common purpose.

"After several days, three of us were initiated as Aryan Warriors, and we pledged ourselves to fight for the ideals of the Aryan Nations. I marched through the opening of the chapel between a group of men on either side of me. I approached the alter where Richard Butler stood with a two-handed, double-edged sword with swastikas incrested on it. I knelt before him. He put the sword on my shoulder. Then I stood and followed him in reciting the oath, pledging my fidelity to Aryan Nations and to the struggle of white racism."

"What followed?"

"I spent a lot of time with the people in the organization, spoke to them, fired weapons with them, and generally exchanged ideas."

"Where did you and other members fire weapons?"

"At a sanitary landfill approximately forty to fifty miles north of Hayden Lake, set up as an urban environment.

There were simulated buildings where one could practice combat tactics."

"And who else from the Los Angeles cross-burning was also present at these urban combat training exercises?"

"Frank Silva, Randy Evans, David Tate, Tom Bentley, Mike Canale, and myself."

"Were there others present?"

"There was Randy Duey and Eugene Kinerk."

"Do you know where these people are now?"

The question drew immediate objections from the defense. Pageant slammed his open palm on the counsel table and rose quickly to his feet. They knew the testimony would reveal the violence that pervades the Klan. The judge summoned us to the right side of the bench on the end away from the jury and witness stand known as the "side bar." As we approached, I knew I had to make this testimony relevant to Lake's expertise.

"Pageant, you keep your voice down, and don't you be slamming your hand in my court. I won't have any of your damn theatrics here. Understand?"

"I apologize, Your Honor, but the prosecutor knows full well that the question he has asked is intended to elicit extremely prejudicial testimony. Each of the men he just referenced is in prison for a violent felony. *They* are not on trial here. The prosecutor is attempting to establish guilt by association, and it's clear misconduct on his part."

"My intent is not guilt by association," I quickly rejoined. "As I said in my opening statement, we're using expert opinion to establish the Klan's true intent in burning crosses. I can assure the court that the defendants will claim they are not *burning* crosses to provoke violence, but are instead lighting the crosses with fire to illuminate them in ritual. Lake will give an expert opinion. I have to qualify him as an expert. He testified in Duey and Kinerk's trial and qualified as an expert. He also knows them as former cross-burners, and I'm entitled to show it wasn't done with a goal of faith ministry but to foster the violence that it did."

"Well, let me ask you this, Mr. Pageant," said the judge. "Are you willing to stipulate that Mr. Lake is an expert and that the Klan burns crosses to provoke a violent reaction? That seems to be the issue here with the unlawful assembly charge."

"I can't stipulate to *that*," Pageant answered.

"Then go back to your seat. Your objection is overruled."

With the objection now overruled, I proceeded to phrase the question with more deliberate emphasis. Call it theatrics, or call it the price the defense paid for their grandstanding. Either way, I wanted the jurors to remember what Lake would say.

"And so, Mr. Lake, *before* the interruption in your testimony, I had asked you 'Do *you know* the whereabouts of Mr. Randy Duey, Mr. Thomas Bentley, and Mr. Eugene Kinerk today?' "

"Mr. Duey and Mr. Bentley have been convicted of murder. Bentley was an accessory. Mr. Kinerk was arrested for bank robberies and was later found dead, hanging in his cell. There was a suicide note. Silva and Evans were convicted of federal racketeering offenses involving the white supremacist movement."

"What types of weapons were they firing in the combat training exercises?"

"An AR-15 assault rifle, twelve-gauge shotgun, Rugar mini-14. I had a .45-caliber semiautomatic pistol. Those were the ones I remember."

"Now, Mr. Lake, as you described the layout of the Aryan Nations compound, you mentioned a print shop that produced literature you described as highly racist. Were any materials printed there present at the urban combat training site?"

"Yes. There were targets that were racist caricatures."

"Do you remember the titles of any booklets for sale at the print shop?"

"Let's see. I remember *The Negro: Serpent, Beast, or Devil, The Hundred Facts.* There was a book by Louis Beam entitled *Understanding The Struggle, Or Why We Have To Kill The Bastards.*

We first established a pattern of murder, robberies, and racketeering, then established the arbitrary nature of intended victims selected simply by race and religion. In my next question I again deliberately used the phrase "cross-burning," asking Lake whom he'd spoken with prior to the inflaming. I anticipated an objection.

As I asked this question, I noticed Metzger tugging at Kearney's sleeve, speaking urgently. In the war of words we had come to an important battleground. The defendants wanted the phrase "cross-lighting," which implied a religious, ceremonial act. I wanted to use the descriptive "cross-burning," because it was an illegal burning, not a religious ritual, we sought to prove. If the judge compelled me to use the Klan terminology, the defense would implicitly be validated by the court.

"Your Honor," said Kearney, "objection to Mr. Phillips's characterizing this as a 'burning.' The witness indicated in a previous response that it was a 'cross-lighting.' I would ask that Mr. Phillips rephrase his question accordingly."

Judge Smith turned toward the witness.

"What did they say it was?" asked the judge.

"They called it a cross-lighting," Lake replied.

"That is their terminology, not mine," I asserted.

"Yes, I understand," the judge replied. "Develop your contention if you can."

"Mr. Lake, is the striking of a match to gasoline-soaked materials something that normally results in a burning of those materials?" I asked.

"Yes, sir. But the lighting of a cross is a symbolic act. As I understand it, this is not meant to consume the cross but to illuminate it with fire. It has, I think, a very different meaning than setting the cross on fire with the intention of having the material consumed by fire."

"But to light the cross in this manner you have to set it on fire. Isn't that so, sir?"

"Yes."

"And it burns?"

"Yes."

"So you understand my terminology if I say 'cross-burning,' correct?"

"Certainly."

"Good. So now, where was it you had your first conversation about this cross-burning?"

"The first conversations I had were in Hayden Lake in mid-November, when I discussed it with Richard Butler, Frank Silva, and Randy Evans. Silva said he would like to have Richard Butler come down and participate in it. That was pretty much the entirety of the first discussions."

"And when you returned to Los Angeles, was it Mr. Silva that you first spoke with on this subject?"

"Yes. We discussed how the plans were coming for the cross-burning, whether Richard Butler would be coming down and who else might be there, when it was going to take place—a rather complete discussion of the whole event."

"Did Mr. Silva ever state reasons why the cross-burning should take place?"

"Silva told me several reasons. One was that he wanted to make a symbolic statement of the presence of the Ku Klux Klan in Los Angeles; another was that he wanted to join his forces with those of Mr. Metzger."

"What was the symbolic statement about the Klan?"

"Frank and Randy believed that Los Angeles had become a cesspool of mongrel peoples. They wanted to assert the supremacy of the white race, and this was the way to do that."

I then asked Lake about the second reason Silva gave for burning the crosses—that he wanted to join his California Klan with Metzger's White Aryan Resistance. I hoped Lake's response would help tie Metzger into the unlawful assembly charge.

"Silva and Evans were both Klansmen, but they had begun the process of joining together with Aryan Nations when we were back in Idaho," Lake replied. "Metzger had been the Grand Dragon of the California Klan, then ran for Congress and actually got nominated. He lost the election, but soon after started a new group called WAR, White Aryan Resistance. Now they were trying to cement all those groups together."

We had now established an express agreement among several of the co-conspirators to commit the illegal burning. The videotape would demonstrate that three of the four defendants on trial—Witek, Riley, and Hofstadler—had actively assisted in the cross-burning. By drawing inferences from this evidence, we hoped to demonstrate that each had agreed to join the conspiracy.

We prepared to show the jury Lake's videotape of the cross-burning. We knew it did not capture the extent of Metzger's participation, or so we would be compelled to argue. Additionally, Lake knew nothing of Metzger's role in prior cross-burning demonstrations. This testimony would come from later witnesses and, we hoped, from Metzger's own mouth when we got him on cross-examination, if he testified.

Three television monitors were placed in the courtroom—one facing the judge, one before the counsel table, and the largest positioned for viewing by the jury. The lights in the courtroom were turned down. Sound first, then a blurry image was transmitted by the monitor. The camera focus was corrected. The jury watched intently as the first scene revealed the Klan inside Silva's home, planning how they would transport the crosses to the site at Kagel Canyon. We then viewed scenes at the second property, the residence of Ron Major, where the crosses would be ignited.

The eye of Lake's camera captured a moonlit night with figures passing between the shadows of overgrown shrubbery. The bare branches of a willow tree swayed in the wind. A clamor of raised voices came from the roadside. Three Nazi Party members threateningly raised table legs, silencing the chastisements of a shocked spectator.

Lake's camera entered the old wooden residence as Butler and Silva pulled satin robes over their clothing. Silva asked Butler if he was going to wear "the mask," a detachable face-piece of the hood. They both decided they would.

Each scene helped prove the commission of a different overt act in furtherance of the conspiracy. First there was the organization of transportation to the cross-burning location, then the distribution of billy clubs and the wearing of "disguised attire."

As Lake walked with his camera to the backside of the residence, he caught a brief shot of Hofstadler constructing torches of rags wrapped around the end of arms-length sticks. A few steps beyond, Silva dowsed the crosses with the flammable liquid, then raised them with the assistance of Riley into previously dug holes. One of Metzger's men, Winston Burbage, jumped atop a knoll and called for the attention of the Klansmen about him. "If anybody gets arrested, tell the cops we're just having a barbecue. They're gonna have a hell of a time saying a barbecue is an unlawful assembly."

Indeed, Lake's videotape showed the lighting of a makeshift barbecue, and on the grill they placed a single pork chop and a can of beans. Then Lake reentered the residence. A clearly audible voice, unmistakably that of Tom Metzger, originated from beside his camera.

"Getting it all down on videotape, are ya?" Metzger seemed more to be expressing an observation than asking a question.

"Well, I'm trying to. It's a little difficult at times with all this helicopter noise."

We knew Metzger to be clever and cunning. He won the Democratic Party's nomination for a congressional seat, publishes a monthly periodical, and produces a cable television show. He was aware the videotape could inculpate the Klansmen. And while Lake was able to gain the confidence of the Idaho group, not for a moment did he fool Tom Metzger.

Within seconds of confirming Lake's camera was taping, Metzger uttered a remark not in context with the conversation that otherwise prevailed.

"Don't necessarily have to have a cross-lighting if it's going to create a major confrontation."

His declaration seemed intentionally self-exculpatory. He made no other attempt to dissuade the other Klansmen from going ahead with the cross-burning.

Despite the police warnings that arrests would follow the igniting of the crosses, Frank Silva steadfastly refused to relinquish his plan. After the previous night's expression of solidarity, the others remained in his ranks. Out of the wood shack residence they filed, one by one, assuming positions before a hastily constructed speaker's stand.

When all were gathered, Silva raised his hands and began to holler over the drone of the circling helicopter. Wearing a black satin robe, red sash, and black hood, Silva manifested a heinous image. Only his eyes showed through the two round holes of the black face mask.

"Children of God, we are gathered here in front of the anti-Christ. We who are Christians, we vow to yield to Yahweh Jesus Christ. We will *never* bow down to the anti-Christ. So long as blood runs through our veins we will never give in. Behold the uplifted cross.

"I welcome you here to the gathering of the Aryan race, those of us who are men. We stand here firm. We have here men of God, Pastor Butler and Pastor Randall Evans. These men have been chosen and ordained by Jesus Christ to be here tonight. This is God's will that we do this. You're all welcome to partake of our simple meal. Now I ask Pastor Butler to offer a word of prayer."

Richard Butler presented an equally terrifying image in his red satin robe, black sash, and red hood and face mask. As he began to speak, he raised his right arm in a

Third Reich salute. The Klansmen surrounding him joined in the salutation.

"Brethren, I come before thee, as the anti-Christ is upon this assembly. We are gathered together tonight to ask that thy power and thy will be with us, Father. We have seen thine enemies face-to-face. May you bless this food, and each and every one who partakes of its nourishment. We ask this in the name of Jesus Christ. Amen."

The others responded, "Amen," and lowered their right arms to their sides. Then Silva stepped forward and cried out, his chin uplifted, again stretching his arm in a Third Reich salute toward the sky, "Hail, Victory!"

The others saluted and repeated his cry.

"Hail, Victory!" yelled Silva again.

The Klan responded in kind.

"Hail Victory!"

One last time they called out, then dropped their arms to their sides.

The voice of Stan Witek came more audibly to the side of the video camera. "The police are organizing on private property. I'd like you to document them before they invade the place."

"Okay," Peter answered. The video image shook with Peter's stride through the brush toward the eastern boundary of the property. He and Witek approached a line of policemen in riot garb.

Lake raised his camera and scanned the officers. They glared into the light, angered by his intent to record them. Several officers shined high-powered flashlights back at the camera lens. Tension quickly mounted.

Lake backed off. He and Witek returned to the cross-burning site. Silva was directing the others to form a circle around the three towering crosses. Once again his arm rose in salutation and he called out his final words before igniting the towering crosses.

"Fellow Klansmen, we are now about to fulfill our obligation to Jesus Christ, and we *will* do it. Remember this, men of the Aryan race. If one drop of Aryan blood is spilled tonight or at any other time, there will be *revenge.*

"Now, some of you live near and some live far away, but remember this. We will be there with you, fighting with you. You have my word. Bless you one and all. Pastor Butler."

Butler cried out to the Klan.

"Aryan comrades, remember. So long as the alien occupies your land, hate is your law, and revenge is your first duty. The alien, this day, occupies your land. This is your land. Wherefore, we in an act of defiance to the forces of Jewry, who now say that they have thrashed the Aryan spirit, we say that before God there lives yet the spirit of true comradeship of the true Aryan. We light these crosses in the name of our God over the Luciferian scum of the earth. We say, Hail to His Victory."

The Klansmen responded, "Hail, Victory!"

With those last words, Silva and Butler stepped toward the crosses with burning torches in hand. Against the burlap they set the glowing flame on one cross, then the others. Up the flames crept, slowly at first, along a single side of the burlap-wrapped center beam. Around the cross the flame swept, moving upward ever faster, and at the horizontal beams it fanned out, reaching upward, challenging the heavens to burst forth from the passing clouds.

Whoops and hollers of joy came from the Klansmen. Lake's camera angle widened as he backed away from the intense heat of the raging inferno.

Small white lights began to flicker in the background of the arena of fire. They grew larger, discernable as flashlights carried by the helmeted officers moving toward the scene. A moment later, they were upon the Klansmen, forcing them to the ground, ordering them to lie face down in prone positions. Peter continued taping. The figure in the white robe and hood was led within camera view, his hands cuffed behind him. The mask face-piece was grabbed by an officer, and the hood raised above the man's head and cast to the ground. Exposed was Jerome Hofstadler, in the foreground of the blazing crosses.

The camera picture suddenly became a blur of motion. From the audio, it was apparent that Lake was being arrested. The camera fell. There was a crunching sound. The picture buzzed with static. There was another crunch. The picture was gone, then the audio. The courtroom was left in dark and eerie silence.

On came the lights. The eyes of all in the courtroom looked for the reaction of the defendants. Witek smiled indulgently, enjoying his celebrity status, however worthy of contempt.

Metzger appeared complacent, with a distinct air of confidence. I suspected that because he had avoided the camera he anticipated the jury would assume his participation was minimal. Hofstadler looked uncomfortable, perhaps embarrassed. He had been attending court nicely attired in a conservative gray suit and blue or red tie each day of the trial. Having his white hood pulled off toward the end of the tape was a stark contrast to the image he was trying to present in court. Riley sipped from a cup of water. None of the defendants conversed with each other.

Later we noticed Metzger befriending Hofstadler. This was predictable. Witek behaved too eccentrically for Metzger to want to be associated with him. Although Witek dressed in a decent suit and tie, there was something about the way he carried himself that made him seem out of touch. Riley was not the sharpest pencil in the box and generally stayed quiet throughout the proceedings. Hofstadler, on the other hand, often took notes during court sessions. If he spoke to his lawyer or Metzger, one could see he was listening and understanding. He was a fairly good-looking young man, about five-foot-ten, with light brown hair and a short moustache. He didn't strike me as a loser. I could not connect his involvement with the Klan prior to the cross-burning in Rosamond a few weeks prior to the one in L.A.. I was beginning to wonder how he had gotten involved with the rest of them.

The judge adjourned court for the lunch hour. I waited for the courtroom to clear before attempting to make my way through the crowd. Metzger walked back to the skinheads. For the first time I noticed that his son, John Metzger, was among them. He had shaved his head and wore combat fatigues. As Metzger approached, the young men smiled and shook the hand of their mentor. He seized the opportunity to address his admirers.

"You all know what we have going here. You all know who the prosecutor wants to convict. But if they don't get *me*, what they've succeeded in doing is legitimizing all of us. If they don't get *me*, they won't ever get any of *you*. If they don't get me, the cops won't ever be able to make arrests again when we do our thing. And I'll tell you what we'll have. It'll be another Skokie, where they tried to stop the Nazis from marching down the main street of the bagel district, and they failed. But because the government called so much attention to it, they made that parade bigger and better than ever. That's what we're gonna have here. And our victory will be a call for members from a thousand miles."

Metzger was right about one thing, now even more than ever before. I wanted very much to convict him.

When we convened for the afternoon session, I initiated my direct examination of Lake by addressing an issue apparent from the videotape. At times, a small metal microphone could be seen attached to the lapel of Metzger's jacket. I wanted to bring attention to this, to force Metzger to reveal the contents of the tape. I figured it had to help our case. It just seemed that if the tape was recording, somebody at some time would have slipped and said something incriminating. On the other hand, if Metzger never produced the tape during the trial, once the jury knew it existed they would assume he'd destroyed the tape to conceal incriminating conversation.

"Mr. Lake, throughout the evening of the cross-burning, did you notice anything attached to Mr. Metzger's jacket lapel?"

"He was wearing a small metal microphone," said Lake. "There was a wire leading down to a little tape recorder occasionally protruding from inside his jacket. After we were arrested, I remember him saying he had a tape that would prove his innocence."

I then needed to attack Metzger's pro forma exculpatory statement, where he briefly discouraged the others from going through with the cross-burning. My perception of Metzger was that he was smarter than he was loyal. He had left the Democratic Party, left the Klan, and severed other personal and political ties as his own needs were best served. He wouldn't have wanted to have been first to grab his hat and leave the party. No, that wouldn't have been gutsy at all. But the spider *never* gets caught in his own web.

"Mr. Lake, do you also recall Mr. Metzger's asking if you were recording, your responding affirmatively, and then his stating an opinion on whether the cross-lighting had to take place?"

"Yes. I remember that clearly from both the tape and from the night of the incident."

"Would you describe Mr. Metzger's demeanor?"

"I would say he was nervous."

"How was it that the comment made by Mr. Metzger came up at that particular time?"

"He came up to my recorder, tapped on the microphone, and then said, 'Is this thing on?' And then he leaned over it and made a comment, the comment that you just heard: 'You don't necessarily have to have a cross-lighting here.' "

"Was the comment within the context of the overall conversation transpiring inside the house?"

"No. It was just out of the blue. My distinct impression was that Tom Metzger was getting something on tape to exonerate him if we later were arrested. It was as if someone were telling another not to dive into the pool as he was already bouncing off the board."

I next wanted Lake's "expert" opinion on the Ku Klux Klan practice of cross-burnings. This was particularly important to the principle charge in the complaint, unlawful assembly.

An opinion of a witness is normally not relevant to the issues of a trial and will be ruled inadmissible by the judge. It is only when a witness has background knowledge beyond the average experience that his opinion is relevant to the jury's understanding of an issue. If such a foundation of knowledge beyond the "lay experience" is established, the opinion is called "expert" and is admissible.

I had asked Lake prior to his taking the stand what his opinion on the cross-burning would be, and I got a mixed read. The underlying problem was that I was asking a nonprofessional witness for an expert opinion. Although this may sound acceptable in theory, a nonprofessional witness has no reason to sort through the depths of his reasoning and may be equivocal in his opinion, perhaps even change it altogether on the stand.

I knew Lake would give a statement favorable to our case, but I did not know how strong. To a limited extent, he accepted the claim that cross-burnings were founded on religious intent. Indeed, there was no denying that the videotape showed Butler leading a prayer prior to the lighting of the crosses, although the "prayer" was knee-deep in the Klan's usual rhetoric of hate and violence.

When I asked Lake's opinion why this cross-burning took place in Los Angeles the night of December 3, a flurry of objections on grounds of relevancy and insufficient foundation erupted from the defense lawyers. They knew the importance of this testimony to the outcome of the trial. Judge Smith ruled without hesitancy. He recited Lake's qualifications as one who had extensively read publications of the Klan, associated with members, and spoken to them on the subject of "cross-lightings." Smith designated Lake as an expert witness and allowed him to give the opinion.

"I do have an opinion," Lake responded. "I believe the cross-lighting was meant to fulfill several different functions. One was to help form an alliance between Mr. Metzger's organization, WAR; the Ku Klux Klan; and Aryan Nations.

"It was also intended to serve notice on people in the neighborhood that if they were not Aryan, there were people who opposed their presence in the neighborhood. That blacks and other minorities should leave.

"It was also meant to establish in southern California a presence of white supremacists and serve as a means of attracting other white supremacists into this movement. Frank Silva and Stan Witek discussed trying to have other cross-lightings in the Los Angeles area if this one turned out to be successful."

I was very satisfied with Lake's statement. It exposed the Metzger connection and the intention that the cross-burning be viewed as a threat by the surrounding community. It was also a continuing threat, and if the jury did not return guilty verdicts, one could imagine there would be more crosses burned in Los Angeles County. I noticed several jurors quickly writing notes as Lake spoke, which he did in a deliberate and articulate fashion.

Brian Pageant started cross examination. More laboriously than artfully, he dwelled on the financial rewards Lake had obtained from his Klan infiltration. Then one by one, the other defense counsel went at Lake in a fury. They hammered at the profit motive, building an impression that Lake needed to sensationalize his infiltration. He had written magazine articles and sold his video to news and talk shows. Lake estimated his financial gain in the area of one hundred thousand dollars. I noticed that jurors wrote notes on these points also.

By the end of the court session that day I felt the kind of mental exhaustion that comes with a long ragtag fight. I sat back in an old swivel chair inside Davidson's office. Perspiration had run through to the lining of my wool suit. Dale closed the door and leaned against the side of his desk. "What's your read on Lake's credibility?" he asked.

"I don't buy into Lake or anybody else trying to make a buck by framing the Klan. I think we're okay with him."

"But what about the jurors?" Dale pondered. "Maybe they see him as a guy willing to take that sort of chance. A hundred thousand is good money, and an opinion is just an opinion."

I was not anxious to concede that Davidson may be right. "Suppose the jurors *do* feel Lake is pumping his testimony to sell himself. We could back him up with a witness who has no profit motive."

"Who's that?" Dale asked.

"I got a guy with the Department of Justice. For half his adult life he's worked on Metzger's group."

◆ ◆ ◆ ◆ ◆

The images seen on video remained seemingly unmistakable proof of participation by Witek, Hofstadler, and Riley. Still, the religious overtones preceding the lighting of the crosses corroborated the defendant's anticipated First Amendment defense. If they successfully developed the constitutional claims, it would not matter how strongly we proved any of the defendants participated.

To overcome the First Amendment defense, the prosecution must demonstrate that the state possesses a "compelling interest" in controlling the conduct associated with the speech and religious expression. The court of appeals would later apply a balancing test between the First Amendment rights and conflicting governmental regulations, if we obtained convictions. The jurors would also apply a balancing standard between state action to protect the public peace and the constitutional rights of the Klan.

For these reasons, we needed strong proof that the burning crosses presented a clear and present danger to the community. We could have done this solely by demonstrating that the Klan intended to provoke violence, but we chose to establish a more viable record by additionally demonstrating the danger of a potentially spreading fire.

To cover this angle, the next witness we called was Los Angeles Fire Department Captain John Stillson. It was his station, located a mile up the canyon road, that extinguished the burning crosses. It was also his station that issued a burn permit to Silva and Miner for a barbecue. Our examination would include both the potential danger of a spreading fire and the inapplicability of the barbecue permit for the lighting of crosses.

Stillson took the oath, sat in the witness chair, and answered questions thoughtfully and articulately. His angular facial features, strong chin, and speckled gray moustache—along with the dark blue uniform of the Los Angeles Fire Department—made him an authoritative character on the witness stand.

After receiving the call from the police officers at the scene, Stillson had driven down Kagel Canyon in a four-person pumper truck. Another truck and crew accompanied his. The firemen were apprehensive, not so much about the fire, but because of the deepening confrontation.

Davidson was taking the direct examination. He asked

the fire captain what he first saw as he arrived. The question was standard and seemed innocent enough. Stillson thought for a moment, then testified to seeing a plainclothes police officer with a bullhorn in hand.

"As we stopped, we heard a plainclothes officer speaking over a public address system. He was saying something to the effect that 'If you ignite the fires, you will be arrested,' and it was repeated several times."

The captain's testimony was entirely unexpected. Neither Davidson nor I had ever heard anyone relate this. My co-counsel glanced over to me. I looked away from him and back at the witness without raising an eyebrow. I wondered if Stillson was right or wrong on this point. He described the plainclothes officer to a match of L.A.P.D. Lieutenant Robinson, but no one else, not even the police, recalled warnings over a loudspeaker. If Stillson was right, the warnings would impute knowledge to all the defendants of the absence of a valid burn permit.

Pageant was seated to my right. He immediately leaned over and tapped my arm. "Where did he come up with this bull?"

"It's what he remembers," I answered.

"And the cops don't?" he said.

The rhetorical question posed by Pageant could easily have passed through the minds of the jurors and damaged Stillson's testimony on other more important points. Davidson moved on, not trying to exploit or highlight it.

Stillson continued, "When we first got there we didn't really know what to expect. The police were positioned around the perimeter of the property in riot gear. The officer in charge told me what was going on. We normally, in that type of situation, defer control of the situation to the police department. And once they determine that it's safe, we go in and do what we have to do."

"Were you concerned that a fire was going to be set in the canyon that night?" asked Davidson.

"Kagel Canyon has been historically bad for brush fires. We normally see long periods of winds during November and December. We naturally feel a little concerned about any kind of open fire in such areas because of the danger of setting a brushfire or of setting on fire one of the many houses with wooden roofs or wood siding."

"Did you eventually determine the exact construction of the crosses that were burned that night?"

"They were each constructed with four-by-four pieces of lumber, wrapped in burlap that was heavily saturated with a flammable liquid. The lab analysis later determined the liquid to be a combination of gasoline and kerosene. The tallest of the three crosses was eighteen to twenty feet in height. The other two stood approximately fifteen and twelve feet above the ground."

"Could you speculate why a combination of kerosene and gasoline was used?"

"Yes. Both are flammable liquids, but the mixture produces a slower burn, one more likely to fully burn the four-by-fours."

"Were you and your men the ones that actually went down and put out those fires after they were ablaze?"

"Yes."

"Do you have an opinion whether these were dangerous fires?"

"Yes, I do. I've responded to many arsons, and this was a similar situation. The flammable liquids caused the crosses to burn with great intensity. The debris wrapped around the wood peeled off, and flames left the immediate scene. These could float down to other areas and cause what we call exposure fires. The winds also have an eddying effect, being at the mouth of a canyon, between dusk and dark. We normally have enough flow of winds during the day, then it starts coming down the canyon at night. And when it equalizes, you get a pretty strong wind."

According to police officers who would later testify, Frank Silva repeatedly displayed a burn permit from the Los Angeles Fire Department. Following his arrest, the permit was removed from his pants pocket and booked into evidence. We knew Silva's permit would be integral to the Klan's "affirmative defense."

An affirmative defense admits the truth of the allegations but claims the conduct is legal under the circumstances. In this instance, the affirmative defense would admit the setting of the fires but claim that the defendants on trial believed they possessed a valid permit. We hoped to counter this defense by making the belief seem so unreasonable under the circumstances that they could not have honestly held it.

Captain Stillson's testimony on direct examination was important in two ways. He refuted the legitimacy of the permit and described the location as a site vulnerable to brushfire. The cross-examination attempted to develop the affirmative defense. Stillson was repeatedly asked questions that sought to establish the validity of the permit. Indeed it was a permit that an L.A.F.D. fireman issued at the local station, but the station's log notes indicated that the fireman on desk duty had been told the permit was for an open-pit barbecue.

Nonetheless, the law would require the jury to acquit the defendants if they honestly believed Silva's permit covered bon fires. The defense is applicable even if the belief was unreasonable, so long as it was an honest and true belief. Pageant desperately needed a concession from Stillson. He placed the document before the fire captain.

"I will ask you to look at this, sir, and tell me what words most immediately come to view."

"The words 'burn permit.'"

"And that's because they are in bold letters, correct?"

"That is correct."

"So if I were to quickly show this paper to another person, or they caught a glimpse of it as I held it, they would most readily notice it was indeed a burn permit. Is that correct?"

"But if they read it closer, they would see it was for an open-pit barbecue."

"But only if they read it closer, wouldn't you agree?"

"I suppose that is so."

On redirect examination, Davidson attempted to demonstrate the defendants' true knowledge. Deftly phrasing questions, Davidson painted a picture of dozens of riot cops surrounding the location, a circling helicopter, and a waiting fire truck. The image contradicted the claim of a true belief in the legality of the fire.

The following morning we received word Doug Seymour had suffered a heart attack. He was living in the Midwest the past two years, trying to find peace and solitude. His doctors told him it was stress related. His wife was adamant that he could not testify.

When I spoke directly to Doug, I didn't want to let on how much we needed him. For twelve years he carried the bitter memory of the night the Klan found him out and tortured him to confess. I wasn't going to let him know that our case against his nemesis rested heavily on his taking the stand. Doug would have come if he knew, but I wasn't going to have this case bury him. There was still one other person who knew more about Tom Metzger. I just had to make sure he would give up his Fifth Amendment right. It was Metzger himself.

◆ ◆ ◆ ◆ ◆

Robert Gentry was scheduled to testify the following morning. Nearly thirty years had passed since his family fled a picnic in 1964 as the Georgia Klan burned its cross on the hillside overlooking his favorite childhood playground. He remembered his cousin wanting to stop them, but not knowing how, and being pulled back by his uncle. He remembered the words of his own dad: "Not here, not now." He never did return to that park. Nor, after moving to Los Angeles with his wife, did he ever return to Georgia. Now he was determined that he would return to his own home, his own family and neighbors in Lake View Terrace, with no less self-respect than before the California Klan tried to steal that away. This was the moment of reckoning for which he'd waited thirty years.

As I walked down the hallway to greet Gentry, who was waiting in the lobby of our office, I heard my name called loudly from a distance behind me. The head secretary hurried to catch me, waving me back to speak with her. "You got a call from your wife. Telephone her immediately."

It was not Diane who answered the phone. "Who's calling?" inquired the male voice. My children cried in the background, but I recognized the voice of a detective assigned to the L.A.P.D. antiterrorist division, Al Taylor. We had met a few times over the past several years. I kept Al informed of the findings of our investigation. He had promised my security, and that of my family, in return.

"John Phillips here. Taylor, is that you?"

"Don't be alarmed. We have the situation here under control."

"What the hell is going on?" I asked. Davidson stepped in and listened.

"There was a package left at your front door. It has a crossed-out label from a Mercedes dealership. There's no other sender identification. It's addressed to you, as a deputy city attorney," he said.

I realized Diane would have immediately thought this suspicious and called Detective Taylor to the home. "I've never owned a Mercedes," I said. "And you know I left the city attorney's office two years ago."

"We telephoned the dealership," Taylor said. "They didn't send you any package. The bomb squad is here. They've secured it. It's out of the house."

"Put Diane on the phone."

She took the receiver. "John?" Her voice was shaken.

"How are you doing?" I asked.

"It's not good here right now. It's not good."

"Where are the kids?"

"They're here with me. They're okay. There's a lot of policemen here. They're closing off traffic down the street. I'm scared, John. I want you home."

Davidson waited patiently, and when I was off the phone he asked what was going on. I told him quickly and left for home.

I honked the horn of my black Ford Explorer to clear traffic as I moved past the shopping center, rounded the corner sharply, sped down tree-lined Westwood Boulevard, and bounced abruptly as I crossed the train tracks before my street. It was just past the morning rush hour—the calm of our West Los Angeles neighborhood contradicted my anxious drive home. As I turned onto our street, I noticed the sidewalks and the front yards of the old Spanish-style houses were completely empty. A police vehicle blocked my path. I slowed. As an officer approached, I identified myself and he let me pass.

I parked and stepped nervously from my car. The police activity was across the street, alongside the railroad tracks. I could see one of them, a bomb-squad officer in a dark blue jumpsuit, carrying the package. It looked about fifteen inches long, a foot wide, and two inches in height and was wrapped in brown paper.

The officers had affixed to it a long wire that led back to the front lawn of my home. The package was placed about sixty feet away, inside an old concrete switchman's box left vacant by the railroad many years ago.

I entered the front door and saw our children, quiet now, standing with Diane in front of the living room window.

"You okay?" I asked, wrapping my arms around her.

"I'm okay. You?"

"No, Diane. *This* is *not* okay."

Taylor entered the living room. "I'm sorry," he said. "I'm going to have to ask you to go to the back of the house. They've decided not to mess with the package. They're going to detonate it."

Diane and I went to the rear bedroom with the children. Taylor signaled from the front door. Moments later we heard an explosion. The windows of the house rattled, as did our nerves. The kids were startled and began to cry again. I went to the front yard and saw that a stripped-down Crown Victoria, the standard unmarked law enforcement vehicle, had pulled to a stop across the street. Taylor stood by me as the bomb-squad officers examined the debris of the package. "I guess you knew the risks when you came back into the prosecution," Taylor said. He motioned toward the Crown Victoria. "Those guys told me this morning you were on the same list as Alan Berg. How come you never told me?"

"List?" I asked. I remembered my conversation in the courthouse hallway the morning I reentered the prosecution. "This is the second time I'm hearing about some list. What's this all about?" I asked.

From the Crown Victoria emerged the two men I'd seen several times seated in the back of the courtroom, behind the skinheads. They had avoided eye contact with me there, and again they turned away, showing ID to an L.A.P.D. sergeant. They wouldn't be so lucky today to maintain their low profile.

"Who are those guys?" I asked Taylor. "FBI?"

Taylor was surprised I asked. "You haven't met?"

"We're going to meet right now," I answered and headed across the street. They saw me coming but said nothing. Taylor followed.

"Good morning, gentlemen." My tone, I'm sure, was decidedly belligerent. "Is there something you've been meaning to tell me?"

"Good morning, Mr. Phillips. I'm Hank Wilson, Federal Bureau of—"

"Procrastination," I added. What's this list I'm hearing about?"

"You were on a list found up in Idaho at Scarborough's place, but we didn't have anything solid. Maybe we still don't. The package contained just a bunch of newspaper and a set of keys. This may be entirely separate from the prosecution of the Klan."

"So what the hell have you been waiting for—a stronger case?"

"This is still investigative," he answered. "There was no need to disrupt the prosecution."

"You stay the hell out of my courtroom. Both of you. Do your damn investigation and get the hell out of here."

By my way of thinking, the federal agents had violated a code of trust between law enforcement agencies. To them, we were *county* prosecutors, not federal. Perhaps the next agents the Bureau would send—and I expected others—would not wait for the axe to fall.

I stayed home until the commotion died down and Diane and the children regained their composure. She asked what I was going to do. "I'm done," I answered.

"Done?" Diane asked disbelievingly.

"I can walk away."

"I don't believe I could *let* you walk away," she replied. "You'll never find peace if you don't finish this."

"Dale doesn't know Gentry. I'd better go in to prep him. I'll see you around six." I was resolved that I would not jeopardize my family, not under any circumstances or for any amount of money, prestige, or other gratification. No one was going to talk me back in. As I left my home it didn't feel the same. I was angry. My home had been violated. We were lucky this time. Very lucky. But I don't trust luck. And this situation was now out of control.

Davidson had managed to delay the trial by asking for time to research a defense motion to limit expert testimony. When I returned to the office he was already aware of what had happened. He asked if any news media had come to my home. There had been none. He asked if I had told anyone at the courthouse about the bomb scare. I had not. Then he asked if I was still going ahead with the trial.

"I'm leaving."

Davidson shook his head. "They're playing poker with you," he said. "They want you to blink."

"I don't *see* this bet. Last week I yelled at my kid because he looked out the living room window. Now they let me know they can get to my home. What am I going to do—have the kids wear bullet-proof vests?"

He raised his voice in a chastising tone. "You've known the stakes."

"Listen, Davidson. I'm here to help you prepare the Gentry examination. I'll interview him, and you take notes." An uncomfortable pause in the conversation followed. I knew why Dale asked if word of the bomb scare had spread. "Does anyone here know what went down?" I asked.

"Only Reiner and Garcetti," Dale responded. "They're keeping a lid on it. Keeping your options open for the next . . . , " Dale looked at his watch, "forty-five minutes." It was 12:45 P.M.

Robert Gentry was seated in an interview room by the front lobby. It had been nearly a year since we'd last seen each other. He wore a dark, three-piece suit. His closely groomed hair and beard, combined with round eyeglasses, completed the portrait of an intellectual. Had there been a hundred applicants for his role as witness, he still would have gotten the call. In truth, he was the only one to come forward.

As Gentry saw me approach, he stood and forced a smile. He seemed apprehensive. Seated next to him was another man, about the same age or just a bit older. He gave me the once-over and stood indifferently as I approached Robert.

"Mr. Phillips, glad to see you, sir." Gentry extended his hand and we greeted warmly. I did not tell him of my decision to leave the prosecution. It made this an awkward moment. I introduced Davidson and told Gentry we would interview him prior to his testifying. Gentry raised an eyebrow. "I thought we had covered all the bases," he replied inquisitively. He introduced his cousin Marcus Gentry, who wanted little to do with Davidson or me.

We sat in the interview room for the next thirty-five minutes. As I asked Gentry questions that prompted the responses I thought most important to his testimony, I looked at Dale to make sure he caught them. He sat with his arms folded, listening, and took no notes.

I thanked Gentry for availing himself so graciously to testifying and let him know I respected his courage and wished him the best. But at these concluding remarks his expression changed, and his cousin became agitated.

"It's not easy for him," said Marcus Gentry, "putting not just himself, but his family, in what could be harm's way." There was an angry tone in Marcus's voice, and the anger was directed my way.

"It's easily figured just where I live," said Robert. "But I knew that was important to this case, that I could see the flames from my home as they burned the crosses."

"I'm sorry, Mr. Gentry, but you're right," I said. "It *is* important that you could see it from your home."

Davidson stood behind me as I faced Gentry. "But they can't touch you as long as you're coming at them, staying visible," Davidson said. "They may try to scare you off, but once your job is done, fairly and honestly done, *no one* is going to get hurt."

I turned as Davidson finished speaking. He was looking at me, not Gentry.

Marcus Gentry became irate. "You don't *know* no one will get hurt. There's no telling what these people may do."

"Oh, I could not stop, Mr. Davidson," Robert Gentry interrupted. "I could not trade a lifetime of remorse for an afternoon of peace." Gentry turned toward me. "You have made me trust, Mr. Phillips. Do you know what that means, for a black man to trust a white man, that he will carry through to prosecute the Klan? Marcus told me early on that I was a damn fool, that the Klan does not get prosecuted in a white society, just as they didn't get prosecuted for what they did to his father. He threw a stone and paid the rest of his life without justice being done. But I trust in you." I could say nothing. Robert Gentry extended a handshake. "I'm sorry to have gone on like this. I'll see you downstairs in court, Mr. Phillips."

As the witness left for the courtroom, I wished I could walk with him as he passed the skinheads, Nazis, and Klansmen. He would be all they needed to become riled up—an intelligent, prosperous black man coming to testify against them. What a brave man Robert Gentry was. I was not so brave a man.

I walked down the hallway and saw the library was

empty. I went inside and found a table in the rear. I sat there with my back turned to anyone who might pass and lay my head in my hands. "Where is he now?" I wondered.

"There are others now who can take up this cross. When I first set out to do this I had no children. I accepted the risk and would have given my life. But I will not give it now. I have responsibilities now, and a love that is greater than any love I can ever have for principle, or justice, or even my own soul. I will not allow their father to be taken from them. I will not allow her to become a widow, bitter and angry.

"Damn me if you will, if I have betrayed you, but I will not stay without a deal. A deal on my terms. You keep me safe. You keep my whole family safe."

◆ ◆ ◆ ◆ ◆

As Gentry took his seat in the witness stand, the only sound in the courtroom was his hand against the metal microphone. He pulled it closer, cleared his throat, and sipped from a glass of water. Gathering my thoughts, I stepped toward the witness stand.

"Mr. Gentry, what is your occupation, sir?"

"I am a computer analyst."

"Where were you born?"

"Savannah, Georgia."

"You eventually moved to the state of California?"

"Yes, about twenty years ago."

"And are you married?"

"I am; to my wife of twenty-three years. We have two kids, both daughters, now thirteen and nine."

"State your area of residence, without relating a specific street address."

"I live in Lake View Terrace. It's in the north-central portion of the San Fernando Valley of Los Angeles."

And so I began the direct examination of this brave man as he faced the national leaders of the white supremacist movement. They rigidly stared, and sometimes smirked at him as he testified. Gentry occasionally glanced over to them, then back to me, neither forcing eye contact with the defendants nor avoiding it. I was proud to take his testimony.

It wasn't easy for me that day. My mind occasionally wandered to Diane and my children. I was not concerned about the "right" thing to do. Now, I was looking for the *best* thing to do, and they were no longer the same. I sensed that I too, like Seymour and Lake and Canale, was playing a survival game.

I asked Gentry to describe the topography of the Kagel Canyon area.

"They call it a city/ranch area where there are horses, and residents are allowed to have some livestock. You know, goats and chickens," he replied. "I'm in about the first row of the residential tract, about half a mile from the Angeles National Forest."

He'd lived there nearly fifteen years, and was very familiar with the residents. He described them as 60 percent black and 40 percent white and other minorities. I asked him to describe the relations between the various people.

"We are a very closely knit neighborhood. It's one of those neighborhoods where you can leave your kids outside and let them play and not have to worry about them because, if something happens, we know our neighbors and they know us and our kids. We play basketball together; sometimes softball or horseshoes. We have what they call block parties where we block off the street and all the neighbors get together and have a party. It is a harmonious community.

At least it was. This Klan episode chilled relations, for a time, between the neighbors of different races. Then we came to realize that our neighbors did not participate in this Ku Klux Klan activity. People from outside our area wanted us to hate and distrust our neighbors, and them to hate and distrust us. I suppose we didn't want those outsiders to succeed in this. We can all smile at one another again and say 'hello' when we pass."

I refrained for a moment from asking the next question, and the witness paused. I glanced to my right and saw Metzger glaring again at Gentry. The pause in my questioning became noticeable, and I could feel the attention of the jury shifting to me. I turned my back to them and drew their attention to Metzger.

I continued with Gentry's examination. He'd heard a commotion that night, went outside, and saw a crowd of neighbors in the street, staring at three large raised crosses on the hillside. Among them were women and children. He'd spoken for a moment with another man, his friend Charles Walker. I asked him what was said. Pageant jumped to his feet and objected that my question called for hearsay. Indeed it did, but I argued that it fell within the state-of-mind exception, and the judge agreed. He instructed the witness to answer the question.

"I told Charles I was angry," continued Gentry. "In fact, I was scared. I had a similar experience as a young boy in Georgia. The Klan had come to this place, this beautiful place I used to play as a child. I remembered my dad was just not up to it.

"I turned around this night, while we were standing in the street wondering what to do. I saw my daughters. They were starting to come out of the house, but my wife pulled them back. They all watched from the windows. I saw the look on my older girl's face, seeing the flames and then looking back at me, wondering what I'd do. It reminded me of when I was a child, of how I remember my father that night. I didn't want to look like that now. I didn't want her to have the same memory of her dad as I had of mine. I loved him so much, but when I think of him, I remember that day. I didn't want to show her my fear. Anyway, in the area that we live in, a fire is a hazardous thing. After talking with some of the neighbors and such, I and Charles decided to take a closer look to see exactly what was happening. We walked up a dirt path closer to the burning crosses."

"Do you recall what you saw as you approached?"

"There were several figures wearing robes and hoods. One or two of the robes were red and black. The others were all white. There were three tall crosses, towering way over the heads of the people there.

"I was determined that the fires were going to be extinguished. I didn't know how, but I knew why. It may sound foolhardy, but I was not going to walk back down the hill to my family and neighbors without the fires having been put out."

"Did you continue to approach?"

"Yes, but two police came up and told us to stay off the

property. The persons responsible were being arrested. I remember just standing there, watching the flames, about twenty feet from one cross. I looked at the Klansmen as they were being taken into custody. I remember thinking how surprising it was that in this day and age there were still people with such small minds."

As Gentry spoke, I recalled his sequence of thoughts from our prior conversation, and, liking these expressions, let him continue answers that sometimes drifted from the scope of my question. Had I directly asked his opinions, objections would have been sustained on relevancy grounds. So instead, at each pause in his response I looked expectantly at him when I wanted more.

We finished with the direct examination midway through the afternoon court session.

The tactic of the cross-examiners was to make it seem that Gentry was too distant to see what he'd claimed on direct exam. He was questioned by each of the four defense attorneys. The questions became repetitious, and on several occasions I could hear sighs of exasperation from the jurors to my left.

We let the cross-examination drag on until shortly before the evening recess. Pageant posed a particularly long question incorporating several areas that had been covered earlier. The timing was perfect. Davidson rose and irately stood with his hands to his hips. "Your Honor," he said, "how much longer must this man endure such endless questioning? If some impact were being made on his credibility or ability to perceive, I could understand it. But this is senseless."

Before Pageant could respond, the judge sustained Dale's objection, making it seem as though he agreed that the cross-examination was overly laborious and ineffective. Gentry wiped his brow and stepped from the witness stand. He'd come across well. His cousin Marcus embraced him as the jury was excused and walked past. Realizing Gentry's long commitment to the prosecution had now concluded, I walked over for a few last words.

Marcus still had his arm around his cousin's shoulder as the last of the defendants left the courtroom. Marcus's eyes welled with emotion. "He's a smart man," said Marcus, beaming with pride at Robert. "He fought fire with water. That's not always so easy to do. My father tried to fight fire with fire—confronted the Klan in the street. God bless him. God bless you, too, Robert."

◆ ◆ ◆ ◆ ◆

The man who would testify next had for over three decades conducted surveillance on the Ku Klux Klan. He'd become a stranger to the beauty of life and an intruder to the dark side of other men's souls. His name was Gene Frice. He contacted me during my early investigation. His background was deep in government operations, both military and domestic, overt and covert. His work for the Department of Justice was now pretty much in the classroom, instructing new agents in the tactics of counterterrorism. Soon, he would retire altogether. The time was right for him to come up from the darkness. I needed someone to back up Lake, and with Seymour gone, only Frice could do it. More important, he could not be tied to the profit motive that attached to Lake's testimony.

Before his work for the Department of Justice, Frice was an army colonel. His hair was silver-streaked, and he had a direct manner of expression. Although Lake's assessment of the Klan cross-burnings helped us prove the unlawful assembly charge, his knowledge of the Klan was too recent for us to be confident his opinion would be persuasive to every juror. Frice could give us something more scholarly and credible.

Since leaving the military, Frice worked with the Department of Justice in its organized crime unit and antiterrorist division. The combination made him the right choice to head an investigation into far-right extremist groups, including the American Nazi Party and Metzger's California Klan. By the late 1960s, the Ku Klux Klan had begun to wield influence in California right-wing politics. His involvement included training in terrorism, reviewing countless police reports of Klan activity, and attending Klan rallies undercover. He'd been personally involved with several hundred Klan-related investigations over the years. He began following Metzger in 1968, and later gathered information on Stan Witek's Nazi group.

We began Frice's testimony with a historical overview of the Klan following the Civil War, their initial contempt for carpetbaggers, and their animosity toward the former slave population. Davidson's questions then focused on the Klan's use of the flaming cross to intimidate those they perceived as enemies. He established the appropriate foundation of expertise for Frice to render an opinion.

"Sir, based on your years in law enforcement, the materials you have read, the videotapes and films you have reviewed, and the Klan functions you have personally attended, do you have an opinion regarding the purpose for which the Ku Klux Klan burns crosses in the present day?"

"I do," answered Frice. "It is intended to bring their cause attention and to announce their presence to others of similar mind whom they may recruit, but its basic appeal and attraction are the ominous threat and intimidation it brings into a racially integrated community. It is a very aggressive act. The intimidation it creates is to all who view it, and let me say, I viewed several—and my skin is not black—and I was intimidated."

At times during Frice's testimony I could easily hear Pageant groan or sigh in exasperation. He hoped at least to distract the jury with this running commentary. It certainly had little impact on Frice, who at times glanced at Pageant but never compromised his testimony. When it came time for his turn to question the witness, Pageant began his cross-examination aggressively. Frice, however, calmly refused to yield ground.

"You state three reasons for the Klan to have a cross-lighting, and you named them in this order: attention, recruiting, and an aggressive act of intimidation. Is that right?" asked Pageant.

"It is," replied Frice.

"Now, would you agree that there is nothing against the law about a group wanting to get attention?"

"Not in and of itself."

"And there's nothing against the law about a group wanting to recruit members?"

"That may depend on how they're going about it."

"Is there anything else you care to add to your opinion of the reasons the Klan performs a cross-lighting?"

"To intimidate, as I said."

"Do you know if there is any religious significance to a cross-lighting ceremony?"

"I have heard so. Ostensibly, at least."

"Isn't it thought to be a religious purification for the participants?"

"That is one of the stated reasons for the cross-burning, but it is truly more intended to cause a purification by frightening those who are rejected by their so-called religion."

"Do you not see any religious significance in the lighting of a cross to the participants?"

"Well, it depends on who's watching. For a Klan member, I feel it is very likely that the burning of a cross has religious significance in the same sense as a pagan ritual."

"So you agree there is some measure of religious expression?"

"In the same sense as an exorcism, where they are trying to expel from society those whom they reject as without a soul. I didn't include that in my opinion, so I thank you for helping me to this analogy."

"Are you aware that the name Jesus Christ is mentioned sometimes quite frequently at cross-lighting ceremonies?"

"The name Jesus Christ is used in many contexts. I understand that Billy Martin used it quite often when the Yankee baseball players he managed made errors."

"And with that in mind, that Christ is prominent at the Klan cross-lighting ceremony, is it still your opinion that such a ceremony is irreligious?"

"I see the 'Heil, Hitler' sign given at the same gatherings, and I fail to see religious aspects of that."

"Isn't that the same salute we have seen in movies to 'Hail Caesar'?"

"Yes, but the Romans did not promote the philosophies of Hitler, as does the Klan."

"Do you know what a menorah is, sir?"

"Yes."

"Is it not lit, sir?"

"The candles are lit. The menorah is not burned."

It was apparent that the strategy of Pageant's questions was to establish religious expression as the primary defense. They had scored some points. We knew we had to *dis*prove the affirmative defense of religious expression, and we had to disprove it beyond a reasonable doubt.

Our exhibits were received into evidence. We rested our case.

Chapter 20

The Defense Case

The colorless concrete walls of the Phoenix federal penitentiary blended into the surrounding desert sands. Within the cells, narrow window slits provided only a passing ray of sunlight each day. After a year within its confines, the inmates also took on the lifeless, pale image of their environment.

Inside cell 2246 was a young man with his future on hold. A couple of times a year, his wife visited with his child. The boy was in diapers when Frank last held him. Now, each visit brought inches of growth. This was his father's measure of time, and the time was long.

Silva was brought to the office of Warden Jim Howe shortly after breakfast. Frank sat comfortably in a leather chair, enjoying the break from his work detail.

"What visits have you had recently, Silva?" asked the warden.

"Only what's in the log."

"Answer me. Who's been to see you in the last thirty days?"

"My wife and my son. That's it."

"Not Metzger? No one from the movement?"

"They must all be in trial."

"Any mail?"

"Not from them. I got some mail from a lawyer by the name of Lyons. Don't you read that, too?"

"I have a request here for you to go on a little trip."

"From who?"

"A lawyer of one of your old buddies. Do you know an attorney by the name of Pageant?"

"He came to see me. May have been not long ago."

"They want your testimony. Are you a flight risk?" The Warden challenged Silva for a strong denial. "I'm asking you straight out because I want to know there are going to be no problems."

"Is this to Los Angeles?"

"You'll get a chance maybe to see some family."

"I'd like that. It's not easy for them coming out here."

"No problems?"

"No, sir. No problems."

◆ ◆ ◆ ◆ ◆

We entered court the following morning, anticipating the defense case. The bailiff whispered to Davidson the news of whom they held in the adjacent cell, waiting to testify.

I didn't know if they would get him. Normally the federal penitentiaries are not so accommodating to the state court systems.

"Oh, I could tell you his testimony right now," said Dale confidently. "It never fails. He's doing a twenty-year sentence and has nothing to lose. He's going to take the rap for them. 'I got the burn permit. I told them all it was good. I didn't show it to anybody.' That's what he's going to testify."

Because a defendant must be acquitted if he honestly believes his conduct is legal, the prosecutor's challenge is to disprove the defendant's claimed state of mind. The only way to do this would be through circumstantial evidence that the defendants did not believe Silva's permit was valid.

"So we attack the belief in the validity of the permit as totally unreasonable," I said, "what with all the cops and the fire engines there. You want to take the cross-examination, or me?"

"I want it," Dale said. "Cross-examination is what I do best. Besides," Dale subtly smiled, "I told the warden to go ahead and send him. I'm going to make Pageant wish he never went to law school."

The jurors took their seats, walking almost cautiously from the hallway. I did not realize until later that a growing number of skinhead supporters were assembling in areas around the courthouse to make their presence known.

The judge announced the start of the defense case and gave the usual instruction that witnesses should be judged by the same standard, whether called by the prosecution or the defendants. He asked Pageant if he would like the bailiffs to bring out his first witness. Pageant nodded affirmatively and looked at us, expecting surprise. The judge turned in his chair, his back to the jury, and looked scornfully at Pageant. J. D. Smith did not like deceit in his courtroom.

Two deputy sheriffs passed through the courtroom to

the adjacent holding cell. I turned my eyes to their point of departure, and a hush came over the packed gallery. The rattle of keys turned a lock, then chains dragged along the concrete floor. Through the doorway stepped Frank Silva, his hands and feet manacled with heavy chain and iron clasps.

He did not look the same. The once vibrant, handsome face exuding cocksure arrogance had paled and hollowed. His blonde hair had darkened to light brown. Two skinheads in the back of the courtroom stood at attention and raised their right hands in the style of a Nazi salute. Frank's eyes glimmered as he restrained a smile, trying to conceal a missing front tooth.

Silva stood beside the witness stand as he was sworn in by the clerk. Then, as is customary, she asked that he state and spell his name. A whistle in his speech was readily apparent. He was self-conscious about this, occasionally placing his right hand at his chin and partially covering his mouth as he spoke.

As Brian Pageant began his examination, my mind wandered to the years behind bars Silva served for his allegiance to this "movement." Was it worth it to him? For all his personal sacrifice, no goals had been obtained, nor ever would. The only difference was the personal suffering that he, his wife, and his child now endured. I looked over to Metzger. He peered forebodingly at Silva, seemingly unsure of him.

I remembered how Mike Canale became disillusioned with his former pals after serving time in the pen for the arson of the temple. Perhaps Metzger feared that Silva would turn on him, as Canale had.

Brian Pageant began Silva's examination with a focus

on Peter Lake. Silva was noticeably bitter that Lake had misled him. Having taken Lake into his confidence made Silva look bad to the hierarchy of the movement. He seized the opportunity to make it look as though Lake was shaping events to dramatize his story. He testified that Lake took the others to a shooting range that Lake had constructed and that it was Lake who directed them in a paramilitary drill.

"What do you recall Mr. Lake doing at the Aryan Nations grounds?" asked Pageant.

"He was pretty much busy doing his own thing with that camera. He said, 'Why don't you guys take some weapons and go shoot at these little shacks over here? I think it would make a really good kind of recruitment tool, to give the impression that this is the kind of activity they could expect.' He asked everybody in general if they wanted to get into the picture. And everybody was just milling around and moving left and right, and we all got taped, I'm sure."

"Was this at the practice shooting range off the grounds?"

"Well, there was no practice shooting range. This was something that Lake pretty much invented in his own mind. He saw the shacks. He said, 'Let's go shoot some guns at them. He put up a target of Menachem Begin's face.'"

Pageant also wanted testimony to bolster the First Amendment defenses of freedom of assembly and speech. To do this, he needed Silva to characterize the L.A.P.D. officers as hard-line and oppressive. As I listened I thought it ironic that Silva would complain of gestapo police tactics.

"I am placing before you a document that reads at the

top 'Agreement to Rent Property.' Do you recognize this?" asked Pageant.

"Yeah. I signed it right down here. This is what I felt was a legal, binding contract to lease the property in Kagel Canyon from Ron Major. It was my right as a citizen, if I had private property, to do what I needed to do on it. And that is why I went the extra mile with Ron Major, to try to make sure that everything I did was legal."

"Did you have a meeting with a Captain Warmoth at the Foothill Station of the Los Angeles Police Department prior to the cross-lighting?"

"Yes. He called me down to the precinct, and I was under the understanding that I would be seeing him on an individual basis, but it turned out he had about thirty officers there with him."

"What happened next?"

"Well, he starts to harass me. He just kept saying, 'Look, if you go on this property, I am going to arrest you for illegal assembly.' His whole demeanor was such that he was trying to intimidate me. Lieutenant Robinson was there, too. He knew both Warmoth and myself. He came by my house later with the same type of attitude, you know, trying to . . . 'If you do this; if you do that; if you do this,' like he was taking my rights away from me, you know, the same way that Captain Warmoth treated me."

Pageant's next objective would be to have Silva take all responsibility for the cross-burning and make it seem the others were completely in the dark regarding material aspects of their alleged culpability. The testimony was carefully orchestrated, but probably this was only apparent to Davidson and me. We could anticipate the arguments of the defense at the conclusion of the trial and the ways this testimony would be used to fit relatively complex jury instructions regarding criminal intent and requisite knowledge.

"Did you tell anyone inside your house what was planned that evening at Ron Major's property?" asked Pageant.

"Yes. I told them we were having a memorial service for Mike Serna, that it would be in fact a Klan ritual cross-lighting and that it was private."

"Did you tell anyone you had a permit to do this?"

"Yes."

"Who did you tell that to?"

"Just if somebody asked me, 'Frank, is everything okay?' I would say, 'Yes. I got the permit. Everything is fine.' Nobody requested to see it, you know. I never showed nobody that."

"Who was the organizer of the December 3rd cross-lighting?"

"I was."

"Did anyone else help you organize that event?"

"No."

"Did you construct any crosses for this ceremony?"

"Yes, two of them."

"Did you wrap any of the crosses in burlap?"

"At least two. Maybe all three."

Pageant followed with a line of questions that were perhaps inappropriate to his representative role as Riley's attorney, but he was determined to attempt to exonerate the big fish. Riley was meaningless to the media. The case against Metzger, along with his defense, was the drawing card for the press. It also proved to be Silva's primary interest. As the questions and answers switched focus to the "Mentor of Malice," Metzger's attorney Daryl Kearney glanced with surprise and consternation at Pageant.

"Did you invite Tom Metzger to attend the ceremony?" asked Pageant.

"I went to Tom, and I told him about it. I didn't invite him really. He wasn't one of the guests. I said, 'Look, I am having this ceremony. If you're in the neighborhood, I would appreciate it if you'd come by.'"

"What was your purpose in wanting Tom Metzger to attend?"

"Well, it was several. Tom was the editor of his newspaper. I wanted it to be carried in one of our press. That was the first.

"Second, Tom was experienced. I knew he would fit in with that kind of thing, and if we needed any help, he would probably give it."

Eliciting this second reason was a tactical mistake from the perspective of Metzger's defense. Establishing that he was experienced would play into the hands of the prosecution's case. We believed it was Metzger who contrived the use of the property rental and the barbecue permit as the ruse for the Klan's assembly. Our theory had become more tangible. I casually looked to see if Kearney picked up on this. He was a good attorney, but perhaps not so good a poker player. He turned irately away from the jury.

Pageant then stumbled into the most common pitfall facing the average trial attorney—trying to establish all aspects of your case with every witness. His next area of inquiry was the religious essence of the "cross-lighting" ceremony. There were better witnesses for this point. Silva knew the right responses, but why have an inmate testify about the religious significance of *anything*?

"What was the religious significance of the cross-lighting ceremony?" Pageant asked.

"The cross-lighting ceremony was initiated five or six hundred years ago. What it means is twofold. One is that it was used in the old days to call clansmen to their kin if there was an invasion from the outside. They would light the crosses to bring people in to secure the tribe.

"The religious implication of this in a Christian sense is that the cross is illuminated to those people attending who recognize Jesus Christ as the light of the world."

"That's all, Mr. Silva. Thank you."

Throughout Silva's direct examination, Davidson impatiently waited. At times he quickly scribbled notes. Occasionally he glanced up from his notepad following a question, so he could see *how* Silva responded. When there was hesitancy, I anticipated Davidson would have follow-up questions.

Most of the cross-examination had already been reduced to notes, at least in general outline form, but it was far from Davidson's style to blandly read his questions. He reacted with every answer and would pursue new areas where he sensed Silva was vulnerable.

"Mr. Silva, you are a practicing Christian, are you?" Davidson began.

"Yes, sir; I am."

"You take your religious beliefs seriously?"

"I do."

"Because of that, you would never consider telling this court or anybody here anything other than the truth; is that correct?"

"That is correct."

"You know Mr. Riley, don't you?"

"I really don't. When I came in, I didn't even recognize him. I guess he is one of the defendants."

"Mr. Silva, if the videotape of the cross-burning shows Mr. Riley helping you erect those crosses out there that night, would that reflect your recollection about knowing Mr. Riley?"

"No, sir; it wouldn't. Randy Evans and I were the only guys that I remember working on the crosses at all."

"Mr. Evans is no longer charged in these proceedings; he is incarcerated on antiracketeering violations like you, and has been dismissed as a defendant from these proceedings. Isn't that so?"

"Yes, sir."

"Mr. Silva, you are no longer charged in these proceedings either; are you?"

"No, but I should be."

"You were at one time, were you not? And then you got into the difficulties that caused your incarceration; isn't that correct?"

"That's correct."

"You were convicted of four felonies in the RICO antiracketeering prosecution, were you not, sir?"

"You will have to be more precise than that, because for the RICO conspiracy you need two predicate acts."

"Besides the predicate acts, you were charged and convicted of interstate transportation of stolen money and also harboring a fugitive—a man named Robert Matthews; is that correct?"

"That's correct."

"Who was Robert Matthews?"

"Just a man."

"Just a man who was alleged as a co-conspirator in the same RICO indictment on which you were charged, who exchanged gunfire with the FBI for thirty-five hours off the coast of Washington on Whidbey Island. Is that correct?"

"It is correct, but you got your numbers wrong. It was thirty-six hours. A female FBI agent tried to shoot him in the back without even calling out her ID letters. Then Bob Mathews returned fire."

"He had no idea they were police officers. Is that what you're saying?"

"He did not."

"Mr. Silva, how many oaths of loyalty have you taken in your life to various white separatist movements?"

"I swore loyalty two or three times."

"Who have you talked to about your testimony? For instance, have you talked to Mr. Metzger about it?"

"On occasion it has come up in conversation, yes. But the prisons have not allowed me to see him except one time."

"Who is the named beneficiary of your will if something happens to you?"

"Objection; relevancy," interjected Pageant.

The judge queried, "Goes to what, Mr. Davidson?"

"Goes to bias in connection with one of the defendants."

"Overruled."

"Who is your beneficiary?" repeated Davidson.

"It would be my wife."

"Two years ago did you fill out a document while you were in prison making Tom Metzger your beneficiary?"

"No, absolutely not."

At this, Silva folded his arms and sat back uncomfortably in his seat. The tone of his responses had become increasingly irate with Davidson's questioning. Although

Silva had managed to maintain the semblance of a repentant convict on direct examination by Pageant, the image tarnished as he debated Davidson's setup points. Davidson, meanwhile, pulled a document from our file and glanced over confidently.

"Your Honor, I have a document I would like to be marked 'People's 32.' I would like to show it to the witness. Mr. Silva, is that your signature on the bottom line of this document?"

"Yes, it is."

"And this is the prison form for the disposition of your property upon death; correct, sir?"

"If that's what it says."

"And you listed Tom Metzger as your beneficiary?"

"That's what it says."

Davidson turned away from the witness stand and looked at the jury to see if he had damaged Silva's credibility sufficiently to now address the material aspects of his testimony. I knew this within the moment of his glance, and I nodded my head affirmatively. He subtly nodded back and then resumed the cross-examination.

"You were at a cross-burning about three weeks before the cross-burning in Los Angeles; correct, sir?"

"It's possible."

"One up in Rosamond, California, at Randy Evans's house?"

"Yes, I believe I was. But let me correct you. It is not a 'cross-burning.' It is a 'cross-lighting.'"

"Would you prefer that I call it a cross-lighting?"

"Yes, I would."

"We're talking about where you wrap a cross with burlap and you soak it with a flammable liquid and it gets lit on fire; is that correct?"

"Yes."

"So will you understand what I'm referring to if I call it a cross-burning?"

"I suppose so."

"Who was at the cross-burning at Randy Evans's house, two weeks before the Los Angeles cross-burning?"

"I believe Mr. Witek, Mike Canale, myself, and Randy. There were probably four or five other people, but they don't stand out."

"How about Jerome Hofstadler? You see him sitting at counsel table here. Was Jerome Hofstadler there that night?"

"It's possible."

"Do you remember some of your guys firing their rifles that night?"

"There was some shooting after the cross-lighting, yes."

"Why were there guns there that night? How does that reconcile with the expression of religious beliefs?"

"I don't see any conflict in it whatsoever. Have you ever shot a gun off after church?"

"On direct examination you testified that you had this lighting, as you call it, here in Los Angeles to honor a slain police officer, is that correct?"

"That was my testimony, yes."

"Because your people were all pro-law enforcement, pro-police; is that correct?"

"That is correct."

"David Tate was real pro-police, wasn't he—

"That is correct."

"—when he gunned down two police officers?"

Not surprisingly, Pageant and the three other defense attorneys rose in unison to object loudly to Davidson's question. After several minutes of legal maneuvering by the prosecution and the defense—which at one point called for a mistrial—the judge ruled that the scope of Silva's current testimony was open to the prosecution, though the question that had prompted the furor was deemed argumentative. After allowing all parties a few moments to regain their composure, the judge asked Davidson to resume his cross-examination.

"Mr. Silva, is it your basic testimony that there was nothing wrong with your lighting fires in that hillside area, whatever the fire department had to say about it?"

"We had no intent to harm anybody, to hurt or damage any property, just to do the ceremony."

"You testified earlier that mostly white people lived in the houses up above Mr. Major's house; is that right?"

"That's correct."

"And the neighborhood down below was mostly black and Latin folks; is that right?"

"If I remember correctly, I said about 80 percent mixed, yeah."

"And you didn't pick that hillside overlooking all those houses to burn your crosses because you thought it might have an effect on those folks? They couldn't have seen the flames of the crosses from their homes down there; is that right?"

"Well, when you say 'flames,' they were not leaping above the trees, if that is what you mean. But it was dark, and it would illuminate the sky, of course."

"And it ought to be up to the Ku Klux Klan to decide where and when they can burn a cross, not the fire department; is that right?"

"Objection; argumentative!" pleaded Pageant.

"Sustained," the judge replied.

"I have nothing further for this witness," Davidson concluded as he strode back to the prosecution table.

Silva's testimony had not surprised Davidson. He was right that more facts would hurt, rather than help, the defendants' chances. Although he tried to shoulder all the blame, Silva had made more than one slipup in presenting Metzger's defense.

I realized our potential to exploit his testimony that he wanted Metzger there because he was "experienced" and if they needed assistance "he could probably give it." In later portions of the tape Metzger's right-hand man, Burbage, is seen advising the others. The barbecue permit, the alibi, the whole bit seemed in keeping with Metzger's former modus operandi as the Klan's director.

Judge Smith asked the defense to call their next witness. We were told he was in transit from the state of Idaho. We recessed for the day.

When the commotion died down, Dale and I made our way through the hallway to the elevators. Pageant was giving his usual end-of-the-day interviews. As one interview concluded he lingered, hoping another reporter would approach him.

Dale and I continued to have no comment to the press, other than to say we would be trying the case in the courtroom, rather than in the media. Although this did not assist the reporters in writing their articles, I sensed they respected it.

Some of the regular reporters would occasionally ask a question off the record, an assurance they always honored. Generally, such a question was asked to gain an understanding of the relationship of a witness or a piece of evidence to the overall case, rather than to obtain a quote.

"Who do you think they're bringing from Idaho?" asked a *Los Angeles Times* reporter. "Don't worry, I won't hold you to it." She smiled. I told her I thought it might be Richard Butler. Dale glanced over with an air of surprise. We walked on farther, away from the crowd.

"Butler is still a defendant in the case we prosecute next," he said. "The defense strategy would be fairly poor to have him testify here first."

"If they want to get this trial knee-deep in First Amendment protections, this is the witness to do it. He always quotes the Bible. And this is the trial they have to win. If they lose, I don't think Butler will ever return to California for his trial. The charges against him are misdemeanors, and they know we can't extradite him from Idaho on that."

"They could use him," remarked Dale. "He makes some religious oratory before the crosses are burned. He *is* their best shot at establishing a First Amendment protection. What's our angle on cross-examination?"

"There're a couple of buttons to press. I remember the outtakes of a news interview some time back. He comes off well until those buttons get pushed. Something about Jesus and Hitler, the apostles wearing the swastika, genocide, and what he calls a "territorial imperative." We have to let them get into the religious philosophy on his direct examination."

That night I searched through hours of news interview outtakes taped by a CBS crew at the time of Lake's visit to Aryan Nations. I also did a bit of soul searching. It started when I pulled my car into the driveway of my house. Again I noticed that my kids were inside, not playing or running or riding bikes along the sidewalk like the other kids I saw in the neighborhood. The backside of our living room couch was positioned against the front window. We were using it as a shield. The curtains were drawn. The experience of the bomb scare was noticeably wearing on Diane, affecting her mood and her routine with the children.

◆ ◆ ◆ ◆ ◆

The next morning, my co-counsel and I waited outside the courtroom in a distant corner of the hallway. Few people would ever approach us there, and it gave us a chance to shoot the breeze. A small clamor began to develop toward the opposite end of the hall, drawing news crews and the curious. The lights went up and on, held by backpedaling technicians. In the midst of it was a tall, elderly man, with deep wrinkles on his long, narrow face. It was Richard Butler. Flanked by young, hometown followers, he maintained a steady stride and stoic focus.

Butler's lawyer—against whose advice Butler had decided to testify—sat stone-faced in the audience section and listened as Pageant began Butler's examination. Butler told about meeting Peter Lake and said that he had trusted him and allowed him to videotape activities at the Aryan Nations compound—"church grounds" as he called it. Later on he accepted money from Lake to finance his trip to California so that he could attend a memorial in honor of a slain police officer. Silva, Butler testified, said it would be a private ceremony on private property. He would do a eulogy. He claimed Silva told him nothing at that time about a "cross-lighting." He traveled from Idaho with David Tate and Thomas Bentley. I knew each of these men to have been convicted of separate murders, Bentley as an accessory. Butler first went to Randy Evans's house in Rosamond, California, about three hours north of Los Angeles. They arrived the night before the ceremony. Pageant then asked Butler questions regarding the ceremony.

"Did you and Frank Silva discuss on the day of December 3rd what he planned for that evening?"

"Well, he mentioned he had a permit for a fire. He suggested that since he was starting a chapter of the Klan, it would be nice to have a cross-lighting for the light of Jesus Christ in recognition of Mr. Serna's sacrifice."

"Did Mr. Silva ever show you that fire permit?"

"No. I just assumed he had it. I didn't question him on it and I believed him to be truthful."

"After arriving at the property where the ceremony was to take place, what was the first thing you did?"

"David Tate and Tom Bentley came in, and we were in the house together. I put on the robe that Mr. Silva had made for me. Then we went out back where the assembly was. There were about another twelve people in the backyard."

"Did you give a ceremony or a eulogy?"

"Yes, I did. I gave the ceremony—or eulogy."

"Pastor Butler, what is the purpose of a cross-lighting in a private ceremony such as this, in your opinion?"

"In a world of darkness, the lighting of the crosses is an old, old ceremony. Jesus Christ is the light of the world. And when everything is dark and then the crosses light up, it symbolizes his word of truth."

"Do you know the origin of the ceremony?"

"It has partly come from ancient Scotland and partly from the Catholic Church in Spain. The priests in Spain used it about the same way we have used it, as the light of the world. And in Scotland during the times of the Viking invasions, they were on the high hills; they would have a cross and some firewood there; and when a watchman would see the Vikings coming to invade their territory, he would light the cross, and then the fellow on the next hill would see it, and he would light it; and this alerted the clans to come together for defense."

"Is the purpose in a cross-lighting to burn the cross?"

"No. It is to light it as a symbolic gesture."

"Have you ever seen anyone arrested at other cross-lighting ceremonies you have attended?"

I quickly rose to object to this question on the grounds of relevancy. I knew no other convictions had ever been obtained in this context, and I did not want the jurors to infer from this that cross-burnings were presumed legal by other law enforcement agencies. Such an implied opinion could seriously damage our chances of getting convictions. I knew no one in Metzger's group had ever been so much as arrested, let alone prosecuted. I needed our case judged on its own merits. Fortunately, Judge Smith sustained my objection, and Pageant was compelled to redirect his line of questioning.

"Have most of the cross-lighting ceremonies you've attended been on private property in secluded areas?" asked Pageant.

"Yes, sir. All of them. It is a private ritual. It is only for those who are amenable to the ritual, sort of like communion in the Catholic Church. It is a ceremony for those who are the communicants, so to speak."

"I have no further questions at this point," concluded Pageant.

I had great disdain for this comparison of the Ku Klux Klan to the Roman Catholic Church. In twelve years of religious education in Catholic schools, I had never once heard of Spanish priests lighting crosses on fire. If a priest somewhere, sometime in history had done this, I can guarantee his intent shared no part of the Klan ritual.

An effective prosecution, however, cannot be made personal. Instead, I would let the jurors decide for themselves if the witness had fairly analogized the Klan to the Catholic Church.

The other key in my cross-examination was to convey that Butler's church was actually his army, and that his congregation were its soldiers. I started by asking Butler to describe his church grounds, which he did in a rather sterile fashion, quite predictably. But I had benefited from an inside view of which Butler was not aware. Lake had videotaped the church itself during a service performed by Butler. Lake had also taped within the social hall, the church office, and the printing press room. I had seen the displays of literature, the artwork, and the artifacts. I had heard Butler's speeches and outtakes of his interviews. It was important that I dissipate the aura of religious innocence that he hoped would provide the impenetrable First Amendment protection.

"The swastika has a very prominent presence in the artwork of the assembly hall and in your church, doesn't it?" I asked Butler.

"I imagine so."

"Now, the name of your church is Jesus Christ Christian; is that correct?"

"That's right."

"How do you explain putting a swastika on an altar to Jesus Christ?"

"The swastika is two thousand years older than the Third Reich. As a matter of fact, if you go back, you will find that the apostles of Jesus Christ used the swastika on their robes. Their robes were decorated with them, and they wore the swastika as a symbol of Christ."

At this the judge turned in his chair and glared disapprovingly toward his clerk, who simply raised an eyebrow, then resumed her work. Pageant continued writing notes, head facedown, as if nothing unusual had been said. I paused until the jurors had an opportunity to take note of the rather bizarre remark. "You're saying the apostles of Jesus Christ wore swastikas?" I asked.

"Yes. It was called the gammadion," answered Butler.

"So then, what *is* the relationship between Hitlerism and Jesus Christ?" I asked.

Butler scowled with indignation. "I would consider Hitler a devout Christian. He probably built and restored more churches than any other leader."

I pressed on, wanting to demonstrate that Butler's religious philosophy incorporated violence that would have been acceptable the night of the cross-burning.

"Were the warfare and genocide Hitler conducted compatible with the teachings of Jesus Christ?"

"I don't know all his acts, but preservation of the church is compatible with any Christian's view."

"How about the genocide conducted by the Third Reich; is that compatible with your sense of morality?"

"Well, the alleged genocide I don't think ever really happened."

"Let's assume that a genocide did occur during the

Second World War. Would that be compatible with the teachings of Jesus Christ from your perspective?"

"If you talk about Luke 19:27, and if you assume the genocide happened, perhaps yes, if you are talking about the Scriptures."

"And how about if we're talking about violence, Mr. Butler? Not violence in the Scriptures, but violence here and now. Is violence acceptable to achieve your sense of morality?"

"Well, again we come back to the law of physics. The only way a race can preserve itself is by separation. It is called 'territorial imperative' in the laws of biology. And no race, no species on the face of the earth, can exist without a territorial imperative."

"And you want to achieve a territorial imperative in the form of a separate state; correct?"

"Yes."

As this line of questioning progressed, I had slowly moved closer to the witness stand. I sensed now that Butler's recital of the "territorial imperative" established that the cross-burning was at least partially intended to drive away unwanted races and ethnicities by the threat of Klan violence. I turned and stepped back toward the podium.

Spencer sat beside his client, Stan Witek, and was riveted to the exchange, plainly not liking the aspersions it cast upon his client. He had not joined with the other defense attorneys in calling Butler as a witness. Although his eyes followed me, I interpreted the angry expression on Spencer's face to be directed at the other three lawyers whose strategies were adversely affecting his client.

I turned again toward the witness stand. "You have a

printing operation at the Aryan Nations' compound. Is that correct?" I asked Butler.

"Yes."

"You print a booklet called *Prepare War,* and one called *The Aryan Warrior,* and another one, *Understanding the Struggle; Or Why We Have to Kill the Bastards.* Do you print these?"

"We do."

"Now, you don't advocate hate against anybody, as I understand from your direct examination earlier this morning?"

"No, I don't. I think we are the cause of our own problems."

"You don't preach hate, and yet you distribute this book here—let's see—*The Negro: Serpent, Beast, and Devil?*"

"Yes, we've sold it."

"Mr. Butler, isn't it true that your use of these materials was intended to cause people like David Tate, Thomas Bentley, Randy Dewey, Stewart Yarborough, Randy Evans, and Frank Silva to hate, to cause them to act out that hatred?"

"No. I think that freedom of speech is one of the hallmarks—and freedom of press—that was brought forth in 1776; and I believe that people have a right to write everything they want, if they are responsible for what they write. And I think it is a right we have lost today."

"Mr. Butler, you distribute books that promote warfare, such as *Understanding the Struggle* and *The Aryan Warrior.* Weren't the actions of these men compatible with those teachings?"

"May we approach the bench, Your Honor?" interrupted Spencer.

I remained at the side of the podium, then I looked

over to Davidson and shook my head reproachingly as the defense attorneys passed. When they were all in place, I stood at the right end of the side bar, watching the jurors as the in-court hearing outside of their presence began. They had no interaction, mostly looking forward, perhaps trying to hear what was being said. I didn't mind if they did. Judge Smith's voice was immediately agitated. He let the defense attorneys know that they couldn't keep trying to silence their own witnesses in the progression of their testimony.

"I said from the beginning that if you defense counsel call these witnesses, don't later object on relevancy grounds. Once they take the stand and testify to their beliefs on direct, then the People have a right to question them on their philosophy. Once you open the door, that's it."

"I suspect that these individuals the prosecutor is talking about committed some crimes," Spencer began, "and I think that counsel is leading up to crimes committed by some people not even on trial here. If that is the situation, I think it should be excluded."

Pageant asserted, "I know exactly where it is going. David Tate is doing a double life term in Missouri, which at the time didn't have a death penalty, for killing a Missouri state trooper and wounding another. The others were convicted in the prosecution of the members of The Order. I only asked this witness about Tate and Bentley and what they did with him on December 3rd. I didn't ask about any of their other conduct."

"Mr. Pageant presented Mr. Butler as a middle-of-the-road pastor of a respectable church," I replied, "but he left out the fact that the disciples of Mr. Butler have gone around the country shooting people, robbing armored cars, and sticking up banks. I think the jurors ought to know where the philosophical justification for these violent acts has come from."

After a moment's reflection, the judge said, "The defense team presented an image of this witness that was intended to bolster his credibility. He talked about Catholics, and different religions and philosophy, and now he is subject to cross-examination. The People can show his true beliefs by his affiliations and his training of others. You called the person as a witness, Pageant, for three of the defendants. Now go back to your seat. You may continue, Mr. Phillips."

I once again approached the witness stand. "For the record, I have in my hands the book *Calling Our Nation*. The words 'Aryan Nations' are printed at the top. Mr. Butler, I would ask you first to take a look at the inside page of the booklet. You see under 'Editor' it says, 'Pastor Richard G. Butler.' That's you, right?"

"Yes."

"And under the words 'Layout and Printing' the names David Tate and Stewart Scarborough are listed; correct?"

"Yes."

"And now, looking at page thirty-five of this book, you see a photograph of two columns of men, ten in each column, and they are carrying rifles and other weapons; is that correct, Mr. Butler?"

"It appears so, yes."

"On the next page, page thirty-six, you see a couple of buildings, several men apparently with rifles moving about, crouched down, and the caption immediately beneath that, Mr. Butler, is—would you read that, please?"

"'Street fighting comes soon at a place near you.'"

"On the following page, page thirty-seven, there is what appears to be a photograph of you; is that correct, sir?"

"Yes."

"And in front of you there are eight men in uniform, and each of them has a rifle in his arms; is that correct, Mr. Butler?"

"That's right."

"And does the caption beneath that read 'Inspection of Arms. Cleanliness is next to godliness?'"

"Correct."

"On the page right next to that you see a group of men in uniform climbing rocks; perhaps carrying weapons, Mr. Butler?"

"Perhaps, yes."

"And would you read the caption immediately below that photograph, sir?"

"'On rappel, death from above.'"

"Now, at the paramilitary training encampment that is close to the Aryan Nations compound where the little facades of buildings are set up, men run from one station to the next firing at targets. Mr. Butler, you know David Tate to have taken part in those exercises; correct?"

"I believe he did."

"You know Stewart Scarborough to have taken part in those exercises as well?"

"I heard he has, yes."

"And Randy Dewey?"

"Randy Dewey, yes."

"Thomas Bentley?"

"Yes."

"Randall Evans?"

"I imagine Randy Evans was there, yes."

"Frank Silva?"

"Yes."

"These men carried through with your teachings, didn't they?"

"How do you mean?"

"I mean they prepared war—a war for social purity—and they carried it out. Didn't they?"

"Not necessarily. If you look at the pamphlet *Prepare War,* you will notice that most all this is out of the Bible."

"Mr. Butler, I am not asking about the Bible. Did not these men prepare war and carry it out?"

"*Prepare War* is out of Bible verses. If you will look and read it and also the other pamphlet, *The Aryan Warrior,* that is from John Locke. Jefferson took part of John Locke's writings to write the Declaration of Independence."

"Mr. Butler, I'm not asking about the Bible, John Locke, or the Declaration of Independence. I'm talking about David Tate, Frank Silva, and Randy Evans. These men prepared war, and they carried it out in a very serious fashion, didn't they, sir?"

"I don't know what was in their minds, but I guess they did prepare war; yes."

I was distracted momentarily by the sound of paper being torn from a notepad and crumpled into a ball. It was Metzger. He pushed his chair away from the counsel table, in the direction of his attorney and away from the other defendants and their attorneys. He spoke briefly to Kearney, his lawyer, then faced the witness with his arms folded. He left a noticeable space between himself and the other defendants. Defendant Kelly looked shyly over at Metzger, like a child fearing the abandonment of his father's affection.

"Sir, returning now to the central question at hand, is

the burning cross a symbol of racial separatism?" I continued.

"Well, I would say that it is a call to a racial family, yes."

"Now, from the perspective of someone who is black and has worked hard to raise a family, worked hard at his job to buy a house, and in his neighborhood sees the burning cross, it would appear to him to be an unwelcome gesture, would it not?"

"I have never viewed it from the perspective of a nonwhite, so I don't know."

"You believe in a purification of society, do you not, Mr. Butler?"

"Yes, sir; I do. I believe that it is good for everybody, for the Japanese, the Chinese, and the Africans. I think we all have that right."

"And you believe in an ultimate race war, do you not?"

"I think we are going to have an ultimate separation. I think we are having it right now, aren't we?"

"That was a beautiful eulogy you gave Officer Mike Serna the night of the cross-burning. Do you recall the eulogy you gave that night?"

"Not particularly. But I—"

"Not particularly, Mr. Butler, because you never gave one, did you?"

"I gave one. Yes. Yes, I did."

"You did? At what point in time?"

"I think it was after Randy Evans spoke that I gave the eulogy."

"Right after Randy Evans spoke, as you were all standing around the crosses; correct?"

"We were standing in front. I was facing them, and the other people might have been standing around. I can't recall."

"Mr. Butler, would it surprise you that there is not a single mention of Mike Serna on the videotape—not his name, his family, or his service to the police force, throughout the entire course of the time period that you have just referenced?"

"It would surprise me if anybody could hear anything said while the helicopter was making so much noise. I could hardly hear myself."

"You believe in a racially pure society?"

"Yes."

"You believe a race war will ultimately decide that?"

"It is inevitable."

"You believe violence is justified to achieve racial purification?"

"It is the nature of the territorial imperative."

"And the lighting of the cross—this is the call to *your* people—the call to prepare war."

"It is the call for racial purification."

I concluded Butler's testimony on this connection of the "cross-lighting" to the call for racial purification, the "territorial imperative," and the violence of the ultimate race war for which he prepared his soldiers. As he stepped from the witness stand, Pageant jovially called over, "Thank you, Pastor." Butler smiled back and shook Pageant's hand as he passed. Judge Smith grinned discreetly toward his clerk, shook his head disdainfully, and slammed his gavel to adjourn the afternoon session.

As we drew closer to the end of the defense case, Dale speculated which of the defendants, if any, would take the stand. We agreed Attorney Pageant would not call his own client, Brad Riley, as a witness. His criminal record indicated various drug busts, and his use seemed to have taken its toll. Our guess was that intellectually he was considerably below average. Also, the videotape showed Riley helping Silva dowse the crosses with the gas/kerosene mixture and then stand the crosses into previously dug holes. There was nothing for the defense to gain from his testimony.

Although physically presentable and mild mannered, Jerome Hofstadler was in a similar predicament as Riley, having actively participated on tape. Also, although I did not learn this until some time after the conclusion of the trial, Hofstadler was no longer among the ranks of the white supremacists.

Witek was too outspoken and volatile to put on the witness stand. He was the proverbial "loose cannon." We would have loved to have had one outburst from him, as we knew he was capable, but the defense knew it too. Metzger surely would prevail upon them all not to testify.

"That leaves only one to speak for all the defendants," I concluded.

Dale shook his head affirmatively. "We know he testifies."

◆ ◆ ◆ ◆ ◆

As Tom Metzger, the former Klan Grand Dragon for the state of California, began to testify, I recalled his publicized predictions that his audiotape would embarrass the prosecution and result in the dismissal of all charges. I was curious—not apprehensive—as our first opportunity to hear it would soon come.

Dale and I believed Metzger would try to shield the

others from blame. He was the most intelligent of the four defendants, and he was an accomplished, articulate public speaker. We thought Metzger would present the defense for all on trial.

We were wrong. He would instead distance himself and claim he discouraged the others from igniting the crosses. It was his personal best play.

Metzger sat at the witness stand completely calm and without display of emotion. His hands were folded, and his suit jacket remained buttoned. He was courteous but in no way condescending to the judge and attorneys. As the defense posed the questions most likely on the minds of the jury, he unapologetically stated his responses to Klan membership, appreciation for racist literature, and other testimony that would have shamed witnesses with average sensitivity.

"Have you ever been a member of the Ku Klux Klan?" Kearney asked.

"Yes. I joined the Knights of the Ku Klux Klan under David Duke and remained a member for two years. He was the national director of the Klan, and I later became the Grand Dragon for the state of California. I prefer to call it the state director.

"I ran for the United States Congress in 1980 and won the Democratic nomination in the 43rd Congressional District. At that time I left the Klan.

"After my unsuccessful bid for the congressional seat, I formed my own organization—White American Resistance, WAR."

"During the time that you were involved with the Ku Klux Klan, did you attend any cross-lightings?"

"Yes. Six or seven while I was with the Klan."

Kearney examined Metzger on each of the prior "cross-lighting ceremonies." The defendant emphasized that each ceremony was the sole responsibility of the local Klan organizer; fire permits were typically obtained by the local den leader; the police were always cooperative, and the ceremonies were conducted in as much privacy as possible. The only violence he recalled occurred at the city of Oceanside, when he claimed his group was attacked by anti-Klan demonstrators. Kearney moved on to other topics.

"How is it decided who stands where at a cross-lighting?"

"Well, if you are a Klan member, you are normally required to have a robe. In the bigger cross-lightings, like Sacramento and Fontana, if you didn't have a robe, you had to stay out of the circle."

"Did you have a robe with you at the Los Angeles ceremony?"

"No. I wasn't in the Klan."

"When did you first meet Frank Silva?"

"It was about six months before the arrests, at a friend's ranch near Fallbrook."

"Did he later discuss a get-together for unity discussions between the various white separatist groups?"

"Yes. He invited me, and I said I was not interested. I didn't want to do the Klan thing anymore. I had no real animosity toward the people, but I just felt we had some better ideas.

"And so then he called and asked me again, and he kept at it. CBS TV came to my place, and they were asking me about this get-together, and I was wondering how in the heck they knew about it. And I said I wasn't going."

"But you did in fact go to this December 3rd cross-lighting, correct?"

"Yeah. He just kept asking me and asking; and I went against my own better judgement because I had decided that I didn't want to have any official activity in Los Angeles. Finally I said, 'Well, I will come under one condition.'

"He said, 'What's that?' He was anxious to reach an agreement with me because he wanted me to write about the meeting in the newspaper we publish.

"I said, 'If I can give a speech detailing that I believe there is a more modern way of going about things,' and cross-lightings that tend to attract a lot of attention, I felt they are passé.

"And he said, 'Just anything you want to say, just as long as you come.'

"Later on, when I met him the night of the ceremony, he told me we were going to have a cross-lighting."

"Now, on that particular day did you have on a microphone and a recorder?"

"Yes, I did. It's something I almost never do, but I got a tip that Mr. Canale had become a bad-news guy, and that Peter Lake was not what he represented himself to be."

"Why did you have concerns about Peter Lake?"

"Silva related to me how he and Lake first met. He said his Klan group was having a demonstration and Peter Lake drove up in a brand-new Mercedes Benz and said he wanted to join the Klan. And I laughed and said, 'Look, he's either an undercover police officer or he's a reporter. And since most police I know can't afford a Mercedes Benz, he must be a reporter.' But Frank didn't believe me."

"What did Frank say was going to take place?"

"He said, 'We're going to have a memorial and a cross-lighting.' And I said, 'Well, that is *your* deal, but have you got your private property?' 'Yeah,' he said. So I asked him, 'Have you got the fire permit?' And he said he did, so I said, 'Well, you had better have, because if you don't, they are going to try to get you.' "

"Was there ever an understanding that the purpose of this ceremony was to unite yourself, Pastor Butler, and Frank Silva?"

"No; none whatsoever. I was only invited for one thing, to give a speech—and write an article for our next month's paper about it."

"Where did you go when you first arrived?"

"We pulled up in our car and just stood outside for a while, because we weren't in charge and no one was telling us what to do. We just stood there for about forty-five minutes. At a certain point I began to say, 'What is happening here?' We were cold. So Burbage, Alcorn, and I moved around to the front of the house where the Klan people were setting themselves up. And I went to the back steps, walked into the house, and said, 'What's happening here? What's going on?' I mean it's cold; it's a mess. And they were all in disarray, trying to figure out what they were doing."

"When you went into the house, was Peter Lake there?"

"Yes. He was taping and I . . . I don't recall talking to him, but they were discussing this cross-lighting ceremony and discussing the fact there were police around.

"I made, I think, one statement. I said, 'Look, if it is going to be a big problem, why light the cross?' So at that point I just sort of turned around and walked out to the backyard and stood there with Irvin Alcorn."

"How long did you stay there before you were arrested?"

"I guess it was about another forty-five minutes before the crosses were lit."

"You were still wearing your recorder at this time; correct?"

"Yes, I was."

"At some point did you turn your tape recorder on?"

"Yes. It ran for about twenty minutes during the entire operation. I turned it on shortly after we parked the car and turned it off after fifteen minutes or so because I thought I might run out of tape. I turned it on again after I walked from the house down to the wall where I was standing before the crosses were lit."

"And when the police moved onto the property, did you or anybody there resist being detained or arrested?"

"No. We just stood there, and they threw us down in the mud."

At this point Kearney requested and was granted permission to play a portion of Metzger's audiotape for the jury. Because of the poor quality of the recording, the judge ordered the portion relating to Metzger's arrest played a second time.

After it was played, I turned to Dale, commenting half aloud, half to myself, "That's not right."

"What's not? No. That was the same part," answered Dale.

"No. I mean that part of the audiotape after they've been arrested. He's cuffed. The tape goes on and off. How could he—"

"Right. That break, that pause just before Kearney shut it off the first time. I heard it, too."

After the playback, the judge said, "My ruling will be that the witness can testify to the words spoken only if he does so from his own independent recollection. I don't want him just repeating what he thinks he hears now."

"Thank you, Your Honor. Mr. Metzger, do you recognize the voices on the tape?"

"I recognize that to be Judge Luros, who was on the stand the other day."

"And what did Judge Luros say?"

"Judge Luros seemed to be quite happy, and he said to Frank Silva, 'Mr. Silva, this is going to be a learning field for you.' And Mr. Silva says back, 'Do you think you can make it stick?' And Judge Luros says, 'Nothing would make me happier.'"

"Now, other than being at Kagel Canyon as an invited guest speaker, were you involved in any of the planning or organization of anything that took place that night?"

"I couldn't. I was not a member of the Klan."

"I have no more questions of this witness, Your Honor." said Kearney.

"Mr. Davidson, cross-examination?" the judge queried.

"There is one matter I would like to address outside the presence of the jury."

"Very well. Approach."

Davidson and Kearney approached the bench.

"I need to have the original of that tape, Your Honor," said Davidson.

"I anticipated counsel's request for a copy of the tape. I have one in my briefcase," replied Kearney.

"No. I need the original," said Davidson.

"Why's that?" asked Kearney.

"Your Honor, I don't think the code requires me to

explain that in detail," protested Davidson. "Let it be enough said that when one side uses any material as evidence of facts it claims to be true, the other side is allowed to examine that material for authenticity."

"You want time to analyze the tape before cross-examination?" the judge asked.

"I do."

"Give him the tape. He has a right to verify it. We'll start with his cross-examination tomorrow."

◆ ◆ ◆ ◆ ◆

We spent that evening listening, over and again, to the audiotape Metzger claimed was in his microcassette the night of his arrest. We mused over the content, and we wondered if the voice Metzger claimed was that of Judge Luros was really the judge. But our real interest, of course, was whether the tape had indications that it was not the original but instead an edited copy.

We studied CBS video outtakes of the defendants being led to the police vehicles and waiting to be transported to the police station. We could hear the cameraman being told to keep the camera zoomed in on Metzger, although he was standing a distance away from him.

Metzger's hands were cuffed behind his back the entire time. There was no imaginable way he could have reached the tape recorder inside his jacket pocket to pause the recording. Was a portion of the tape erased that incriminated Metzger? Dale vowed to uncover the truth during his cross-examination of Metzger the next morning.

◆ ◆ ◆ ◆ ◆

"Good morning, Mr. Metzger. Let's get right to this tape recorder you were wearing that night. As I understand your testimony, you turned the machine on when you went where the crosses were. You were standing there; the crosses got lit; the cops came down and arrested everybody; and you had the machine running that whole time; is that correct?"

"Yes, I did."

"And you were then handcuffed, were you not, sir, as it's shown on the videotape?"

"Yes, I was."

"And you had this recorder in your jacket pocket; is that correct?"

"That's correct."

"So you couldn't turn it off; is that right?"

Metzger paused in thought, then looked coldly at Davidson. Kearney stopped writing notes and glanced from the corner of his eye.

"I don't believe I could."

"Mr. Metzger, correct me if I am wrong. I want to play it again for you. This is the section of the tape involving Judge Luros that was played yesterday. Tell me if this sounds right to you."

Davidson played the tell-tale portion of the audiotape for Metzger and the jurors.

"Mr. Metzger, that was the part of the tape that was played yesterday, wasn't it?"

"Yes."

"What I noticed is a long pause immediately after that comment by Judge Luros. Then there is a big gap where it is obvious that something has either been edited out of that tape—"

"Excuse me, Your Honor—" Spencer leapt to his feet.

"Let's play it again," Davidson continued.

"—if counsel wants, he can take the witness stand."

"Let me hear the tape again," the judge replied.

Davidson played the same portion of the audiotape again.

Glancing toward the court reporter, the judge said, "The record should reflect that there is about a five-second pause."

Metzger, coming a little undone, broke in, "I can tell you exactly what that break is. This case has been going on for years and was once thrown out of court. At that time we figured it was all over, and so the tape didn't have great importance to me. So one time it was on my desk, and either I or one of the kids hit 'record' accidentally, and that is what happened. I was very upset about it because I thought it might be important someday, and I knew you would think this."

"Yeah, you're right," Davidson agreed. "Mr. Metzger, was it your understanding that Frank Silva took care of the coordination with the police?"

"Yes. This is the first time that I had depended on a person that was not under my control. When I ran the Klan I made my negotiations, and I never had a big problem. I assumed that Mr. Silva had everything squared away."

"You are a very cautious, careful man, and you didn't become a national leader of the white supremacist movement by letting the Frank Silvas of the world lead you around by the nose, did you?"

"No, I didn't feel I had been led around by the nose. I was asked to speak. I told Mr. Silva that I didn't care about their cross-lighting. I was simply going to give a speech that I was interested in giving."

"On your own tape you said you knew the police were getting ready to enter the property and make arrests; you knew there was a problem with the police. Their helicopter was circling above; and somehow, all along in your testimony, you don't think anything illegal was going on. I just don't understand that, Mr. Metzger."

"Well, besides the point that I was not involved in the cross-lighting, I do believe there are severe constitutional issues here and that it was a religious ceremony. There were three crosses, as were the crosses of Calvary, and a minister present to give a eulogy."

"Mr. Metzger, you brought Winston Burbage with you that night; didn't you?"

"Yes. He drove the car."

"And Mr. Burbage is shown on the videotape giving orders to the other participants. Do you recall seeing that?"

"I saw it on the video."

"And he was your right-hand man at that time, your aide; is that right?"

"Well, he is a good friend of mine."

"And yet he is down there very clearly talking about the *barbecue,* and saying you can't be arrested for unlawful assembly if you say you're having a *barbecue.* Are you saying you don't have any idea how he knew about the permits being for a barbecue?"

"Winston Burbage was in the restaurant when he heard Frank say he had the permit."

"But did Silva at that time say he had a *barbecue* permit?"

"No, a fire permit."

"You don't know how it is that Mr. Burbage was down there talking about 'Say it is a barbecue and you can't be arrested'? You don't know where that thought came to him; is that right? He didn't share these thoughts with you, Mr. Metzger?"

"No, he didn't. But I will say that Winston is young and impetuous, and sometimes he took off like that. When I heard about him being down there, not knowing what he had done, I said, 'Get back here. That's not our thing, and stay with us.' And then he did."

"Mr. Metzger, correct me if I am wrong, but it seems to me you're telling this jury that nothing wrong happened that night; nobody broke any laws. You're saying all the participants share your views, but you deny any participation. You seem to be trying to distance yourself from all this activity that you think is so absolutely proper. Isn't that what you are trying to do, sir?"

"I have testified already that I was not interested in a cross-lighting. I was not going to participate in it. And I was not going to set it up. I was to come and give a speech, and that was it."

"You were shown on the videotape arriving at the cross-burning site just at the point in time when the participants began circling the crosses; are you not, sir? Isn't that exactly the point in time you decided to go down there and join the party?"

"I didn't join any party. I walked down halfway and just stood there with Mr. Alcorn."

"And how is it, sir, that you picked just that point in time to go down there and join the others, when the crosses were in the process of being burned?"

"I don't know."

Davidson pursued Metzger's denial of philosophical

attachment to the Klan by reviewing various hate messages he published in his WAR newspaper. Then, one by one, the prior cross-burning incidents that Metzger staged during his reign as Grand Dragon were reviewed. We introduced photographs of the cross-burnings staged from the Mexican border to Sacramento, each demonstrating the usual armory of weapons. The pattern of Klan activity became apparent, culminating with the Los Angeles cross-burning. The photographs and videotapes of the burning crosses surrounded by hooded Klansmen carrying clubs and rifles were chilling proof of the Klan's intent to provoke surrounding communities into violent confrontations.

My mind began to wander to what our society would be like if Metzger, or someone like him, ever did control it. Of course, there would be no tolerance for racial or religious minorities. But it would not stop there. If Metzger, Butler, or any one of them put in motion the quest for "racial purity" they professed, their job would never be finished. They would keep finding arbitrary distinctions and new levels of discrimination. Butler had already bifurcated the Caucasian race into Aryans (which includes only Nordic peoples) and "the others." They would continue to prioritize people on finer distinctions of ethnicity, specific religious membership, and physical characteristics. And they would do this until only their particular bloodlines remained in the hierarchy, eventually establishing an aristocracy and a monarch.

As I refocused my attention to the trial, Davidson was standing directly before the witness stand, irately pointing at an eight-by-ten-inch, black and white photograph of the Klan demonstration at Fontana. I was familiar with the evidence. What I took notice of was Davidson, pounding away with question after question. Metzger was equally resilient. He would not back down nor concede the smallest premise. By the fourth hour of the cross-examination, the two of them were still going toe-to-toe, like boxers trying to win the last round of a grueling title fight.

Later in the afternoon, I happened to glance over as Pageant nodded a greeting toward the back of the courtroom. I turned and saw a tall gentleman with a closely cropped beard, dark hair, and glasses, wearing a dark blue, three-piece suit and red tie—the standard attorney dress. I thought little of this, thinking the trial would conclude with Metzger's testimony, until Kearney later informed the judge that the defense had one last witness, an "expert witness," whom they would call to testify in the morning. When court adjourned, the man was hurried away, safe from our inquiries.

"Who do you figure he is?" asked Dale. "Do you remember his face from any of the videotapes?"

I didn't, and we had little time for guessing. We walked to a private lunchroom on the same floor as the court that the attorneys were using as an interview room. We knocked on the door. Borowitz answered and seemed a bit put off that we had followed them there. "What do you two want?"

"I'd just like to speak to your expert witness for a few minutes," I responded.

"Maybe he doesn't want to talk to you." Borowitz looked back to the witness. He was seated with Kearney, Spencer, and Pageant, all of them listening.

"Of course he does." I smiled at the witness, and he acknowledged with his own. "He's an expert. There shouldn't be any reason for him to preview his opinions with only one side."

"I have no problem speaking with the prosecuting attorneys." The man rose cordially from his chair. "Is here okay?"

I introduced myself and my partner, then waited for his name.

"I'm Kirk Lyons." We shook hands and went to sit by a table in the far corner of the room.

We talked for a while about his background—he was indeed an attorney. Then we discussed the opinions he understood would be elicited from him when he testified. Cross-lightings from this man's perspective were traditional, religious rites, and he articulated his opinion as a professional would. If Metzger could have chosen his own court-appointed attorney, as he wanted at our first arraignment hearing, it would have been Kirk Lyons.

I needed to speak with my contacts who might know the kind of information Lyons wouldn't want to volunteer. When we finished talking, I returned directly to the office and began making phone calls.

The next day, Lyons's direct examination was taken by Kearney. In the usual meticulous manner that Kearney favored, Lyons was prompted to recite his academic training and professional background. He had a degree in social and behavioral sciences from the University of Texas at Austin that he described as basically a history degree. He related that he almost had enough credit for a minor in German. He graduated from Bates College of Law at the University of Houston where, although he became a lawyer, he attended numerous history seminars.

He testified that he had given lectures to school children for the past sixteen years on various aspects of American social history. Although he had a relatively pleasant demeanor, his perspective on the Klan made me wonder if this was the best instructor the children could have. He also taught several college and graduate classes specifically on the American Civil War and the Reconstruction Era.

Lyons testified that in his legal practice he had represented a number of individuals associated with white supremacist organizations. As he answered Kearney's next questions it became apparent that Lyons was the principle criminal defense attorney for the Klan and related organizations. Among his clients were Lewis Ray Beam Jr., a former Grand Dragon of the Ku Klux Klan affiliated for a time with Aryan Nations; Jim Wickstrom, who was one of the prime movers of the Posse Comitatus; Douglas H. Sheets, of the White Patriots Party in North Carolina; Thomas Robb, the national director of the Knights of the Ku Klux Klan; and Stephen Ray Nelson, with Aryan Nations. He also admitted having recently represented Frank Silva. Lyons testified that in the course of each such representation, he had discussions concerning the philosophies of their various organizations. The apparent purpose of this preliminary portion of his testimony was to build the foundation for his opinion on the purpose and intent of a cross-lighting.

Lyons denied membership in any white supremacist organizations. Oddly enough, he testified that he belonged to the ACLU.

He related that he had been to the Aryan Nations compound in Idaho on about four occasions, and that he had attended four or five cross-lightings. Kearney asked him to relate some of the details.

"The first example of a cross-lighting was at my school in 1974. The school was integrated, and someone burned a cross in front of the school. The FBI was swarming all over the place. The scuttlebutt was that the Klan in Menard, Texas, had done it, but to my knowledge there was no Klan there.

"The next was sponsored by Thomas Robb on his own property in Harrison, Arkansas. There were fifty to sixty people, half in Klan garb. I believe it was Robb who ordered the torchbearers to lead the procession in a circle around the crosses, three of them."

He continued to describe in detail the events at this and the other "cross-lightings" he'd witnessed, reciting names, dates, and places. He was making them sound like the good ol' boy social routine and, other than for the FBI at the school cross-burning, there had been no police intervention in any of these Southern jurisdictions. After next establishing that Lyons had read the daily transcripts of the testimony in our trial, and that he had reviewed the photographs and videotape made by Peter Lake, it was now time for Kearney and Lyons to try to make the L.A. cross-burning fit into place.

"How does the Kagel Canyon cross-lighting compare to the other cross-lightings you were present at?" asked Kearney.

"Well, they've all had the three crosses, which is a recent innovation in Klan ritual. The religious symbolism is still there, and by and large it doesn't seem to differ significantly from the ones that I have seen."

"What is the purpose of the lit cross?"

"The cross symbolizes light into the world, lighting the darkness, lighting the ignorance. It is the altar of the Klan, wherever it meets."

"Is there a distinction between a cross-lighting for religious or organizational purposes and a cross-burning to intimidate somebody?"

"There is definitely a difference. As I understand the term, a 'cross-burning' is an act of intimidation that is put by somebody's house or a direct threat to an individual to warn him of some specific conduct. So there is a distinction."

"Mr. Lyons, based on your reading of the transcripts of these proceedings and your review of the videotapes and other material, are you able to formulate an opinion on the purpose of the cross-lighting at Kagel Canyon?"

"Yes, it was a religious ritual; it was not intended as an act of intimidation but as a means of exercising their right to assemble peaceably and to practice their beliefs on private property. That is my opinion of that event."

Kearney should have left well enough alone at this point. He'd gotten "the company line" on the meaning and intent of the cross-lighting, and the absence of police intervention in the prior examples implicitly supported their claim of First Amendment protection. He should have ended on a strong note but instead took the bait on the Nazi salute tangent we raised with some of his other witnesses.

"In the tape that you saw, do you recall hearing a salute with the words 'Hail Victory'?"

"Yes, I do."

"Could you tell me the significance of this, also?"

"'Hail, Victory' is basically a Teutonic salute. It evolved from the Teutonic Knights of Germany with roots going back to biblical times. The Germans translate it into 'Sieg Heil,' which the Nazis adopted and borrowed from Teutonic mythology in the 1930s. But it has a many-hundred-year history before that. In the contemporary Klan, 'Hail, Victory' signifies the victory of Christ's kingdom. That's what it's used for."

"Is there anything further to it than that?"

"No. In conversations with several different Klansmen and members of the Church of Jesus Christ Christian, that is what they have consistently told me. If they'd wanted to indicate something involving Nazi Germany, they would have said, 'Sieg Heil.' It is the same as 'Ave Maria,' which means 'Hail Mary' in Latin. 'Ave' and 'Heil' and 'hail' are the same word."

"Could I have that answer read back, please?" I interjected. "Just the part about 'Sieg Heil' and 'Ave Maria.'"

I had heard both the question and answer just fine. I only wanted to make sure that the judge, an Irish Catholic, had heard it as clearly. As for those jurors who may have prayed that prayer known as the "Hail Mary," well, I guess I wanted them to hear again this witness tell them their prayer was the same as "Sieg Heil." Lyons shifted uncomfortably in his seat. The judge quipped that he'd like the answer read back too, as if he couldn't believe the comparison. And so, we all listened again as the court reporter dutifully read the testimony. With that, Kearney's examination of Lyons ended. I began my cross-examination.

Lyons waited for me to place my notepad on the podium, then cordially said, "Good morning, Mr. Phillips," and smiled as if we were friends. He was trying to influence my perception of him to warrant good treatment. It was a smart move, one that I would expect of only a skilled attorney, but he wasn't going to play it out with me.

I smiled back at Lyons and returned his greeting. My reply, though, was deliberate, and the smile faded as I addressed him.

"Mr. Lyons, you are actually quite a believer in this white separatist movement, are you not?"

"I wouldn't characterize my beliefs as that, no."

"Don't you call your law office the American Patriot's Defense Foundation?"

"Yes, I do."

"Do you remember being quoted in some of your local newspapers as saying, and I quote, 'A lot of these people's values are not that much different from mine. I just don't think they should go into a gunfight without a gun. Our foundation is providing the gun'?"

"That is correct. I did say that. That is not a blanket approval of all their beliefs and philosophies, because I myself couldn't pin down one belief or philosophy in any of these groups."

"And do you also recall speaking before the Aryan Nations Congress a couple of years back?"

"I did appear at the Congress, yes."

"Do you remember throwing a piece of meat on the floor in front of the audience as you were speaking, taunting informants to come out and retrieve it?"

"Yes, I did. I knew they were there."

"The 'Congress,' as they call it, concludes with a cross-lighting. Did you attend that?"

"I did witness the cross-lighting."

"Do you recall that at that 'cross-lighting' the participants formed a line down the aisle and out the door of Mr. Butler's church? They approached the altar one by one as a sword was lifted and pledged themselves to Aryan Nations."

"That is called the Soldier's Ransom."

"You participated in that swearing in, didn't you?"

"I did participate in that function. Yes, I did."

"In fact, Mr. Lyons, you were married by Mr. Butler, were you not?"

"Yes, I was."

"Now, you are not going to tell this court you don't share the beliefs of that organization.

"I will tell you I fell in love when I went up there and I married a girl up there, yes. I am not anybody's man except my own. I have my own beliefs, my own values; and I see these people as persecuted legally and socially for their unpopular views."

"And you have a lot of friends in this movement?"

"Yes, as I've testified earlier."

"Among them you named Lewis Beam and Robert Miles?"

"Yes."

"You know, of course, that Lewis Beam was the Grand Dragon of a Ku Klux Klan chapter in Texas that was found liable in a civil court for the arson of a Vietnamese immigrant's fishing boat off the gulf of Texas?"

"Yes, he was. That is where he came to prominence."

"And your other friend, Robert Miles, was convicted of conspiracy to burn school buses, wasn't he?"

"Yes. He spent five years in Marion Penitentiary."

"What percentage of your income is derived from monies paid to you by your American Patriots Foundation?"

"It would be hard to calculate, but the bulk of my

income comes from the money I receive monthly from the Foundation."

"And isn't it true, sir, that you are seeking donations for Tom Metzger's appeal in a Portland, Oregon, civil case, in which his WAR group was found liable for the bludgeoning death of a black exchange student?"

"We have considered that a very crucial First Amendment case. And, yes, we are attempting to raise money for the appeal."

"And there has also been the Frank Silva representation; correct, Mr. Lyons?"

"Yes, just recently."

"And you were part of the defense team in a sedition trial against Richard Butler, Robert Miles, and Lewis Beam at Fort Smith, Arkansas; isn't that so?"

"Yes."

"And you may also represent Randall Evans on the appeal from his RICO conviction."

"That's so."

"And you know, of course, that he, along with Silva and Butler, was one of the principles in this case, this cross-burning that took place in Kagel Canyon, don't you, sir?"

"Yes."

"So you have represented quite a few people connected with this cross-burning on other matters, haven't you?"

"I suppose that's so."

"You have heard the expression 'lawyers are advocates for their clients'; have you not?"

"Yes, I have."

"There is a dichotomy in your testifying here, isn't there, Mr. Lyons?"

"A dichotomy?"

"Yes. On the one hand you are the lawyer, the advocate, for five principles in this case whom you either directly or prospectively represent on other matters, and on the other hand you are on the witness stand as an expert witness—"

"That's right."

"—to give an objective opinion."

"And I am trying to do that."

It was my impression at this point that the jurors would see the conflict inherent in the roles Lyons was attempting to play. I had also succeeded in eradicating any suggestion of professional cordiality Lyons implied to our relationship by his friendly greeting. His tone was still contained but becoming aggravated. He sensed that his credibility was harmed by his representative capacity for so many of the defendants, and by his participation in Aryan Nations activities. He seemed taken off guard by our knowledge of him.

"You testified that the first time you saw a cross-burning was in 1974 at a school in Austin, Texas, that had just been constructed. Could you tell us about it?" I asked.

"It was a brand-new school. Schools had already been integrated in the Austin school system, I believe, two years before, and this was a school that was built in a mostly white neighborhood. And it was named after the old black high school that had been closed down due to integration. And so there was a lot of rancor in Austin at that time, the blacks wanting the name back for their school and the whites feeling that they didn't get the name they wanted for the school. And a cross was burned in front of the school."

"And you were so inspired by the meaning and symbolism of the burning cross in front of that school that you decided in the future you would celebrate other cross-burnings as well?"

Borowitz rose. "Objection, Your Honor; argumentative."

"He's an impartial expert witness, Your Honor," I replied. "I'm sure he can handle this."

"We don't need the cynicism of the prosecutor in this courtroom, Your Honor," Borowitz retorted.

"Overruled, Counsel," the judge intoned. "The witness will answer the question."

"What impressed me most was the covey of FBI agents that descended upon the school the next day over what I considered a mere act of vandalism." said Lyons.

"That's interesting, Mr. Lyons. You have a bachelor of arts degree in social and behavioral sciences, don't you?"

"That's correct."

"In view of that background, what impact do you think that burning cross had on the black students that were coming to the campus that day?"

"I think the administration officials probably covered the situation up, but they couldn't stop the FBI agents from coming in. If attention was brought to it, it was the fault of the FBI."

"Let's talk about a burning cross on somebody's front lawn."

"All right."

"Legal or illegal, Mr. Lyons?"

"I would say illegal."

"Why?"

"Because it is an assault. It is an act of potential arson if the house catches fire, and it is trespassing on private property."

"So you acknowledge the fire danger caused by a burning cross?"

"Oh. Well, certainly I acknowledge there is a fire danger."

"The state has a right to protect against fire danger, doesn't it, Mr. Lyons?"

"Of course. As long as it doesn't trample First Amendment rights of people peaceably assembling."

"So there are laws that relate to a cross-burning situation that the state may constitutionally enforce, aren't there?"

Lyons realized that he had been led to an inescapable trap. Of course the state is entitled to enforce fire prevention laws, even where there is First Amendment activity. He slumped back in his chair, and his voice dropped.

"I assume they can."

"Thank you, sir. What I'd like to do now, Mr. Lyons, is talk with you about your opinion on cross-lightings. They are, in the summary of your opinion, fraternal acts of Christian expression. Would you say that is a fair assessment of your opinion?"

"That's a fair assessment."

"Would you agree that opinions are all relevant to their context?"

"How do you mean?"

"Well, if you were speaking to World War II vets on the dropping of the atom bomb, you would be likely to express a different-sounding opinion than if you were speaking to survivors from Hiroshima."

"I would still be truthful, but yes, of course, one would consider his audience in how he expresses his opinion."

"And in your opinion today, well, you haven't thrown any raw hamburger meat in front of the jury."

"That would of course be out of place here."

"You've relied on a number of publications as the basis of

the opinions to which you've testified in court. You provided a list of those publications. Is that correct?"

"Yes, it is."

"I'm going to read a passage from one of those books, titled *Invisible Empire.* You are familiar with that book; aren't you?"

"Yes, I am. I listed the book."

"Reading from page 127 at the very top: 'In 1940, the Ku Klux Klan finally held a meeting with the pro-Nazis at Nordland, New Jersey. Speakers from each side praised each other's efforts for "the master race" and enthusiastically recalled battles waged against communists, Jews, blacks, unions, and foreigners. The swastika and the *burning cross* were then united on New Jersey soil.' Was there anything religious in that *cross-burning?*"

"I differ from the author in my assessment of that meeting."

"Well, Mr. Lyons, aren't there expert opinions that very much differ from the ones you have expressed?"

"I would be the first to say that."

"Let me read another passage from page 121: 'The Klan cross regularly burst into flames when black families almost anywhere in the United States moved into white neighborhoods.'

"What is your reaction to that assessment of the Klan's cross-burnings? It doesn't seem to me that the Klan was holding a religious ritual in those situations."

"My reaction is that we lived in a racist country then and we are living in a racist country now, as any black citizen can tell you. You cannot lay that necessarily at the door of the Klan."

"Excuse me, sir. Are you saying we cannot necessarily lay racism at the door of the Klan?"

"They did not invent it."

"So this passage from the writings of another expert and published author on the Klan does not in any way affect your opinion that the burning cross is used as an act of intimidation?"

"The burning cross is an act of intimidation. The lit cross at a Klan ritual on private property intended to give pride in membership to the participants is not intended as an act of intimidation."

"Mr. Lyons, are you familiar with a book published by your friend Lewis Beam, former Grand Dragon of the Ku Klux Klan in the state of Texas, titled *The Klansman's Handbook?*"

"I am."

"And in that book he refers to Tom Metzger as the master of what Beam calls 'the guerilla theater,' doesn't he, Mr. Lyons?"

"Yes, he does. Mr. Beam is very aware of Mr. Metzger's ability as a public speaker. That's all he means by it."

"And the definition of 'the guerilla theater' stated in Beam's book is 'where the plot is carefully planned, the actors know their parts, and the scenes are carefully rehearsed,' correct, Mr. Lyons?"

"Yes. That is what he is talking about."

"*'The actors know their parts.'*" I repeated. "I have no further questions."

Kirk Lyons stepped from the witness stand. He glanced to the jurors, nodded, and smiled. They did not react to him. As he walked passed the counsel table, Metzger looked away. Lyons continued to the rear of the courtroom, hesitated a moment, then departed.

The defense had no further witnesses, and they rested

their case. The jury was excused. Brian Pageant walked to the back door, but before he could leave the judge called loudly to him. "So, Pageant, 'Sieg Heil' is the same as 'Ave Maria.' That's the most goddamn offensive thing I've heard come from that witness stand. Next time have an idea just who you're calling to testify." Pageant stammered as the judge stormed to his chambers.

All that now remained were the closing arguments of counsel. We would begin Monday morning. Dale and I agreed to split the two-part argument allowed the prosecution. I would do the opening and, after the defense arguments, Dale would do the rebuttal. We considered our personal styles appropriate to these roles.

The prosecution's closing argument is most effective when used as a methodical recount of the most salient evidence. To open, I would state the applicable law and the prosecution's basic theory of how the evidence satisfies the proofs necessary for convictions on each count. I had gathered the evidence, and I remembered the details of interviews and testimony.

Our opening argument should set forth fully the People's case without arguing against what we anticipate the defense will contend. This is standard for experienced prosecutors. The prosecution gets the last shot with its rebuttal argument. If the criminal defense bar could change one aspect of criminal procedure, this would be it. The prosecution should always save some punch for its rebuttal argument, when the defense can no longer answer.

Rebuttal argument requires oratory skills that play well with a bit of rage and indignation. Davidson considered this to be one of his finest trial skills. We also anticipated the defense would personally attack whichever of us delivered the opening argument. It's a common defense tactic to shift the jury's focus from the defendant's crimes to the prosecutor's ethics. So we would both go to bat, and Davidson would be ready to argue in my favor.

Chapter 21

Opening Argument of the People

I had done the opening argument a hundred times—in the shower, driving to work, in the middle of the night as I lay awake. This morning I would do it in court.

I wondered if all those clever little lines would flow as eloquently as they had in my mind's eye. I needed to keep my head clear and be able to draw upon the mental index cards of points and phrases. I don't use notes. I never had in any trial. I speak to jurors as if they were guests seated in my living room.

The right suit for closing argument is a light-gray, and that is what I wore. Bad guys dress in black. There are subtle messages communicated by the clothes we wear. The colors have to be right.

I arrived early downtown, before the clerical staff. The door to Davidson's office was open. His back was turned as I entered. He was deep in thought. When he heard me come in, he turned and looked at me.

"I've reflected a lot on this case," he said. "I'm sure you

have too, John, as strange as it's been. I mean—fate played an unusual role.

"I think back to how we became friends, the very first day we watched that tape. Then their screwball motion to compel a felony prosecution and the case comes to this office. No one's ever made that motion.

"Then the case gets assigned to me, and they hire you in as special prosecutor. This office has never hired a special prosecutor. What were the chances of this all happening, John; things that hadn't happened before? I'm not a believer in coincidences. What has happened here hasn't happened by mistake or chance.

"You see, we do not control this case, John. All along we thought we did, but we don't."

I reflected on the day that I returned to the city attorney's office with all the evidence I had gathered on Metzger's Klan. "I thought once that I did control it—that I *was* in control," I replied. "It was the night before Judge Cherniss blew his cork and dismissed it. Was I ever wrong."

"This is like no other case." Dale shook his head as he spoke. "It is a will—a will that has joined us all in its servitude. Even the defendants are role-players in the service of this will—a very powerful will."

The hallway was filled with cameras, cables, news people, monitors, and spectators. We looked beyond it and passed through the courtroom doors.

To shield myself from the distraction of the camera inside the courtroom, I busied myself with preparation. I took the exhibits admitted during trial and placed them on our counsel table in the order of my argument. There were still a couple of minutes. The defendants were each seated beside his counsel. They were silent, having thoughts of their own, no doubt. I remained numb to all beyond my sphere of concern.

I sat down beside Dale. He looked over, then back ahead, and spoke softly. "Good luck, man."

"This is the easy part."

Dale looked back over, with a slight air of surprise. "For you, really?"

"No, not really," I replied. We looked again at each other and nearly burst into laughter.

"Try not to have too good a time," Dale said.

The jurors took their seats. The bailiff called the courtroom to order. The judge stepped from chambers. He read the title of the case and looked down to us.

"Are we ready to proceed?" he asked.

"We're ready."

He turned to the jury. "Mr. Phillips will start with the opening argument for the People of the state. Because the People have the burden of proving their case beyond a reasonable doubt, the People will address you twice, once in opening argument, once in rebuttal. After Mr. Phillips argues, Mr. Spencer and then the other defense lawyers will argue their case."

"Thank you very much, Your Honor." I began. "First, I would like to say on behalf of Mr. Davidson and myself that we very much appreciate the efforts of this jury. You have been exemplary in your attentiveness as the testimony and evidence have been presented in this case.

"Soon you will be starting a different function in your role as jurors. You will no longer be passive listeners. It will be your job to discuss the case and reach a verdict.

"I've organized what I'm about to say by first discussing

the exhibits and testimony; then I'll discuss the law. Finally, I'll discuss the application of the facts to the laws that deal with your verdict.

"The first category of evidence relates to prior cross-burnings in which some of the defendants engaged. We presented photographs that depict each of these incidents.

"The photographs numbered twenty through twenty-four depict Tom Metzger at a cross-burning in Fontana, California, three years prior to our incident. He is standing in the company of two others; one is carrying a rifle, and the other is carrying a handgun.

"The same is true of subsequent cross-burning incidents at Ceres, another at Fontana, and at a demonstration that resulted in a riot in the city of Oceanside. The photographs taken at the Lopez Lake cross-burning show shields, helmets, and different types of blunt striking instruments, including ax handles, baseball bats, and clubs.

"At each of these incidents Mr. Metzger was present. He had no reason to think the Los Angeles cross-burning was going to be any different.

"The next series of photographs in evidence were taken at a cross-burning at Rosamond, California, only two weeks before the Kagel Canyon incident. These show Silva, Witek, Hofstadler, and Evans. Hofstadler is holding a rifle, and Silva and Evans have handguns in their possession.

"This first category of evidence was presented to demonstrate that when these individuals came to Los Angeles, each was fully aware that his actions would create a tumultuous, inciteful, confrontational situation. They came looking for a fight, and they were prepared to win it, just as they had been on the previous occasions.

They knew their actions would incite terror in the neighborhood. They knew some people who lived in that neighborhood would react to their provocation. They brought those table legs for the sport of their hatred. The First Amendment of the United States Constitution does not protect such inflammatory conduct. It was not designed so and it never has been interpreted in that way.

"The next category of physical evidence reveals the character of Richard Butler's Aryan Nations. Mr. Butler reviewed portions of his books on cross-examination. He was the editor. David Tate, the man who gunned down two Missouri state troopers in cold blood, was listed in the credits for layout and printing.

"One drawing here shows the Star of David, the Nazi swastika, and the symbols for Aryan Nations and the Ku Klux Klan. The Star of David is depicted with a snake with horns at the top of its head. It's not against the law to display this drawing. But we submit that it shows an antagonistic predisposition, one that is likely to lead to a cross-burning as an antagonistic rather than a religious act.

"What is it that these groups have in common—the Ku Klux Klan, Aryan Nations, WAR, and the American Nazi Party? It's a common hatred.

"And as much as Mr. Butler would have liked to have his organization characterized as a peaceful, religious group, we saw that it was not as we reviewed the photographs and captions in the books he edits. I recall asking him about a photograph that shows men crouched down in a combat exercise with a caption beneath it that says, 'Street fighting. Coming soon at a place near you.'

"And on the next page is a photograph of Mr. Butler inspecting a group of paramilitary soldiers holding rifles, and adjacent to that is a photograph depicting a group of men climbing a small hill. The caption below that reads, 'On rappel, death from above.'

"The implications are the same in Metzger's publications, such as People's Exhibit number fifty, which offers for sale books of a violent orientation—various books on guerilla warfare, explosives, and demolitions; army tech manuals; books on the chemistry of explosives and booby traps.

"We have introduced these materials published by Butler and Metzger to show their predisposition and that of their followers to commit the crimes charged: to create a racial confrontation and carry out that which is printed in their publications. The questions become, Are these men immune from prosecution because they call themselves members of the Ku Klux Klan or the Church of Jesus Christ Christian, and Do these religious views, as they call them, remove them from compliance with the laws to which the rest of us must abide?

"We have the burn permit itself, People's Exhibit four. Under the Los Angeles municipal code, a person can apply for a burn permit under any of several clauses. One of these clauses is for a bonfire by any legitimate religious or fraternal group. That's how the ordinance reads: 'any legitimate religious or fraternal association.' Did the Ku Klux Klan apply under this clause? Answer: no. Instead it applied for its burn permit under that clause claiming its fire was an open-pit barbecue.

"Now if they really believed in the religious character of their actions, they would have applied under the clause for legitimate religious or fraternal association use. Instead, they chose a ruse. The barbecue they set up was just a little makeshift thing. They stuck one pork chop on it and a can of beans. When Mr. Silva testified on this point, even he laughed at the notion that this was their dinner.

"The language is very clear on this permit. The words 'barbecue pit' clearly identify this permit to be for a barbecue, not a cross-burning. And here it says at the top of the reverse side, 'Barbecue Permit Instructions.' There could have been no mistake whatsoever.

"Consider Metzger's testimony that he used to get burn permits for Klan barbecues. Of course, we know from the photographs of those prior gatherings that those barbecues were actually cross-burnings. But he had gotten permits for those gatherings as barbecues. Is it so mysterious how Frank Silva now has that type of burn permit for his cross-burning? Remember that Silva testified he wanted Metzger present because he was 'experienced with these kinds of things.' This is the very kind of advice Silva would have been seeking. He eventually wound up with the type of permit Metzger had obtained in the past. Why? Because Metzger advised him so, and in this alone Metzger is an aider and abettor to the crime of unlawful assembly.

"These table legs were among the first exhibits we presented. They were identified by Mr. Lake as items that Mr. Witek transported to Kagel Canyon on the night of December 3rd.

"They were also identified by Mr. Lake as having been inside a van that transported Witek's Nazi group to a Nazi/Klan demonstration at the Ontario Courthouse a month earlier. During that ride, Witek said they may have to use these against antagonists. We know from that comment that these table legs were intended to be used as powerful, blunt, striking instruments.

"On the night of December 3rd, these items were again passed around, as the Nazi Party members set up a security perimeter for the Klan to burn its crosses. The table legs are seen in the videotape and a still photograph. Witek himself was holding a long pickax handle. He is charged with a violation of penal code section 12020 for the possession and distribution of billy clubs. There is no defense to this charge. We must not allow this type of weaponry to be carried into street battles of the American Nazi Party.

"Although Mr. Hofstadler, Mr. Riley, and Mr. Metzger are not charged with this crime, the presence of these weapons is important in relation to these defendants as well. They knew as they entered this neighborhood that they were traveling with a band of men that had so armed themselves. And as they prepared to inflame the crosses in this racially mixed community, they knew their group was prepared to confront people who might come on that property to investigate that fire, perhaps to put it out, whether they realized it was a Ku Klux Klan cross-burning or not. They lived in a neighborhood where fires are a danger.

"Those residents had every right to approach that fire to see if they could be of assistance in extinguishing it. And in fact, two residents were doing just that. One dreads to think what would have happened to Mr. Gentry had he entered that property with men carrying these clubs there to meet him.

"Then we saw the videotape, ladies and gentlemen. While this conclusively proves issues that, in its absence, may have been in contention, it does not show every conversation, act, and behind-the-scenes planning. We rely on more conventional forms of evidence for the proof of many of these issues.

"What is shown on this tape that *is* very important are the commission of the overt acts and the true circumstances of the burning of the crosses. The tape shows Mr. Hofstadler kneeling as he wrapped a piece of material to a stick to construct a torch, a torch that was later used to inflame the crosses. And at this time the crosses were lying just to his side. He surely would have known that he was assisting the lighting of the fires.

"The tape shows Mr. Riley assisting Mr. Silva in dousing the crosses with a flammable liquid, then raising them and planting them into the ground, constituting a clear act of aiding and abetting the setting of the fires.

"At the conclusion of these arguments by counsel, the court will read instructions that are the applicable law. One of those instructions defines those who are 'principles' in the commission of a crime. You will be instructed that principles includes 'aiders and abettors,' ones who in any way give advice, encourage, or facilitate the actual crime itself. These acts of aiding and abetting by each defendant demonstrate their role as principles in the commission of the crime.

"Finally, I ask you to consider the audiotape made by Tom Metzger that night. Portions seem deleted. The helicopter noise is clearly audible at certain points, and then suddenly it stops.

"At one of these times Mr. Metzger was definitely handcuffed. This was during the conversation between Frank Silva and Judge Luros. Yet, there is a break in the tape. Mr. Metzger's explanation is that his kid accidentally recorded over it. But if that had really happened, there would have been a new audio portion there. You might have heard a kid talking, or somebody saying, 'Shut that off.' But all you hear is one set of noises immediately followed by another, both from Kagel Canyon. So you know he isn't being truthful when he testifies that somebody accidentally turned the tape recorder on and off.

"The Metzger tape is also significant in that it refutes the orchestrated testimony of the defense witnesses. According to them, this cross-burning was a ceremony in honor of slain police officer Mike Serna. On this tape you hear absolutely nothing about Mike Serna. Nor do you hear one word from Tom Metzger advising the others not to burn the crosses, as he claimed.

"Among our witnesses was the investigating officer, Sergeant John O'Neil. He's from the Foothill Division of the Los Angeles Police Department. Yes, ladies and gentlemen, the Foothill Division is the same station as the one in the Rodney King case.

"Well, I'm going to tell you this: these L.A.P.D. officers did everything *right* on the night of December 3rd. They told these people, 'Do whatever you want so far as meeting and saying what you want to say, just don't burn the crosses. You have to have the right permit to burn the crosses, and you don't.'

"Well, that wasn't good enough for the men on trial here and the others among them. They had to take it one step further. If Sergeant O'Neil had said, 'Do whatever you want to do, just don't spit on my boots,' they would have spat on his boots. It was with that type of arrogance they intended to accomplish their objective. After all, isn't that psychologically the whole point of being a Klansman, to take it one step further, push it a little more? That night they took it too far.

"Sergeant O'Neil had more conversations with Frank Silva at his home that afternoon, advising him again not to burn the crosses, and saying that if he did, arrests would be made.

"I ask you to imagine being inside a home with a group of men doing something that attracted a great deal of police presence. One of you has a conversation with the officer in charge, and then comes back inside the house. Would you just sit there and not ask him what the conversation was about? *Of course* you'd find out what the conversation was about.

"The appearance and circumstances of the Kagel Canyon location have been described and shown to you on videotape. There were thirty police officers, three fire trucks, and a helicopter circling above. There could not have been a greater amount of warning to anybody about to commit a crime that they were violating the law and would be arrested if they persisted.

"But in spite of that knowledge, they wouldn't quit. Instead, they would try to outsmart the law by following through with the Klan ruse that their party was just a barbecue. As Winston Burbage, Mr. Metzger's right-hand man, told those standing by the makeshift grill, 'Just tell them it's a barbecue we're having. They're going to have a hell of a time saying a barbecue is an unlawful assembly.'

"Well, it didn't work, at least not up to this point. It's now your decision. You see, when the Klan decided to try to outsmart the law, it wasn't just the cops they had to get past. Now, you tell us. Were the defendants having a barbecue, or were they burning crosses in violation of the law? Let them know the Ku Klux Klan is responsible to the same laws as the rest of us.

"The next category of evidence was testimony of expert opinion, elicited from Gene Frice and from Peter Lake. Mr. Frice has an extensive history in law enforcement. With both the Department of Justice and the California Specialized Training Institute, he has followed and studied the Klan. We elicited his opinion on why the Ku Klux Klan burns crosses. His conclusion was that the cross-burning is intended to create an atmosphere of intimidation; that it is, at best, a pagan-like ritual; and that it is to stake out Klan territory. Lake's opinion was very similar. Both men testified there was definitely an intent to intimidate. As Mr. Frice testified, they use intimidation as a means to drive away those they dislike—to achieve their state of racial purity.

"And let's use our common sense with this, because we all know full well what the burning cross represented the night of December 3rd and what the tradition of the burning cross has represented in this country for more than a hundred years.

"Kirk Lyons, the defense's expert, expressed an opinion that flew in the face of common sense. But view his testimony in the overall context of its circumstance. Mr. Lyons, the lawyer, represents five of these co-conspirators in other matters related to their activity in the white supremacist movement.

"For five of them he has been an advocate, and now he asks you to accept him as an objective witness with an honest and fair opinion on the Klan's intent in burning crosses.

"Well, he *is* an advocate, and he knows it. He's their lawyer. He represented them in the past; he will represent them in the future; and in these proceedings he has represented them now. He created a foundation to establish himself as the national Klan attorney. He was so favorably impressed by the burning of a cross at a school that he attended others thereafter. He is a man with a degree in social and behavioral sciences, but he refuses to acknowledge the negative impact of that cross-burning on the school children. Should we accept his testimony as credible? Should we give weight to his opinion?

"It is the same thing the defendants are trying to say here, that the neighboring residents did not even know of the supposedly private Klan ceremony. It's all absolute nonsense.

"But there was some significance to his testimony, concessions that were unavoidable. One of these was his admission that the government is constitutionally allowed to enforce laws that restrict Ku Klux Klan cross-burning activity. The Klan is charged with violation of a law that is intended to prevent the spread of fire. It was a true and an unavoidable admission.

"This brings us to the last witness I want to talk about. He represents, in many ways, what this case is all about.

"Mr. Gentry described that night when he, from his bedroom window, could see the orange glow of the fire as the crosses were inflamed. He went to the street in front of his house and there, he testified, were fifty to sixty people, half of whom were children.

"You know, when one empathizes, putting yourself in the position of the people who saw what was happening that night, it must be acknowledged that the actions of the

Ku Klux Klan create lasting emotional scars. Peaceful residents and children—these are the victims. They have done nothing to deserve this ugly act of intimidation.

"They are not alleged in any portion of the complaint as victims, but they are the real victims in this case. We cannot ignore, we cannot make secondary, our responsibility to the rights of these people.

"Why should you care? Why should I care? I can tell you this. You can choose to let prejudice exist today, but you *cannot* choose who it exists *against* tomorrow.

"Now I'll discuss the laws that apply to this trial. Count one alleges a violation of penal code section 408, unlawful assembly. An unlawful assembly can occur in either of two ways. The first is for two or more persons to come together to commit an illegal act—the illegal act in this case being the igniting of unlawful fires. The second form of unlawful assembly is the coming together of persons in 'a violent, boisterous, or tumultuous manner.' The legal definition of 'tumultuous' is 'conduct likely to incite terror in others.'

"Ladies and gentlemen, we ask you to find that when these members of the Ku Klux Klan, Aryan Nations, WAR, and the American Nazi Party came together to burn crosses, their acts were inherently tumultuous in nature. They knew their actions were confrontational and provocative. A band of men, some in robes and hoods, some armed, setting fire in a residential canyon, arrogantly challenging the dignity of the people who lived there. There is no better example of conduct likely to incite terror.

"Count two of the complaint alleges a violation of Los Angeles municipal code section 57.20.19, unlawful burning. An 'unlawful burning' is any open, outdoor fire without a valid burn permit. It would be a defense if they believed they had a legitimate burn permit, but only if that belief were a true and honest one. Consider the circumstances: the police poised and ready for arrests, the fire trucks, the circling helicopter. None of these men could have truly believed the burn permits were valid. They wouldn't have needed an alibi, a makeshift barbecue, or their hoods and masks.

"This brings us to the conspiracy charge. The legal definition of 'conspiracy' is an agreement between two or more persons with the specific intent to violate the law, with the commission of at least one overt act in furtherance of the objective of the conspiracy. That overt act may be committed by any one of the conspirators after the formation of the agreement. Here, our theory is that the law they intended to violate was the unlawful burning. The overt acts committed in furtherance of this objective were the preparation of the crosses by Riley and Silva, the making of torches by Hofstadler, the organization of transportation by Witek, acquisition of false permits by Silva, the distribution of billy clubs by Witek, the announcement of an alibi by Burbage, and the wearing of disguised attire—the Klan masks—by Silva, Butler, and Hofstadler. You saw these acts on videotape or have credible testimony with hard physical evidence to substantiate.

"I recall that during the testimony of Kirk Lyons, we discussed the 'guerilla theater' about which his friend Lewis Beam, the notorious Texas Klansman, wrote. It is 'where each of the actors must know his lines, each of the scenes must be carefully rehearsed, and the plot must be carefully carried out.' Such was the night of December 3rd. The conspiracy has been proven.

"Do you wonder about the application of the First Amendment? Of course you do. Are there elements in this case of free speech and religious expression? There are. What, then, is the state's right to regulate in these areas?

"The state may regulate speech that constitutes a clear and present danger of immediate violence. Although not allowed to control the substance of speech, the state may regulate the form of expression where legitimate safety concerns exist.

"We do not ask you to convict the defendants on the basis of *what* they were saying, but instead for the dangerous and inflammatory manner in which they were saying it.

"I would like to make a couple of concluding remarks. One thing I think needs to be said—because there has been twisting and mischaracterization of the truth on what may be the central issue in this trial—and it regards the significance of the cross itself.

"What is the symbol of the cross? What is the meaning of the cross? Well, Christ died on the cross in an act of forgiveness and of love. This group uses that very same symbol in an act of intimidation and hate.

"You get a concluding instruction, ladies and gentlemen, defining reasonable doubt and the state of the evidence that establishes a case to that level of proof. 'Proof beyond a reasonable doubt is that state of the evidence which leaves, in the minds of the jurors, an abiding conviction, to a moral certainty, of the truth of the charges.'

"Many times I have sat in court and listened to interpretations of the phrase 'an abiding conviction.' I must say that 'an abiding conviction' means a lasting belief. It means that ten years from the day that you render your verdict you will look back and think that verdict was right and right to a moral certainty.

"There is but one verdict that this jury can return to capture that moral certainty, that abiding conviction. It is that Mr. Witek is guilty of violating the Los Angeles municipal code provision prohibiting unlawful burnings; that he is guilty of conspiracy for his conduct in aiding and abetting to further that violation; and that he is guilty of transporting, distributing, and possessing billy clubs in violation of penal code section 12020.

"That verdict is that Mr. Riley is guilty of unlawful assembly, conspiracy, and unlawful burning. It is that Mr. Hofstadler is guilty of unlawful assembly, of conspiracy, and of violating the fire code provision. And it is that Mr. Metzger is guilty of unlawful assembly, of conspiracy, and of the municipal code section prohibiting the unlawful burning.

"You will look back on this case, I think, for the rest of your lives. And one day you will recall that you did the right thing by returning these verdicts. You will know that to a moral certainty, and you will hold this conviction as an abiding conviction, surpassing the test of time.

"It is your right and it is your responsibility to protect that community, this city, and this state from that type of conduct."

Chapter 22

The Defense Argument

Attorney Spencer had sat quietly at the end of the counsel table through most of the trial, rarely objecting to our questions and conducting little examination of the witnesses called either by us or the other lawyers. He was the tallest of the four defense attorneys—thin, midfifties in age, short curly hair, wearing glasses. Somehow he managed to keep a lid on his client, Stan Witek. He not only separated himself physically from the three other defense lawyers, but he also did not join in the witnesses they called or the motions they made. From a philosophical standpoint, there was no reason for him to have taken this case. He was Jewish, and, ironically, was selected from the appointment panel to represent Witek, the head of the American Nazi Party. But Spencer had an intellectual and idealistic view of the application of the First Amendment and a realistic perspective on his role in the trial and his relationship to his client. For these reasons, he was the best choice to deliver the first of the defense arguments.

"We are back in session," stated the judge. "All parties are present. We will now start with the defense argument. Mr. Spencer, please."

"Thank you, Your Honor." Spencer rose and faced the jury. "At the end of the prosecutor's argument, he started talking about the meaning of the cross, and for a while I thought I might be in an ecclesiastic court. It concerned me because that isn't what we're here for.

"As the trial was going on, I thought I was at the Salem witch trials prosecuting people because they have bizarre thoughts, but that isn't what we're here for, either.

"I am not going to talk to you about the philosophy of individuals. I am not going to talk to you about whether you should agree or disagree with anybody. I don't expect you to be agreeing with the defendants in this case. What I do expect you to do is to try to apply the facts to the law in this case and figure out what to do with it.

"As I sat here in this trial, I looked at the jury and I did the same thing you do; you look at the way the defendants are dressed, how they're paying attention; and then my mind wandered, as I am sure yours does on occasion.

"I kept asking myself, 'What brought us here?' I look at my client and I say, 'Are we here because of Stanley Witek?' But it was just hard for me to accept that we are here because of Stanley Witek.

"Then I look at Mr. Riley. 'Are we here for Mr. Riley? Who is Mr. Riley that anyone should care?' Then I look at Mr. Hofstadler. I said, 'Gee, maybe we are here because of Mr. Hofstadler. Nah.' I really couldn't figure out, at first, why we were here.

"But as I sat here listening, I heard something different from what I usually hear in these cases. There was testimony, day after day, saying that these individuals are rotten people, not much testimony about whether they violated the law; just a lot of appeal to emotion.

"There was a lot of appeal to you not to do your job. There was a lot of suggestion that 'Gee, if you don't convict these guys, you are somehow a racist; you are somehow doing harm to society; you are somehow rejecting values that are really important.'

"Let me offer a few comments on the prosecuting attorney's argument. 'They want a race war,' he says. If one of them was Attila the Hun, it doesn't change the evidence. He always refers to them as 'they,' even though they are all four individuals. One thing apparent here is that these are individuals with different connections. They may have some similarity of ideas—the ones that get everybody mad—but they are different individuals. The prosecutor says that they have a unity of hate. What is he appealing to when he says these things? Is he asking you to give a careful evaluation of the evidence?

"You know, the role we all play in these types of trials really doesn't change through the years. There appears to be an effort here to think that, by locking up these individuals, you will lock up their ideas and never hear them again. I would suggest that you can lock up the individuals, but you can't lock up ideas. You can't lock up people's thoughts.

"I remember in the 1960s when the civil rights movement was starting in the South and the civil rights workers were being thrown in jail. Somehow it didn't lock up their ideas. And the people who did the locking up were just as offended by those civil rights workers' ideas and goals as the People here are offended by these defendants' ideas and goals.

"You say, 'But the civil rights workers were right and these defendants are wrong.' That is the thought that goes through your head; right? But how do we know? Maybe when you go into the jury room you can select one person to decide what ideas are right and what ideas are wrong.

"There are many ideas thought of and expressed every day in our society. Only by airing those views and not being afraid to listen to the ideas and thoughts that other people have can we deal with them.

"They are not going to be dealt with by locking people up, by hiding from them, and by convicting them of crimes they shouldn't be convicted of because you don't like their ideas.

"Now, this is not the first jury to face this type of situation. It comes up over and over again. We can look back in history and see a lot of it.

"We can look back to Boston, March 5th, in the year 1770. Somebody had started thinking. The British didn't like the thoughts, and so they decided to put another tax on the colonials. Bostoners hated taxes, so they started throwing rocks, started rioting. And the only people who could maintain order were the British troops who were acting, in effect, as police officers. They couldn't take this rock throwing anymore, and they panicked and fired into the crowd.

"Five people died. But did it stop all the activity of the colonials by doing that? Well, I guess it didn't. The British couldn't stamp out the ideas.

"But something else happened there, and it is noteworthy because it relates to your duties. After the incident, Captain Preston, who ordered the shooting, found himself in threat of being arrested. So he sent out one of his sergeants to a local lawyer, a colonial, by the name of Josiah Quincy.

"Quincy was a great man. You may have never heard of him, but he was great nonetheless. Mr. Quincy's wife answered the door.

"Now, Quincy, in the eyes of the British, was as obnoxious a character as they could deal with. He was so odious that when his wife opened the door and saw the sergeant there, knowing what had happened, she assumed her husband was going to be arrested. She felt relieved when she and her husband realized he had a new case, which was to be one of the lawyers to represent the British soldiers.

"We have a bit of insight into what happened because Quincy's grandson told us. He had looked at some letters that were written. Quincy's father was a prominent man, too, and he got upset with his son. He wrote a letter to Quincy and said he was mad at his son for taking the case. He says, 'Those citizens charged with the murder of their fellow citizens, good God. Is it possible? I will not believe it, that you could represent these people.' That is what his father wrote to him.

"Mr. Quincy replied to his father that his professional oath committed him to give legal counsel and assistance to the men accused of a crime but not proved guilty of it. Adding, 'I dare affirm that you and this whole people will one day rejoice that I became an advocate for the aforesaid criminals, charged with the murder of our fellow citizens. I never harbored the expectation, nor any great desire, that all men should speak well of me. To inquire my duty and to do it is my aim.'

"I like that letter because it describes what lawyers do. And I also like it because it shows how self-centered lawyers were in 1770, just like now. He took himself seriously in doing his job.

"But here is what Quincy's grandson wrote: 'There is no

more honorable passage in the history of New England than the one that records the trial and acquittal of Captain Preston and his men, in the midst of passionate excitements of that time, by a jury of the town maddened to rage but a few months before by the blood of her citizens shed in her streets.'

"You think these guys, sitting here, are bad? Can you imagine how the people of Boston felt, in a small town, about those soldiers?

"It was a jury of citizens from Boston. They didn't have a Bill of Rights, and there was no United States then. They didn't have television and the knowledge we have now. But even then they understood. They did what was right; unpopular, but right.

"So even before the creation of this country, juries have been asked to stand between the forces of the government and the forces of public opinion to do what is right. And usually they do.

"I stand here and ask you to apply those same principles. It doesn't matter whether you perceive the defendants as rotten sons of bitches or good guys. It is a matter of applying what you are supposed to do, because our system only holds itself together by the action of the human beings within it.

"Let me now discuss the defendants' involvement in the alleged unlawful fire and the conspiracy to ignite an unlawful fire. These are counts two and three of the complaint.

"There are a few elements that must be present for them to be convicted of anything. The first thing relates to the crime itself. We know that these men are being prosecuted on an aider and abettor theory because they didn't actually set the fires themselves.

"And you will be instructed that a person aides and abets the commission of a crime 'whenever he'—and then the next line is, 'with knowledge of the unlawful purpose of the perpetrator.' I will read that again, 'with knowledge of the unlawful purpose of the perpetrator.' So he has to know that there is something unlawful going on.

"The conspiracy is the same thing. You will be instructed that 'A conspiracy is an agreement entered into between two or more persons with the specific intent to commit the public offense of violating the fire code ordinance.' So they have to specifically intend to violate that law.

"Then there is another instruction that is called 'Ignorance or Mistake of Fact.' I will read that to you: 'An act committed or an omission made in ignorance or by reason of a mistake of fact which disproves any criminal intent is not a crime. Thus, a person is not guilty of a crime if he commits an act under an honest belief in the existence of certain facts and circumstances which, if true, would make such act or omission lawful.'

"An example of how this works is that if you ask someone if he has a driver's license and he says 'yes,' you are not breaking the law by giving him the keys to your car and letting him drive, even though he really has no driver's license.

"So there are two issues with this trial. Did the defendants really aid or abet an act they knew to be unlawful? And the second issue is, Did the defendants believe they had a valid burn permit?

"Simply being there at the scene of a crime does not make one an aider and abettor or a coconspirator. We have to ask what was said to these people with regard to the permit. Review the conversations. This is what we know: Silva got the permits. I think that is fairly obvious.

"But we also know that Mr. Silva was telling people about the permit. It seems at times, from the testimony of Peter Lake, that Silva was referring to the permit as a 'burn' permit rather than a 'barbecue' permit.

"Now, I want to read to you the last words in the opening statement that the prosecutor gave at the beginning of the trial: 'The constitutional rights of the residents of that neighborhood must be protected by this jury.' Those were the last words he gave when he summarized the case at the beginning of the trial.

"I will tell you how you can protect the constitutional rights of the residents of that neighborhood: by giving these defendants a fair trial. And if the time came, to give residents of that neighborhood a fair trial if they were in like position; and by telling the people of that neighborhood that we are not going to use our system of justice to squelch bad ideas. Because I can tell you that in any neighborhood there are plenty of people with ideas that are unacceptable to their neighbors. And if you went back into that jury room and you started getting into all your personal beliefs, you would find that each of you probably has beliefs that are totally unacceptable to some of the others.

"So much for the idea of protecting the constitutional rights of other people in the neighborhood. You can do that by looking at the evidence here and considering only that which you are supposed to be dealing with.

"Just to tie up that story I told you about the trial in 1770, Josiah Quincy died in March of 1775, a year before the American Revolution. That is why you never heard of him. His co-counsel, though, you did hear of: John Adams, one of the architects of our Constitution and the second president of the United States.

"The point is this: when you sit here, don't allow yourself to be controlled by the human tendency to ask, 'Would they give me a fair trial?' And 'Gee, I don't know if they would give me a fair trial, so why should I give them a fair trial?' You have to decide not what they stand for, but what you stand for, and whether you stand for what is proper and right, and whether it meets your obligations and duties.

"In order for you to convict any of these defendants you would have to believe, first, that he was somehow a participant in the fire. You would have to believe this beyond a reasonable doubt.

"The second thing you would have to believe beyond a reasonable doubt is that they didn't think they had a valid permit.

"Now, proof beyond a reasonable doubt is the highest degree of proof in our system. This is intended to protect the truly innocent. All reasonable doubt concerning the guilt of a defendant is to be resolved in his favor.

"The question in this case is, Did the defendants violate the law? And that is the sole question. That is all I'm asking you to take a look at. I am asking you to act as responsible jurors and responsible citizens in looking at that. That is all we can ask of you.

"This is my last chance to talk to you. I don't know what else may be said. I won't be able to respond to it. But I think if you take a look at what has been presented against each of these men, I think you will find there is at least a reasonable doubt they were connected to the cross-burning. And more, there is certainly a reasonable doubt that they had an honest belief the permit was proper.

"I just ask you give these men a fair trial. Thank you."

The remaining defense attorneys in their arguments joined Spencer's appeal to freedom of speech and assembly, breaking little new ground. Pageant read judicial opinions that criticized conspiracy charges as "the dragnet of the prosecutor," and he quoted the Wendy's hamburger lady of years past who complained, "Where's the beef?" They attacked Lake's credibility, the perceptions of Robert Gentry and fire captain Stillson, and the opinion of our expert, Gene Frice.

I did not know what Davidson planned for his rebuttal argument. It had been my impression he would endeavor to restore the focus of our case. But as Pageant and Sortino assailed the prosecution, my good friend seethed like a bull at a picador.

Chapter 23

The Prosecution's Rebuttal Argument

We are back in session. All parties are present, said Judge Smith. "Mr. Davidson will now present the prosecution's rebuttal argument."

"Thank you, Your Honor." Davidson rose, walked toward the jury box, and smiled. "Good afternoon, folks. As I was sitting here listening to the defense arguments today, I was wondering if we were all in the same courtroom and if they had sat through the same trial that I had sat through, and I was beginning to have my doubts.

"Ladies and gentlemen, this case is very much about our Constitution and our freedoms in this country; but it is not about the freedoms as the defense has perverted them and tried to present them to you like they have many other things in this trial. This case is about your freedoms and my freedoms; it is about Mr. Gentry's freedoms and his neighbors' freedoms.

"The Ku Klux Klan, you see, don't want the rights the rest of us have. They wish to be privileged. If you or I or any of our friends went into a residential area and erected eighteen-foot wooden structures of some sort, wrapped them in burlap and soaked them in gasoline, then lit them on fire, we would all know that we are going to be arrested. We would know we are going to be charged with a crime. We would come into court and we would plead guilty.

"But it is not the same for this group. Their position is 'We are the Ku Klux Klan. We can go out and do whatever we want and we are not responsible to the same laws as everybody else.' That is their basic position. The Ku Klux Klan has spent 125 years with the same goal, the same motives. It has never changed. They've spent 125 years trying to make their interests and their rights greater than those of everybody else. That is what they are still trying to do.

"Nobody is on trial here for their beliefs. Nobody is on trial here for their speech. You see, in our country we all have the right to certain freedoms. We have the right to freedom of speech. They do, too. They can say anything they want to say. They can assemble and do what they want, as long as they're not interfering with other folks' rights.

"But their rights end where your rights begin, my rights begin, and the rights of the citizens of that neighborhood begin. They can say whatever they want, and they can have whatever beliefs they want to have. But when they take their crosses into that neighborhood and burn them in a canyon without the required permit, that is a crime. It is as much a crime for them as it would be for you and me, period.

"Count one of the complaint is unlawful assembly. The way a complaint is drafted is that count one is the essence of the prohibited conduct; it is the most important of the allegations. There are two alternative ways of proving an unlawful assembly. If either one is proven, the defendants are proven guilty. If they assembled together to do an unlawful act, in this instance to violate the fire code, they are absolutely guilty of unlawful assembly. As a defense, they have the burden of raising a reasonable doubt that they in fact had a valid permit. They didn't have a valid permit, period.

"The other alternative method of proving an unlawful assembly is that they assembled and engaged in tumultuous conduct. You will receive an instruction from the judge that 'tumultuous conduct' is that conduct that incites terror in others.

"Now, contrary to what one of the defense counsel said in his closing argument, this case is very much about cross-burnings. That is what they burned. They chose to burn their crosses at the fringe of a white neighborhood overlooking a predominantly black neighborhood. Coincidence? Of course not. They made the crosses fifteen to eighteen feet high. A private ceremony? Not in the least. Did they know their conduct might incite terror and provoke a reaction? Your answer lies in the fact that they brought their clubs and bullet-proof vests. They'd been there before, at cross-burning demonstrations throughout the state. They knew what they were doing. They engaged in tumultuous conduct, and they are absolutely guilty of unlawful assembly.

"The conspiracy charge is the most serious in the complaint. It should be. The reason is a recognition under the law that when people combine into a group to commit a crime, it is more dangerous than any one of them individually committing the crime. What could be more fitting to allege as a conspiracy than this: men passing among themselves these large table legs, setting up patrols organized for setting fires in a canyon area, and flagrantly provoking neighboring residents.

"A conspiracy is proven by demonstrating an agreement and an intent to commit the crime, then an 'overt act' committed by any one of the co-conspirators in furtherance of the criminal objective. The overt act need not even be by any one of the defendants, just any one of the co-conspirators. It can be Silva. It can be any one of them.

"In fact, the overt acts that we have charged are absolutely proven on the videotape. What you have to do to return a guilty verdict is just find one of them, just find any one of them true.

"These guys will not even admit what is shown on the videotape or in the photographs. None of them. Nobody saw Witek with the clubs. Nobody saw Riley with the crosses. Nobody saw Hofstadler with the torches. Nobody saw anything, even if it is shown on the videotape. They know all that went down. But anything that might implicate somebody that is on trial here, they didn't see.

"And, you see, the reason they are so free to disregard that oath they took from the witness stand is because of something else you learned during this trial. Their only loyalties are to each other. And besides their feelings about minorities and those who disagree with them, the only other strong hatred they harbor is the hatred they have for our Constitution.

"Look at Metzger's speech printed in his own publication when he holds up a forty-five-caliber handgun and tells his adoring skinheads, 'Don't follow the Constitution; follow this.'

"They have their own constitution, the Robert Matthews Order Constitution, that arose from the conspiracy to overthrow our government. That is what they worship.

"You see, that is the perfect irony of this case. That which they hate the most, our Constitution, which grants rights and equality to all regardless of color, is what they hide behind. They come in here and try to portray themselves as being persecuted for expressing their speech and religion. That is absolute nonsense.

"You can say what you want, as long as it doesn't provoke immediate violence. You can have any religious beliefs, no matter how absurd or how bizarre, and that is your right as a citizen. But you are not entitled to force your beliefs down somebody else's throat, and you are not entitled to infringe another's rights in exercising your own.

"You see from the videotapes and from the testimony that the defendants had a unity of action. You see a unity of purpose. You see them all working together. Do they have a better word for it than 'conspiracy'?

"Now, part of the defense as I'm hearing it is that the defendants thought they had a valid permit. Could anybody in their right mind who was out there that night think they had a valid burn permit to torch three large crosses in a residential canyon area? Could any human being have believed that? You have the police all around, the fire trucks, the helicopter; all just watching and waiting. I am sorry, folks, but I just don't think so, and I don't think any person could honestly say so.

They say this case is not about Robert Gentry. Well, this case is very much about Robert Gentry. Here is a man who has worked hard all his life to build a life for his family. He hasn't come in here asking for any special rights or favors. He has come in here under a sense of obligation—obligation to his children and to his neighbors. When the

Ku Klux Klan came upon them that night, the neighbors did not respond with bats and table legs. Mr. Gentry responded by giving his name as a witness, and by waiting for justice to be prescribed by the courts.

"This is an important case. It is very important from a societal standpoint. It is much more important than any single murder case. It is the test of our will to protect our own from those who would prey upon them.

"Mr. Phillips has done what he can about this, and I have done what I can do about it. The final test is what you folks do about it. Do what is right."

Chapter 24

The Verdict

The judge read the instructions to the jurors constituting the law they were to apply in deciding the issues before them. We then began the long wait.

The first day passed with no indication from the jury—no questions, no read-backs. On that first day you hope for a quick verdict, like a boxer wanting a knockout as he leaves his corner for the first round. If you thought you had a good case, you expect it. But when it doesn't happen that way, you figure they have to pick a foreperson, maybe review the instructions, and this takes time.

The second morning passed. Still, no indication from the jurors. We watched them from down the hall as they reentered the court after lunch. They were getting along well; politely at least. This seemed a positive sign.

The third and fourth days passed, still without a verdict. We tried to persuade ourselves that the number of defendants and the multiple counts had slowed the deliberation process, and that there would still be verdicts.

On the fifth day, the jurors asked for a read-back of testimony, that of witness Peter Lake relating to discussions at Silva's home regarding the fire permit. We speculated on the reason for the read-back of these conversations. We wondered if a rift had developed over the defendants' beliefs in the authority of the permit.

On the sixth day we were no longer patient. In fact, I kept my distance from the immediate vicinity of the courtroom to avoid any show of hostility at the jurors for their apparent indecision.

I returned to the Criminal Courts Building on the seventh day to organize the remnants of unused photographs and duplicate copies of reports. I was sifting through some old files while Davidson sat at his desk, his hand propped against the side of his head, deep in thought. Without turning toward me he inquired, in a humble, introspective manner, "Have you ever lost a trial you really wanted to win?"

I chuckled for a moment when I first heard Davidson's question, but not in mirth. Perhaps it was time to face the possibility that we had lost this trial. Then I thought for a moment. "No. *Winning* has never been the key in the criminal prosecutions I've done. I only hoped the verdicts would be just, whatever form that took."

Dale turned his chair toward me. "Why did you want this trial, John? For you it was just a one-shot deal; no promotion, no pay raise. You lived on the boiler plate, and all for what? You only had to say 'no.' "

I appreciated the sincerity of Dale's concern. Other than my wife, no one could have known how unnerving the routine had become. He deserved the only answer I knew to give. "I believe we are each judged on the basis of what we do with the strengths life has given us. For a man who is physically strong, it may be pulling someone from a fire. For a mother, it may be caring for a sick child. This is what I do best. I got to come back for one last trial."

Dale gazed somberly. I realized he understood, but did not feel it the same. I wondered, and so I asked him what was it that made him take this case.

Dale leaned back into his chair and rested his foot on the side of his desk. "It was my second year in the office. Only my second year. I prosecuted the rape of this pretty, young girl, eighteen years old. She had beautiful long dark hair and innocent brown eyes. She looked like the kind of girl who would inspire a knight to ride his stallion a hundred miles without sleep to drive his sword through the heart of a dragon. But she was tough." Dale looked over at me, breaking the trance of his memory. "I knew she was rough around the edges. I won the case. I had to drag witnesses to court and do a retrial, but I did it.

"A few months later I was assigned a mayhem prosecution. A fifteen-year-old girl had her face slashed up. She was scarred. Badly scarred.

"My defendant? Well. My defendant was the victim in the rape case. Yeah. The princess who could inspire armies. She discovered her younger cousin had slept with her boyfriend. I prosecuted her." Davidson grimaced with anger. "I sent her to prison."

His expression relaxed a bit as he continued. "I realized then there were no princesses, no knights in shining armor, no Holy Grail. Not in this city.

"Then one night I sat beneath a sky with a thousand glistening stars. I don't know exactly what it was, but maybe it was the magic of a child born. Something new, pure and hopeful. I listened to a fool swept away by this moment in his life. A moment that let him dream, and believe the dream could be his life.

"As I listened I looked away, back to the stars, and when I looked again at him I no longer saw a fool. I wanted to be part of his dream."

There was a rapid knock struck upon Davidson's office door. It was his secretary.

"The judge wants you right after lunch," she said. "The foreman wrote a note saying they've finished their deliberations."

Judge Smith peered down from the bench to us and smiled courteously. "We are back on the record in the matter of *People of the State of California versus Thomas Metzger et al.*, case number A790456. Mr. Davidson and Mr. Phillips are present for the People. All counsel for the defense and their clients are also present." He turned to his right. "Ladies and gentlemen of the jury, do you have a verdict?"

The jurors looked to the gentleman now seated in the first row, far right, the seat that the foreman traditionally assumes. Dryly he answered. "We have verdicts on eleven of the thirteen counts."

"On the two counts on which you did not reach a verdict, how many times did you vote?" asked the judge.

"Twice. Once today and once two days ago," answered the foreman.

"Tell me the numerical count, without telling me whether it was for guilty or innocent."

"It was ten to two, today."

"Is there anything the court can do, such as further

instructions or read-back, that would assist the jury in reaching a verdict on those two counts?"

"We don't think so. We have exhausted our efforts, all of our resources."

"Give the verdict slips you have signed to the bailiff, please. You've worked on this a long time. The court finds the jury is hopelessly deadlocked as to those two remaining counts."

The bailiff handed Judge Smith the verdict slips. He viewed them one by one, tapped them on the desk top of his bench, and looked at me emotionlessly. I heard Davidson sigh in anticipation. The judge handed the verdicts back to the bailiff, who walked them to the court clerk, standing ready for her reading.

"Madam Clerk, would you read the verdicts, please?" said the judge.

"In the matter of *People of the State of California versus Thomas Metzger et al.*, case number A790456, 'We the jury in the above entitled action find the defendant, Thomas Metzger, *guilty* of the crime of unlawful assembly, as charged in count one of the complaint.'

"Title of court and cause: 'We the jury in the above-entitled action find the defendant, Stanley Witek, guilty of the crime of unlawful assembly, as charged in count one of the complaint.'

"Title of court and cause: 'We the jury in the above-entitled action find the defendant, Brad Riley, guilty of the crime of unlawful assembly."

And on she read, for each of the eleven counts: Witek, guilty of conspiracy, possession and distribution of billy clubs, unlawful assembly, and unlawful burning; Riley, guilty of unlawful assembly, conspiracy, and unlawful burning; and Hofstadler, guilty of unlawful assembly, conspiracy, and unlawful burning. With the exception of the two hung counts on Metzger for conspiracy and unlawful burning, it was a clean sweep. Having convicted him of unlawful assembly, count one of the complaint, we were thoroughly satisfied with the outcome of the trial.

For me it was a bittersweet moment. Well-wishers and news media slowed our passage through the courthouse hallways. It was a relief to be able to speak openly and smile. It had been a while since I felt simply good inside. I wanted to celebrate, but I knew I had reached the end of a part of my life that I would miss dearly.

When I returned to the office upstairs, I was approached by Reiner's chief deputy, Frank Sunstedt. He asked me to stay with the D.A.'s office, to head a newly created unit prosecuting hate crimes. Mr. Reiner was waiting for me with his press secretary. It was an opportunity I had always wanted, and the feeling could have been euphoric. But it wasn't. Someone very special was missing, and it was with her that I had to be. I went home, and I promised Diane that I'd return to my private law practice in Woodland Hills.

I was relieved this battle was over. We had played it clean and won. I hugged my wife and children that night, knowing I was no longer a threat to anyone, and no one any longer was a threat to me.

Epilogue

Tom Metzger, founder of WAR and one-time Grand Dragon of the California Knights of the Ku Klux Klan, was sentenced to six months in jail. Word spread in the white supremacist movement that in his testimony he sought to disassociate himself from the other defendants, the "cross-lighting," and the Klan. It was perceived that he had betrayed his co-defendants and the white supremacist movement. Although he continues to spew racism over the airwaves to those who will listen, it is viewed as racism for profit. Metzger is no longer a credible or viable force in the white supremacist movement.

Stanley Witek, head of the American Nazi Party, was sentenced to eighteen months in state prison. Due to his apparent and deep-set paranoia regarding Jews, Dale and I recommended that Witek be treated in the psych ward of the prison medical center. His counsel readily joined in our recommendation. Witek has been inactive in the movement since his release from prison.

Brad Riley was provided little actual representation during the trial by attorney Brian Pageant, who involved himself more with Metzger for his media appeal. Unfortunately for Riley, Pageant's lust for the media spotlight continued during the posttrial sentencing phase. While publicly decrying Metzger's six-month sentence, Pageant seemingly didn't notice his actual client got a full year. Having been betrayed by cohorts and counsel alike, Riley has publicly renounced the movement.

Jerome Hofstadler disassociated himself from involvement with white supremacists and was granted special consideration.

Richard Girnt Butler fled prosecution; a warrant was issued for his arrest; and he has not since returned to California where the warrant can be executed.

Frank Silva and Randy Evans remain in prison on antiracketeering offenses. David Tate and Thomas Bentley remain in prison for murder.

The convictions of each of the defendants have been upheld by the California Court of Appeals.

In the years following this prosecution, there have been no Ku Klux Klan ceremonial cross-burnings in the state of California. Klan demonstrations, which in their peak had attracted hundreds of participants, have ended.

If the state of Georgia or Alabama had prosecuted the Ku Klux Klan as vigorously the first time it showed itself in those jurisdictions, many innocent people may have been spared victimization at the hands of the Klan. Children here, for this place in time, will have to ask, "What is the Klan?" rather than know it from personal experience.